ANGELS' TOWN

ANGELS' TOWN

Chero Ways, Gang Life, and
Rhetorics of the Everyday

RALPH CINTRON

Beacon Press
Boston

Beacon Press
25 Beacon Street
Boston, Massachusetts 02108-2892

Beacon Press books
are published under the auspices of
the Unitarian Universalist Association of Congregations.

03 02 01 00 99 98   8 7 6 5 4 3 2

Text design by John Kane.
Composition in Berthold Akzidenz Grotesk and Adobe Garamond by
Wilsted & Taylor.

Library of Congress Cataloging-in-Publication Data

Cintron, Ralph.
    Angels' town : chero ways, gang life, and rhetorics of the everyday /
Ralph Cintron.
        p. cm.
    Includes bibliographical references and index.
    ISBN 0-8070-4636-1 (cloth)
    ISBN 0-8070-4637-x (paper)
    1. Hispanic Americans—Illinois—Chicago Region—Social life and
customs.   2. Hispanic Americans—Illinois—Chicago Region—Ethnic
identity.   3. Chicago Region (Ill.)—Social life and customs.   I. Title.
F548.9.S75C56   1997
977.3′110468073—dc21   97-21673

Dedicated to
K
above all

& to Josefina, Rafael, & Josie
& most preciously to Jane & Colleen

CONTENTS

PREFACE

More than twenty years ago while walking through a Mexican-American neighborhood somewhere in San Antonio, Texas, a good friend and I passed by a house whose front yard had become a cluttered gallery of homemade concrete folk art. Scattered within this fantastic scene were real mesquite trees, shrubs, vines, a dwarf tree or two, and potted plants and flowers. Narrow paths tried to make their way through the clutter but were soon defeated. The lot was small, but oh so intense. The clutter wrapped around both sides of the house to create an even bigger heap of the backyard. This scene was from long ago, and now I cannot remember if the figurines and other odd, concrete sculptures contained a set of themes that may have unified this enormous, wild collection. Such a poor thing my memory is, but what I distinctly remember to this day was a sign over the doorway of the house. It announced the artist's name, and this was followed by the word "MAKER." Makers; the process of making; made things as cultural displays or performances; the economic, social, and political contexts of made things; the circulation of such things through the imaginations of a community and a culture—these issues intrigue me, and thus they constitute major themes inside this book.

This book addresses at least two levels of "making." At one level, I critique the making of ethnographic texts, this book in particular. For instance, at times the book negotiates a dialectic between assertion and simultaneous criticism of that assertion. Such a negotiation might all too easily become a kind of tortuous path, but, fortunately, I do not follow such a route throughout. Indeed, what interests me more is how humans "make" an order. In order to explore this idea, I compare rather glibly the "ordering" of a text and the "ordering" of a society. I find both sorts of ordermaking paradoxical. I assume that there is always a need to make an order, and yet the process entails ordering something out. The result of this action is that a flaw, a fault line, is implanted in whatever has been ordered, and the flaw has the potential to collapse the structure that harbors and maintains it, whether that structure is the self, a text, or a social system. This assumption weighs almost mythically for me, and so I have never fully unearthed how it directs much of my thinking.

At a second level, this book explores how a variety of people made or displayed themselves and how these makings were influenced by systemic power differences. For instance, one of the book's controlling questions is *How does one create respect under conditions of little or no respect*? Where I did fieldwork, it seemed sometimes that the difficulty of conditions—or their perceived difficulty—encouraged a kind of hyperbolic need for respect. The result was that some versions of creating respect were incompatible with other versions. Indeed, the book might be understood as a series of vignettes representing how different people created different kinds of respect and then disagreed with each other concerning what was respectable or not.

At this level, as I explore how people made and unmade themselves and how these makings were received by different audiences, the book is traditionally ethnographic. I call the book, then, an ethnography, an ethnography of a Latino/a community approaching thirty thousand who lived in a city I call Angelstown, a city of approximately a hundred thousand located close to Chicago.[1] However, I would like my readers to consider the book a project in the rhetorics of public culture or the rhetorics of everyday life. The first term in particular is my own, but both terms try to name an approach that, consistent with the discipline of rhetoric, is interested in the structured contentiousness that organizes, albeit fleetingly, a community or a culture. I came to this approach because while doing fieldwork it occurred to me that not only uses of language but also a wide range of artifacts and bodily gestures became consistently mobilized during the making of disputes. Those interested in the performative dimension of human action should find considerable compatibility with my analyses of these public ways of displaying disputes. For instance, I interpret the surfaces of public culture—hairstyles, clothing, car decoration, musical styles, talk, the geometries of city streets and street names—as performances, as rhetorical gestures emerging from the desire to persuade others of the propriety of certain identifications and, implicitly, of the impropriety of other identifications. So, the performance perspective evident in both sociocultural anthropology and rhetorical studies is akin to my own mode of analyzing public displays, displays that are deeply connected to asymmetrical power relationships.

A project in the rhetorics of public culture or the rhetorics of everyday life, then, suggests a set of mixed interests in which sociocultural anthropology and rhetoric shade into each other. For instance, like most ethnographers, I attempt to evoke a macro-world by synthesizing a plethora of information. But sociocultural anthropologists will notice a difference between this work and their own, a difference that runs deeper, I suspect, than a reliance on a certain amount of rhetorical vocabulary. That difference has much to do with looking at cultures and communities as systems of contention in which a contentious position does not exist without its structured opposite and the two together have much to do with generating the specificities of everyday life. At any rate, it is my hope that readers will find their sympathies adequately represented in my preferred terms, namely, "a project in the rhetorics of public culture" or "the rhetorics of everyday life." But beyond my interests in both sociocultural anthropology and rhetoric, there are other intellectual interests: for instance, the empirical research of social scientists in general, Marxist theory, and literary theory and analysis, particularly as these have come to be influenced by cultural studies scholars who excavate the political in public and literary discourse. In short, I see a project in the rhetorics of public culture as a somewhat new approach, one that adopts the fieldwork methods traditional to sociocultural anthropology and blends these with the cultural critique now common among critical ethnographers and theorists, and picks up as well ideas from an entire lineage of rhetorical theorists stretching to classical Greece and Rome.

And speaking of that classical tradition, let me say a few words about the notion of making and how it may have been viewed by Aristotle and Plato. For Aristotle, *tekhne*, "art" or "craft," was associated with "a reasoned habit of mind in making something." For Aristotle, rhetoric was an art, and so was architecture. For Plato, gymnastics training and shipbuilding were worthy arts, but rhetoric, instead, was more of a knack that offered cheap gratification.[2] But let me amplify this notion of *tekhne* further because I find the concept important. For Aristotle, *tekhne* was associated with ability, capacity, and skill. Most significantly, art "as a reasoned capacity to make something" was concerned with that something's "coming-into-being"; hence, art was "not the product of artistic skill but the skill itself."[3] I am skeptical of our ability to capture fully Aristotle's perspective on these issues and even more so his entire culture's, and I am even skeptical of using Aristotle or Plato to represent the bulk of classical rhetorical theory. Despite my caution, I still hear a valuable hint coming through that might be of interest to many: Has this ancient concept of *tekhne* or art devolved in the modern world into something more debilitating, a cleavage, say, between artistic skill and other skills? The detritus of romanticism, particularly the idea of the alienated and sacred artist, survives in the modern fetishization of the art object. With such fetishization, art becomes aggrandized, a product of the mysterious, irrational, creative, and individual mind; in contrast, mundane skill becomes a product of generic minds.[4] I am using the notion of *tekhne* here to level that fetishization and to see the art in mundane skill and, more significantly, in day-to-day life. And there is, of course, the *tekhne* of doing fieldwork and the *tekhne* of writing ethnographies. I haven't heard this concept of art represented in the acrimonious debates that have occupied some sociocultural anthropologists, for instance, the so-called scientists versus the so-called postmoderns, the empiricists versus the subjectivists and/or literary types. The notion of art that gets pitched back and forth among these debaters is the more modern, narrow variety: art as high art or art as fiction.[5] Why not, instead, level the concept of high art and recover another sort of art, one that is not dressed in prestige but that names, nevertheless, an intrinsic aesthetic or crafting that underlies the practices of everyday life, including the making of research. Call it *tekhne*, "a reasoned habit of mind in making something."

A few words about the title. There were two gentlemen in the community whose real names were Angel, and so it is for them that I have titled the book (*Angels' Town*) and named the community. I have chosen to write openly about one of these men, Don Angel, but the other Angel must remain obscure, although I have named him in this paragraph for the first and last time. I met the first Angel in 1990 at the beginning of my second stage of research; I met the other Angel toward the end. The first Angel, a more traditional man, a *chero*, was described as a saint by the retired priest who had hired him to tend the garden that flowered a grotto next to the church buildings. The other Angel would never be called a saint, for he has spent much of his life as a powerful underworld character. These two figures represent the lightness and darkness of this text—its comic side, its tragic side. Their lives, however, have been much too complicated to be imagined as allegories of lightness and darkness, and, therefore, it is important not to reduce their remarkably different worlds to just those categories. Everyone else in this text has a pseudonym, including the second Angel who will soon acquire one so that he can hide like the others, but perhaps for more significant reasons, from prying eyes. By naming the town after both of these gentlemen, I hope to celebrate their lives in a small way, lives that have received, by their own accounts, not much celebration. But these acts of naming also entail subversions that can be played out on the plane of language if not the plane of reality. For instance, Don Angel, as will be seen, was the only person I came to know in Angelstown who had never read a book. Nevertheless, he is the only one truly named inside a text that is itself largely about the written word and about a man who did not need to read extended texts. Further, because he reads English with great difficulty, he himself will probably read very little of this book. There are ironies here, but in replacing the real name of the town with both of their names, I hope to suggest a kind of symbolic conquering of the city itself. In one sense, the book might be read as an extended tragicomedy in which both Angels stage for a short period of time an elaborate role reversal in which they rise up from the obscure depths of the city to rename the city itself with their own lives. The comic part is that such things can be performed scatologically in the spirit of carnival inside the playful possibilities of a text; the tragic part is that, with the disappearance of night and the return of bruising daylight, the playful text evaporates and the old order reemerges. This symbolic conquering is particularly important in the case of Don Angel since he has experienced not much power in his life but less important for the second Angel, for he moves through a rough-and-tumble world gathering respect from both enemies and, as he might say, his "associates" even as he generates fear within the status quo.

But this action of ironic naming has another purpose as well. I hope also to mirror a certain ambiguity that I experienced in Angelstown, an ambiguity that will be explored intermittently throughout the book. I along with my two research assistants, Edmundo Cavazos and Dan Anderson, both of whom helped shape this text in extraordinary ways, were often perplexed by the soft underbelly of what appeared to be true but wasn't—or was it? In short, ethnographies typically contain pseudonyms, but in the case of *Angels' Town* I hope readers will sense through the pseudonym a larger trope that has helped me to understand the fieldwork problem, quite pronounced in Angelstown, of the difficulty of finding the truth inside the lie, the lie inside the truth.

ANGELS' TOWN

1

STARTING PLACES

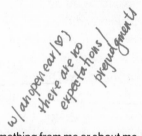

For some time now, a favorite image of mine has been the collection basket. When I was a little boy growing up in the Rio Grande Valley of south Texas, my mother would take us to Sacred Heart Catholic Church, the town's "Mexican" church in Mercedes.[1] Inside the church, the main statue was that of Christ with an oversized heart fully exposed, dripping blood. His left arm gestured gently away from his body; his gaze looked just beyond the gesture. In another context, the vividness of the statue would have been tasteless, a bit overdone, perhaps campy in the eyes of some. But the purpose of such vividness—as I reflect on it now so many years removed—is to reanimate that which is no longer noticed. The hope, I suppose, is to startle an audience from its slumber: Christ as throbbing heart opens into the present, alive, in order to recover the vividness of a past message before the present can close again over its own wound, as it always does, to become the forgotten past, again.

we forget (implying we make same mistakes again)

is a human who follows ♥ and that way is successful

But I particularly remember the collection baskets in the church, their long handles. When the time came, four men, two per pew, would thrust them before us at chest level, and we would drop our money and envelopes in. The collection basket becomes a metaphor of an individual who moves at the level of the heart, and so much is dropped into her or his life.

I remember one Sunday a very drunk man at some point during the service started walking on his knees from the back of the church. He was filled with catastrophe and perverse ritual. He chanted something, perhaps the rosary, in Spanish, of course. Perhaps he beat his chest rhythmically. I do not recall now. He kept shuffling forward on his knees until he reached, more or less, the front third of the church. We were astonished. The men who wielded the baskets, always so dutiful, came finally to pick him up and remove him from the church. Our layers of propriety rustled back into place on the surface of our lives, and our vulnerability was once again clothed.

The collection baskets and this man—who, seemingly, sought deliverance from brokenness through ritualized penance—are now juxtaposed in this text. They tell me something about the ethnographer. I have passed like a collection basket before the lives of others. During interviews and conversations, during incidental moments, others placed something inside of me. This book is an emptying of the basket. What purpose will their donations serve? But the image of a basket as passive receptacle collecting reality is, of course, unbelievable. In contrast to the basket image, much of this chapter will describe me as somewhat like that muddy, distorted man making odd gestures, this book being one.

So in essence everyone is a collection basket

Let me now expose something of my own ethos by making an autobiographical gesture in this chapter, the sort that ethnographers have been requesting for over a decade.[2] I want to do this because, as a rhetorician, I am always concerned with the densities of a text and how to open these to scrutiny, and certainly one of the most significant densities concerns the writer's ethos, which is typically understood as a person's moral character or disposition.[3] Before exposing my own particular disposition, however, I want first to look more carefully at the concept of ethos itself. By calling ethos a characteristic of texts, I am calling attention to the crafting of ethos and suggesting that a writer's ethos is the "appearance" of ethos and that I do not know what ethos might be as a "reality" somehow separate from its appearance. As one might expect, in the discipline of rhetoric the problem of ethos is muddy with ancient and contemporary commentaries. For the purposes of this chapter, however, what I wish to emphasize is how ethos is bound up with *logos* (in its most ordinary sense, "word," "reason," or "rational argument"). In other words, the rational argument does not necessarily persuade when reason is made pure. Indeed, rationality, the pure kind, does not exist outside the soup of human affairs.[4] In matters of persuasion, then, character plays an important role. In some cases, one might even say that the carefully deliberated argument is itself a sign of character. However configured, the central point is that ethos and logos—or character and a rational knowledge claim—are linked so that knowing something of a person's character helps us to judge that person's knowledge claims. We can say this more enigmatically: logos is layered with ethos and ethos is layered with logos.[5]

In the discipline of sociocultural anthropology, the weave of logos and ethos is tighter than anyone, to my knowledge, has fully explored. If a kind of reconceptualization of sociocultural anthropology were to occur via rhetoric, it would entail much more than an examination of the rhetorics of ethnographies. Clifford Geertz's *Works and Lives* and James Clifford and George Marcus' *Writing Culture* are two texts along with others that have entered anthropology rather flamboyantly and confrontationally by pointing to the importance of the textual dimension in the creation of anthropological knowledge.[6] But a full mobilization of the discipline of rhetoric, if it is to serve/disturb anthropology, entails more than a rhetorical examination of texts. Such a mobilization would also see rhetoric operating outside the text, for instance, in the helter-skelter of fieldwork. If we think of fieldwork as thick with representations and displays— as anthropologists interested in performance often do[7]—and if we further note that the discipline of rhetoric has been historically concerned with display, calling it an entire branch of rhetoric, *epideictic*, we might begin to sense how we might talk about the rhetoric of artifacts, rituals, cultural institutions, informants, texts, architecture, public and private spaces, silence, and so on.[8] Sociocultural anthropology, then, is rhetorical long before its texts, its ethnographies and theoretical treatises, come into being because the cultural stuff that becomes a fieldnote is rhetorical, as is the fieldnote itself.

In being noticeably rhetorical, sociocultural anthropology, more so than the natural sciences perhaps, is defined by the dependence of logos upon ethos. For instance, data gathering may have as its purposeful end the creation of logos, but it can only get there through the creation of an ethos. In fact, sociocultural anthropology carved out its distinctive procedures in large part because of the problem of ethos. By "distinctive procedures," I refer to the fact that the modern ethnographer is now largely defined as one who lives with others over a long period of time, and this definition acknowledges that the process of coming to know a people—hence, the right to make a knowledge claim—is deeply intertwined with the creation of ethos, an ethos that is acceptable to the Other. One's credibility or character is created during miniscule moments of interaction, each moment interpreted consciously or not so consciously by others. Within this corpus of interactions, interpretations, and reinterpretations, the organic shaping of an ethnographer's ethos occurs. Obviously, such shaping takes time, and the apparent shape of the ethnographer's ethos will tell the Other, who is also always establishing his or her ethos, what to share and what not to share from the otherwise secreted community. In fact, I have often suspected that the reluctance and inability to fully systemize ethnographic inquiry in order to make it more machinelike in the production of anthropological logos has much to do with how ethos saturates the moment of inquiry, and this is a condition that the natural sciences face differently and less conspicuously. My central claim, then: The persuasiveness of the ethnographic knowledge claim is constituted through and through, both in the moments of fieldwork and the moments of the final text, by ethos.[9]

I do not remember the book, author, or when I read it, but part of the lore of ethnographers is that their ethos, in part, is a product of living and viewing from the periphery. Their peripheral status is often evident when in their fieldsites, but it is also evident in their relationship to their own culture. Perhaps this feeling of living at the periphery is part of the cord that connects ethnography, embarrassingly or otherwise, to nineteenth-century romanticism and twentieth-century alienation/cultural critique.[10] The drunk man shuffling up the center aisle was also on the periphery. But his peripheralness became most evident as he performed one of the central grotesqueries of Catholicism. What is more central to Catholicism, images of the compassionate Christ or the tortured Christ? The drunk man chose the tortured Christ as center, moved himself bodily into it, and at that very moment placed himself outside the limits of propriety. Said differently, as outsider he was drawn to the iconography most deeply inside a particular community, and in finding that private center not often made public, he set off a communal shock wave that exposed everyone's private longing and suffering, and for this he was pushed even further toward the periphery and literally placed outside the church. This reaction, more than likely, only intensified his self-definition as tortured outsider and his longing for redemption. Of course, my interpretation is but a projection of his originating motives and the public's reactions to his bit of theater. In my scheme, this man had a special and brave, albeit fleeting, knowledge that emerged in part because of his conflicted role as insider/outsider. Ethnographic knowing is a different sort of knowing; nevertheless, there is a shared theme of outsiders coming to know the insides of things, and I find this theme compelling.

I want to make clear that my own ethos contains a certain socioeconomic and cultural nervousness. These are odd demons that have helped place me on

Ethnographies

the periphery of two groups of people. I believe that much of this book's ethos is entangled with these demons. I was born of Puerto Rican parents and raised in south Texas. I was the son of a farm manager, a Ph.D. horticulturalist, who was pragmatic and a highly skilled technician. The workers on the farm were Mexican, and they called my father *el patrón*. To this day, I retain a mostly Puerto Rican accent when I speak Spanish, which means I kept myself apart from the Mexican-American Spanish around me, and now I do not speak Spanish as easily as I speak English. Here are clues of human distances that even now cause me discomfort.

My family embodied a more or less patrician sensibility. The desire to be patrician is, perhaps, more accurate. Imagine this set of colonialist-like images, images that may have seemed odd in a United States context but approximated the images in which my mother and father were raised in Puerto Rico: Our large house on a hill at the eastern corner of two thousand acres of citrus trees, twenty to thirty workers and their families living at some distance in a kind of village where the farm equipment was located, the wife of one of the workers becoming an occasional housemaid, and a worker occasionally coming up the hill, embarrassed, with some personal problem. Unlike my family, I had trouble with the role I was to follow. When workers would be sent by my father to do yard work around the house, I would hide. Until my midteen years I was noticeably ashamed of my "workless" state, embarrassed by class differences even though I acted them out daily by simply being who I was. Because the owners of the farm lived five hundred miles to the north in Dallas, we were, in effect, the source of authority for a number of people. Our authority was less than it appeared, however. For instance, we did not own the house. It too was farm property, and our infrequent visits to the Dallas owners were awkward, for the owners represented real American wealth and power that far surpassed possibilities in Puerto Rico, and this realization seemed to undermine our authority back home in Mercedes. I remember my mother as deeply self-conscious of her Spanish-accented English, a sign of her difference, or afraid that her actions would betray a lower station in life and somehow reveal in front of all the Dallas owners some essential *bochinche*-like (disorder, common gossip, typically associated with the uneducated) qualities that in her mind followed Puerto Ricans wherever they went. These at least were the feelings of a young boy, and now these are the thoughts that those feelings have become.

I write least well about reality and much better about the perception of reality, the perceptions mentioned here and many more: for instance, perceptions of my schooling successes in contrast to the schooling disappointments of others whose *latinidad* I shared but with a difference; perceptions of Dallas as very white, rich, and air-conditioned—again, a difference, but this one generated a different courtship in which we were the petitioners and they the granters of white-gloved favors. I was then and continue to be a nerve attached to these sorts of differences. Then, I had mostly feelings at my disposal. Now, I also have theory and lots of words, words that want justice to weight them. This book is attached to the other side of the same nerve. One of its desires is to make amends for the distances that placed our family on that hill, many more families below, and precious few families five hundred miles to the north. Surely, if this book is able to make amends, it is because of certain negotiating skills that were cultivated under conditions of difference and distance.

I do not wish, therefore, to critique the distances that I have described by arguing for utopian brother/sisterhood. Distance serves a purpose. Besides, I rather like distance, perhaps because I have accommodated myself to it. To a certain extent, distance has become a way of life that enables tenderness. One starts to find the inside of what it means to live at a distance, and there is at that moment a kind of bounty, for we are in contact with one of the deep wounds of everyone. By voyaging through the feeling of distance, one can start to understand the intensity of the drunk man at Sacred Heart Church, if not the specifics of his life. Was he not distanced from himself, perhaps someone else as well, and a community to which he wished to belong?

This distinction between intensity and specifics interests me. This ethnography contains a set of specifics that I could not have understood if I had not lived ethnographically in a particular place at a particular time, but how does one understand, indeed, experience, the emotional intensities of people, their desires, envies, and resentments? Renato Rosaldo talks of having to experience the intensity of personal grief before fully understanding the motives for head-hunting among the Ilongots.[11] I am saying something similar here, although I do not wish to compare anyone's experiences, much less mine, to those of Rosaldo and his extraordinary encounters with grief. But I have been elaborating in this chapter a set of emotional intensities that did not originate at the fieldsite but long ago, at the moment of birth. Indeed, the fieldsite first magnetized me because of these intensities, and so I cannot remove them from my text, nor do I wish to. In short, in this book the analyses that at times look hermeneutical and at other times like social science, are deeply embedded in the intensities of particular feelings that over the years have not dissolved but have become, to a significant degree, the core of a worldview, an interpretive frame, a heuristic. These intensities, then, have coursed through this project, from fieldwork to text, and through this ethos I have made a certain logos.

But there is still more to talk about concerning ethos than what I have recounted here. In particular, I would like to broaden further the notion that ethnographic logos depends on ethos. My strategy for doing so will be to examine three recent fieldsites as exerting a special magnetism, or, if one prefers, as answering a deeper pattern in an ethnographer's life. This deeper pattern, I take it, is part of the ethnographer's character or ethos. What I wish to maintain is that my description above of a connection between early-life experiences and a later fieldsite where professional work gets done is not just a subjective account. Other ethnographers, I believe, have said something similar.

I note, for instance, Nancy Scheper-Hughes in *Death Without Weeping*: "[I]n writing about the [sugar] cane cutters and their families of Bom Jesus de Mata [Brazil], I am also trying to reach out and touch the fading images of those sugar workers I knew as a child" growing up at the foot of the Domino Sugar refining factory in a working-class neighborhood of Brooklyn, New York.[12] I note also Ruth Behar in *Translated Woman*: "[M]y work with Esperanza, the Mexican street peddler, was also a bridge to my own past [one of her grandfathers was a door-to-door peddler of blankets and men's suits in Havana, Cuba] and the journey my family has made to shift their class identity."[13] I note, finally, Smadar Lavie in *The Poetics of Military Occupation* who describes her work among the Bedouin of the South Sinai as being, in part, an attempt to recuperate the heritage of her grandmother, a Yemeni Bedouin, a heritage that had almost disappeared beneath the family's identification with its European and Jewish origins.[14]

I could go on with many more examples, but what is one to make of these ongoing patterns connecting early life to professional life that ethnographers of late are willing to see? Uncovering the connection between fieldsite and some deeper life-pattern of the ethnographer's has become a minor trope in the current moment of ethnographic writing. Does it suggest the emergence into ethnography of a certain sentimentality, or at least confessionality, that violates an older positivist or a more recent Marxist sensibility? I don't think so. The ethnographies mentioned above are too clearheaded, too politically committed, too aware of power differentials to sustain the glaze of sentimentalism. Moreover, the confession is a genre whose self-absorbed persona never leaves center stage—and, again, this mode is very different from the sorts of ethnographies that I am thinking about.[15]

I suspect that what I am pointing to—fieldsites that ethnographers acknowledge as somehow continuous with or answering some life-pattern—is part of the unacknowledged history of ethnography. For it would seem that the ethnographic process of observing the world and making sense of it requires making tenuous negotiations between knowledge claims and memory, partic-

link own experiences to their studies re ethos

ularly the memory of very old experiences whose details have been forgotten, a memory that functions more as a sounding board for recognizing what is important and for providing an assurance, probably based on feeling, that a given claim is true or real. Knowledge, then, would seem to get made in relationship to the sort of memory that I am pointing to here, one that functions very deeply, and would seem to be inseparable from one's character or ethos. This sort of memory or character or ethos that helps to verify and shape knowledge suggests that knowledge is, in part, autobiographical and, similarly, that the fieldsite in very subtle ways, not literally so, is also autobiographical. Let me broaden my argument even further: The real fieldsite observed by a knowledge-making ethnographer eventually becomes the fieldsite of a text, which is the only fieldsite an audience comes to know. Part of the transformation of the first fieldsite into the second is through negotiations that become explicit between observation and memory, between brand new experiences and very old experiences, and it is through processes like these that real fieldsites become understood both as objects of knowledge and as extensions of a life-pattern or ethos. A fieldsite, yes, is a real place to make a certain logos, but as this real fieldsite becomes the fieldsite of the text, which is a somewhat different thing, all kinds of sense-making machinery gets mobilized, machinery that is meant to persuade through any means available. Logos is one means, and ethos, which saturates the moment of inquiry in the sorts of subtle ways that I have tried to outline in this chapter, is, for most readers, its largely invisible partner.[16]

Let me shift from one kind of autobiographical gesture to another, from a set of notes about my own ethos in this text and the role of ethos in ethnographic inquiry to a brief explanation of how this text was made. There were two distinct stages in the making of this project. The first stage began with fieldwork, which lasted from February/March of 1987 to August 1988 and was completed as a dissertation in the English department of the University of Illinois at Chicago. The second stage, which I will discuss shortly, began when I returned to the fieldsite during the summers of 1990 and 1991 and has continued off and on to the present. My involvement in Angelstown, however, started in 1981 when my family and I moved there while I attended graduate school in nearby Chicago. Living in Angelstown, I was an active member in several Latino/a organizations. As a representative of these organizations I participated, for instance, in more mainstream organizations, such as one school board committee and, for a very brief time, on a city-sponsored Image Task Force. In some ways, my research began as an extension of my activism, but I should also say here that throughout my life my own activism has always been compromised by a certain desire to know as completely as possible the positions of the other side and a willingness to sympathize with the Other.[17]

One project that helped launch the first stage of fieldwork and continues to influence my thinking was an oral history project of Mexican immigration to Angelstown that was funded by a small grant from the Illinois Humanities Council. Two other researchers, Irene Campos-Carr and Susan Palmer, who in different ways were more knowledgeable than I of Mexican immigration history and Angelstown's Latino/a communities, and I used this grant to construct a portrait of the history of Mexican immigration to Angelstown.[18] This material plus more has been radically transformed in order to produce the second chapter of this book.

The first stage of fieldwork was devoted to understanding the oral and written language characteristics in the homes of three *mexicano* families. I focused on the children in these homes and how they were acquiring language, particularly English, but I was also interested in adult language uses. Working with the English department's sociolinguist, Marcia Farr, I had acquired an invaluable understanding of the language characteristics of American communities and their similarity or lack of similarity to the language of schooling. Following the leads of Shirley Brice Heath in *Ways With Words* and Ron and Suzanne Scollon's *Narrative, Literacy, and Face in Interethnic Communication*,[19] my work was directed mostly toward an audience of literacy specialists and was meant to have educational implications, although I decided early on to spend almost all of my time inside the homes of these families rather than in the schools. With each family, I took on different social roles: a child's tutor, one who takes children to a park to play baseball or to a museum in Chicago, a builder of Halloween masks, a translator for adults, one who helps adults compose official letters, a friend who passes the time talking or watching TV, and so on. In time, I gathered over three hundred pages of elaborated fieldnotes, ninety-one cassette tapes filled with formal and informal interviews or ongoing conversations, and over a hundred documents consisting of children's writings and drawings or items read and/or written by adults.

In the summers of 1990 and 1991 and as a member of the rhetoric faculty at the University of Iowa, I returned to the fieldsite for lengthy stays, and the second stage of fieldwork began. During these stays, a series of transformations occurred. These transformations continued during shorter trips, which typically occurred over weekends after the summer of 1991. All of these trips were made with Edmundo Cavazos, my research assistant, who is Mexican and, hence, far more fluent in Mexican Spanish than I am. Edmundo's personal skills and his sensitivity toward the verbal art of Mexican Spanish have deeply influenced this text. When we made visits, our base for conducting research was a rear apartment rented by Don Angel, a main character in this text, and a variety of his male roommates who came and went over the years. Don Angel was renting from one of the original families from the first stage of fieldwork. By 1991, another research assistant, Dan Anderson, joined us. Whereas Edmundo helped me understand the Mexican aspects of this text, Dan helped me understand theoretical aspects as well as city leadership.

My original intention for reentering the fieldsite was to broaden my understanding of the workplaces of the adults I had come to know and to reconceive the community more richly by, for instance, doing research inside many of the community grocery stores and businesses. My intention, at first, remained sociolinguistic, but I was quickly losing interest in educational implications because literacy as a scholarly concentration did not seem to allow the broader cultural examination that I aspired to. In short, I found myself moving away from sociolinguistics and toward what I have already described as a project in the rhetorics of public culture or the rhetorics of everyday life. Increasingly, I began to practice semiotic and/or rhetorical readings of cultural material, emphasizing how one set of cultural materials (Latino/a) interacted with other sets (Anglo, African-American, and so on). Moreover, I realized more clearly the porousness of communities and the slippery task of defining such theoretical constructs as "culture" and "community."[20] In sum, I began to imagine ways of talking about socioeconomic and power relationships by reading rhetorically the minutiae of life. If in 1987 I had seen written texts as discrete objects, in 1990 I began to see a written text as a sign system embedded in other sign systems and interpreters of the text as both signs and signers.[21] In addition, I began raising questions of representation, not only my representations of others in a book but also the representations of one people by another. In short, I was abandoning the gaze of the educational expert who measures an instance of oral and written language according to its proximity or distance to a schooled norm. In contrast, becoming a rhetorician of public culture was more satisfying because it entailed a sensitive detailing of the minutiae of life as these get divided by the borderline of power difference. In short, Heath as a theoretical lens had been replaced by Michel de Certeau.[22] This new perspective generated more than two hundred pages of elaborated fieldnotes, over two hundred slides, approximately sixteen hours of videotape, another eighty hours of formal and informal interviews and ongoing conversations, and an uncountable number of city documents, newspaper clippings, and street gang texts (to name only a few).

Earlier, I listed the researchers—Edmundo, Dan, and I—and one of the

text's main figures, Don Angel. In so doing, I wish to emphasize the conditions
that led to a very male-oriented project. The researchers were male, those
whom we had easy access to were males, and the crowded living conditions encouraged a male humor and worldview. In one sense, although I do not wish to
make too much of this, the male in Angelstown's Latino communities was very
conspicuous. For instance, those who had amassed noticeable wealth—namely
grocery store owners and owners of small businesses—were by and large male;
similarly, those who were most noticeable among the youth—namely street
gang members or those who drove "thumpers" (cars notable for their loud
sound systems, particularly the "thumping" bass that sometimes can be heard
long before the car is seen, and sometimes notable for "hydraulics," which
allow the body of the car to move in a number of directions)—were also typically male. In this sense, the fieldsite had an obvious and accessible surface:
maleness. Accessing that which was beyond maleness was sometimes difficult.

 An anecdote: One afternoon I decided to take pictures of teenage girls who
"put up the bangs." "Putting up the bangs" referred to a hairstyle distinguished
by a high crest of hair that rose from the forehead and curled just at the top of
the peak. The style at that time was a semiotic marker quite popular among
teenage girls in the neighborhood, and sometimes it indicated alliances to male
gang members or female street gangs. Typically, the hairstyle was part of an
overall wardrobe. I was trying to collect a series of these pictures to juxtapose
with the equivalent male style. After "cruising" a variety of neighborhoods, I
saw a group of five or six girls with "bangs up" and dressed, moreover, in the
colors, black and gold, of the Almighty Latin King Nation. I turned the block
and came around again. I stopped the car, got out, and approached, camera in
hand. My highly direct walk, age, clothes, gender, and the fact that they knew I
had turned around were my semiotic markings—and they bolted. For me, the
scene summarizes how I remained on the periphery of many forms of female-
ness. I knew many adult women, those who worked on assembly lines and the
daughters of several families, but I never came to know as wide a range of
women as I knew of men. Moreover, I suspect that gender differences explain
why I rarely entered the same depths of conversation with women. If the fieldsite's surface of life, maleness, was relatively accessible, another surface, a more
oppressed one (I leave the word "oppressed" even though it does not capture
my experiences in Anglestown with more subtle male/female relationships)
was less accessible.

 In admitting that in this project the ramifications of gender difference are
not as clear as they might be, I hope to further emphasize my skepticism about

the essentializing instinct that lies behind such phrases as "a culture" or "a community" and the effort to "interpret a culture." Such phrases are empty, such efforts futile. Better put, such phrases and efforts are rhetorical tropes and ploys by which ethnographers create their images of a stable *logos*, "rational argument," "rational knowledge claim." Michele Rosaldo, for instance, was very aware of how these key terms function rhetorically to construct knowledge: "'Cultures,' like 'personalities' are descriptive tropes, lent conviction by their power to illuminate the activities of individuals or groups and organized by our assumptions concerning people and society."[23]

I suspect that to do research in an urban fieldsite characterized by immigration is to give up concepts and interpretive schemes that evoke images of stability. In the field, knowing males better than one knows females is just one sign that one's interpretations are skewed and not as richly conceived as possible. And yet the mind is constantly provoked to conceive and make sense, or, as I described earlier, "make an order." Moreover, the very existence of the social sciences depends on the possibility that one can make sense. In my text, I try to make sense, but I also try to deflect the essentializing tendency by openly admitting that my story/analysis is less about a group of people and the meanings inside their heads, as might be found in a traditional ethnography of a people bounded geographically, linguistically, ritually, and so on. Indeed, I have not searched for a collective set of practices, language habits, or inside-the-head meanings that will help me identify the Mexican immigrant community in Angelstown. At most, I have made use of individually nuanced practices, but even these are not central to what I am writing about. In a strong sense, this text is about the conditions of in-betweenness, an almost unlocatable place. If, for instance, Don Angel and others had interpretations about the practices and beliefs of *curanderos*, "folk healers," those interpretations were important to me and were, in fact, distilled from a variety of interviews, but these interpretations did not tell me much about how *curandería* was imagined by the Anglo middle class, how *curandería* became a semiotic marker arrayed alongside other semiotic markers pointing to Mexicanness, and how the accumulation of these markers became a political problem for those in charge of the economic revitalization of a city. Nor do these interpretations tell me how the children of Mexican immigrants simultaneously despised yet romantically honored the traditional markers. For the Latinos/as in Angelstown, living the in-between life was far more than experiencing the polarity of Mexican versus Anglo. The in-between life also occurred somewhere in the complexity of many socioeconomic levels, the assortment of Latino/a communities, the assortment of eth-

(makes note)

nicities, the varied mix of urban and rural backgrounds, the varied styles of language, the varied levels of education, the varied amount of time spent in the
United States, the varied age levels, the varied subcultures—sometimes determined by gender, sometimes determined by one's legality or illegality, sometimes determined by the split, particularly among youth, between life at home
and life on the streets—and all this within the subculture itself of *latinidad*. It
is as if the in-between life consisted of a density of shadows, a density of nuances, traces of the past and present that were difficult to track. My goal in this
text is to talk of these contradictions and nuances as they appeared in individual
lives. Making matters even more complicated, Arjun Appadurai frames what I
call the "in-between life" inside a broader net of cultural flows circulating in a
global economy.[24] When looked at in this way, the in-between becomes something more than the middle of oppositions; it is more like a locus registering
variables that originate nearby and far away, and it is the mission of this text not
only to consider the nearby (the individual within the community of Angelstown) but also the far away (the global circulation of goods and images).

Exploring the in-between life requires that I concentrate on the proliferation of images and representations that circulated through Angelstown and
constantly search out what might structure the perceived attractiveness or un-
attractiveness of a given image or representation for a particular person. The
main structuring device, as I have said, was a power differential that was largely
socioeconomic and divided one set of images from another, thus making them
mutually attractive. However, where power resided was also sometimes a matter of individual interpretation, and by saying that power was largely the perception of power, I am saying that power too was not essentialized but part of
the network of circulating images and representations. In making such a claim,
I emphasize an interest in epideictic rhetoric broadly conceived, an interest that
I described earlier and one that will become clearer via the details contained in
chapter after chapter.

But I wish to return to where I began (this chapter), to Mercedes, Texas; to a
church there; to a citrus farm about three miles north, just off of Baseline Road;
to return to the lower Rio Grande Valley, the Magic Valley or the Tip o' South
Texas (as its promoters like to call it), or, as it is also called by those who feel a
certain difference, *el valle*. This location on the American landscape, perhaps
not so different from other locations, is a large swirl of social and economic
problems that tightens like a corkscrew into the core of almost every Valley in-
habitant. Like other places American, however, it is also other than this, for the

consumerism that keeps the American bag of tricks afloat has soothed, ameliorated, and masked here as well. The ethos that appears in this book owes much of its making to *el valle* of the fifties and sixties. In one sense, the Valley has never been a fieldsite for me, but, in another sense, because so many of its details prepared me for the real fieldsite that became Angelstown, I suspect that it continues to act as a kind of filtering mythos and pathos, a way of seeing Angelstown, of feeling it, of speaking its languages, of knowing it.

2

MAPPING/TEXTING

"The city is a huge monastery," said Erasmus. Perspective vision and prospective vision constitute the twofold projection of an opaque past and an uncertain future onto a surface that can be dealt with.
—Michel de Certeau, *The Practice of Everyday Life*

the lay of the land

I begin with a meditation on a map. A map is a representation, an abstraction, "a surface that can be dealt with." It is the product of an exacting rationality, and it furthers the conquest of system-making over the melange of the everyday. It satisfies what the poet Wallace Stevens called the "blessed rage for order."

Today, I have a map of Angelstown spread out on the floor in the office where I sit writing. The map is a ward map—and it is large: six and a half by four feet. As I write, I construct a representation of Angelstown, and the map itself is another constructed representation. In short, here are two representations of the same town, a town that has become vaguely exotic because it exists almost two hundred miles away from this office and, most importantly, because it is the "fieldsite."

For those who read and write ethnographies, the fieldsite is an ethnographic trope that generates both the spell of the exotic (romance) and resistance (science) to that spell. Long ago, ethnographers might have begun their accounts of the exotic with a "utopian scene of first contact."[1] Consider this opening from Raymond Firth's account of his landing on the South Sea island of Tikopia:

> In the cool of the early morning, just before sunrise, the bow of the *Southern Cross* headed towards the eastern horizon, on which a tiny dark blue outline was faintly visible. Slowly it grew into a rugged mountain mass, standing up sheer from the ocean; then as we approached within a few miles it revealed around its base a narrow ring of low, flat land, thick with vegetation. The sullen grey day with its lowering clouds strengthened my grim impression of a solitary peak, wild and stormy, upthrust in a waste of waters.
>
> In an hour or so we were close inshore, and could see canoes coming round from the south, outside the reef, on which the tide was low . . . . I wondered how such turbulent human material could ever be induced to submit to scientific study.[2]

The classic ethnographer, like a god or a balloonist descending from the clouds (or, like Firth, approaching from the sea), began his or her account with an overview of an exotic reality. I, instead, begin with an overview of something less, a worn map, whose apparent mundaneness, in comparison, seems comical. This map deflates the exotic and, in so doing, amplifies it. The breadth and width of Angelstown, its complexities and conflicts, the shooting at the corner of Front and Jefferson, Don Angel's small apartment at the corner of Lincoln and Superior—all these particulars that belong to the exoticness of Angelstown are displaced by a text roughly the size of a double bed. Instead of a conflicted hymn to the Tikopia, which was Firth's project, I write a conflicted hymn to a large and somewhat shabby map. My "utopian scene of first contact" concerns not Angelstown itself but something a bit less, its thin representation on paper. This writing strategy, less idealistic and, perhaps, more jaded than the strategies of the past, seems appropriate for this era of sociocultural anthropology, which for a number of decades has mourned the loss of an erotic and conflicted ideal: the desire to witness the incomprehensible and simultaneously to report on it without sterilizing it. That desire, magnificently embodied in Lévi-Strauss's *Tristes Tropiques* and, perhaps, Firth's *We, the Tikopia*, has entailed something dehumanizing in so far as it exoticized/eroticized its object—made it alien, different, distant—in order to appease the restless, possessive, envious, God-abandoned spirit of the West that needed, for its own salvation, contact with what it thought were the messages of raw primitivism. But what if we were to write, in part, an ethnography about exacting rationality, system making, and the kinds of texts that further such projects? Where would we start? Would we not have to dispense with the conventions of nature writing—those sunsets, sunrises, wild storms, towering mountains, impenetrable forests, desert landscapes, barren white snows, the play of light on water, in short, the exoticness of strangers and their environs when first contacted? Indeed.

This map is a kind of text or, better yet, a good example of the discourses of measurement.[3] Measurement, of course, is central to a map since everything is drawn to scale. A certain length of real space becomes one inch of map space. With this reduction, then, we understand a whole system of reductions: for instance, on this map height and depth disappear and become flat; details of the terrain—trees, alleys, sidewalks, houses—disappear, and the ways to traverse a city become prominent. In a sense, numerous locales are washed of their reality, and what is left is their abstractness held in relationship to each other. It may be easier to "see" relationships when realities are executed for the sake of heightened abstractions. If this map, then, reduces real and ever changing particulars, it amplifies abstract relationships—and this is the service it performs. Loss and gain perform their eternal dance.[4]

One of the clearest relationships displayed on this map is the difference between the oldest parts of the city and its newer, outlying areas. The city streets in these two areas have different geometries. The city proper, for instance, old and in many parts decayed, particularly where we did our fieldwork, is laid out in gridlike fashion. But the grid is not absolute. A winding river splits the city, and, in response, the grid adjusts itself, more or less, in order to maintain right angles to the river. The dominant impression is of orderliness, of city blocks cut into more or less uniform dimensions. This orderly laying out of the city, which occurred almost at the city's founding, allowed traffic to be regulated and enabled the first parcels of land to be more easily bought and sold so that the first commercial enterprises and industries could be built along the banks of the river.

In contrast, the outlying areas of the city contain new housing developments whose streets snake circuitously. Many of these areas were annexed by the city in the early 1970s, 140 years after the founding of the city. History, then, separates the city proper from the outlying areas. The recent and the old follow different geometries. Why is this? Does circuity signal an escape from the immediate past (the temporal dimension) as well as older geometries (the spatial dimension)? The grid as confinement—think here of the phrase "the straight and narrow"—is broken by circuity. Indeed, circuity, in this case, is associated with a whole range of escapes: the accumulation of income, the ownership of more space, the relative assurance that similar price tags on property mean similarity of outlook among property owners, and the zoning guarantee that one's residence will be free of commercial noise and traffic.[5] The meander that sometimes ends at a cul de sac has become the geometric design associated with those who manage the goods and services of society. The meander signals a break from more routinized behavior, particularly that of work. It is one more symbol of an escape from the city grid and its management of space, movement, and large populations. If the city grid is a synecdoche for the social controls that manage so many of our moments, then we can understand the allure of escape and how the geometry of circuity can further a fantasy.

We can explore this distinction between the rhetoric of the grid and the rhetoric of circuity by considering their histories. For some urban planners and architects—Le Corbusier, for instance—the grid as symbol of rationality was a visionary revolution. He imagined a kind of modernist order, itself ordered to the logic of the cosmos, as having the power to sweep away a past characterized by inefficiency, pestilence, unhappiness, and disorganization. Writing in 1924 in *The City of To-morrow* , he despised what he called the "Pack-Donkey's Way," emblem of all that was wrong with the contemporary city:

> But a modern city lives by the straight line, inevitably; for the construction of buildings, sewers and tunnels, highways, pavements. The circulation of traffic demands the straight line; it is the proper thing for the heart of a city. The curve is ruinous, difficult and dangerous; it is a paralyzing thing.
>
> The straight line enters into all human history, into all human aim, into every human act.
>
> We must have the courage to view the rectilinear cities of America with admiration. If the aesthete has not so far done so, the moralist, on the contrary, may well find more food for reflection than at first appears.
>
> The winding road is the Pack-Donkey's Way, the straight road is man's way.
>
> The winding road is the result of happy-go-lucky heedlessness, of looseness, lack of concentration and animality.

Gridlike layout of an area close to the downtown of Angelstown.

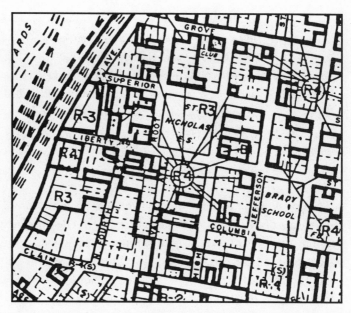

Winding streets and cul-de-sacs of a recently developed area of wealthy homes on the far eastern perimeter of Angelstown.

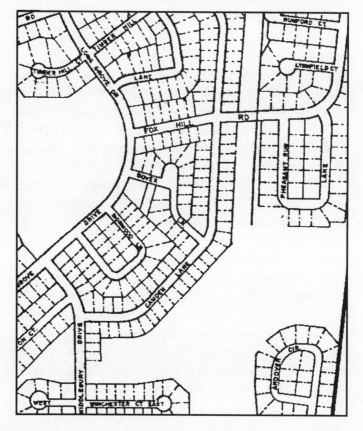

> The straight road is a reaction, an action, a positive deed, the result of self-mastery. It is sane and noble.
>
> A city is a centre of intense life and effort.
>
> A heedless people, or society, or town, in which effort is relaxed and is not concentrated, quickly becomes dissipated, overcome and absorbed by a nation or a society that goes to work in a positive way and controls itself.
>
> It is in this way that cities sink to nothing and that ruling classes are overthrown.[6]

At one point in history, circuity would seem to mean everything that is backward—or that is how Le Corbusier saw it. But decades later, after his revolutionary logic ran itself dry, a kind of romanticization of circuity emerged: not a circuity of some necessarily "real" past but, more than likely, some invented past. The circuity in these suburbs, then, is not by happenstance (the Pack-Donkey's way) but just as rationally conceived as the city grid—and maybe more so. Hence, because circuity was specifically chosen by builders and buyers, we are given the opportunity to explore their motives. In short, the builders have seized some cultural trope or theme that animates their customers, and this shared trope that I am calling "circuity" means that both builders and customers are connected rhetorically.

One way to explore this shared trope is to consider the rhetoric of place-names. The city proper, by using the names of its founders for parks, streets, and certain buildings, assures that its history stays present. Of course, such naming came into being through rivalry and malice as well as honorable intentions, but how do we make sense of the street names of the newer and circuitous subdivisions? "Castlewood Ct.," "Montclare Ct.," "Carriage Ct.," "Asbury Dr.," "Cheshire Dr.," "Brookshire Ln.," "Briargate Ln.," "Heathgate Dr.," "Seasons Ridge Blvd.," "Greenbriar," "Queens Gate," "Windemere Ct.," "Autumn Ridge Dr.," "Tudor Ct.," "Andover Ct.," "Regency Ct.," "Knightsbridge Ct.," "Normandy Ct.," "Essex Ct.," "Buckingham Dr."—I have made a selection, of course, but many of these names seem devoid of both local history and local landscape. What sorts of images are these place-names meant to create? There is the suggestion of escape into an English countryside with castles, shires, and gates, of remote pasts and natural environments. And these images seem to be in keeping with a geometry of circuity: a life that wants to free itself of gnawing necessity wanders through history and nature—or so the associations might go. But this suggests too easily a dichotomy between the names of city streets and those of subdivisions. Remember, city street-names too conjure images of inspiration ("Lincoln," "Liberty," and "Superior") and pleasantness ("Grove" and "Rosewood"). The rhetoric of place-names everywhere on this map, then, is part of a network of idealizations that enable the buying and selling of property. The map itself is a subjugation of reality that makes place-names and their conjuring idealizations/evocations—English countrysides, founding fathers, high ideals, and sentimentalized nature—salient. These names that idealize and evoke create the imagery that buyers desire for themselves—so it is that a cash economy is like a sail blown by the wind of imagining desire.

However, the reality behind the idealized surface of the map is a different story. For instance, significant sections of "Lincoln," "Liberty," "Superior," and "Grove" (all within the grid of the city) are also known as the territory of the Almighty Latin King Nation, a street gang and chapter of a national organization. The Latin Kings, with their selling of cocaine and their rhetoric of a separate "nation" that articulates the imagery of autonomy, frighten the status quo by shattering the image of a single and stable national culture. It is the intent of the police, then, to "recover" the streets—or, in the language of this argument, to recover the mythic stabilities, to restore a collapsed ideal that place-names all across America articulated and manipulated in order to sell local real estate.

Outside the city grid and the circuitry of the subdivisions is further hope. These are the open lands within the boundaries of the city. At first, the opposition between open land and already occupied land seems to be that of blank space versus delineated space, of absence versus human presence. The map suggests that in these open spaces human action has yet to detail its desires. But the need to maintain economic health so that life will be improved keeps driving the colonization of the formless. (Land is only one version of the formless; the mind, body, and society are other versions. All represent different focal points, objects of knowledge to be colonized by the encompassing intellect—through a discourse of measurement—and all are improved by colonization—or so the thought goes—so that land is made more productive and the mind, body, and society become better understood.)[7] Therefore, these blank spaces on a map, these areas of formlessness, are not really formless, for city planners have already worked over these empty spaces, projecting and calculating. These are the future industrial parks and the commercial and residential centers that are coming, and for a city trying to pull itself out of the kind of local economic problems that became most noticeable during the 1970s and 1980s, these locations represent a golden future.

An abstract rendering of the city's layout, 1980s–1990s

W	West Side	Near West Side	Downtown and river	Near East Side and fieldsite	Open land	Far East Side, newer mall, and wealthy subdivisions	E

Angelstown's "Comprehensive Plan, Industrial Land Use," which was prepared by the Department of City Planning and dated December 1980, provides insights about these blank spaces that the map that I have been examining cannot. The words "Comprehensive Plan" are significant. They continue to echo Le Corbusier's loud insistence fifty years earlier in *The Radiant City* that cities must have a "Plan." All these instances reiterate the notion of the overview and the actions of shaping and managing through the discourses of measurement. The pamphlet opens, interestingly, with a map of Angelstown. This is followed by eight statistical tables "mapping" since 1950 the city's population, labor force, industrial work force, and industrial acreage and projecting the same for the year 2000. These tables, like maps, are another set of reductions of thick particulars, guiding us, this time, not through physical space but through time, both past and future. In table 2.1 I reprint a series of numbers from the first table in the Comprehensive Plan in order to suggest that, as with a map, under apparent fixity lies a palpable elusiveness:

Table 2.1

Statistics from Angelstown Comprehensive Plan

	1960	1963	1970	1973
Population	63,700	66,850	74,200	75,955
Labor Force	27,632	28,043	32,836	35,267
Industrial Workers	11,360	17,456	21,230	26,141

Puzzle 1: How do we define "labor force" and "industrial workers"? Do the terms include part-time workers? Are teenagers counted? Are people who work more than one job double-counted? What sizes and what kinds of businesses and industries are included and excluded? Are the self-employed included? What political and economic motives underlie the gathering of these particular statistics?

Puzzle 2: How do we explain the appearance of 6,096 industrial workers between 1960 and 1963 but not see a comparable growth in the labor force? Did, for instance, a comparable number from other segments of the labor force simultaneously flee? The ratio of labor force to industrial workers during the other years seems reasonable, and this suggests that the numbers for 1960 and 1963 may be correct. If they are, it suggests that large numbers of people are strangely present for one category but strangely absent for another. Who were these people and where were they?

Puzzle 3: Another anomaly again appears between 1970 and 1973. Population growth is small, only 1,755 (the city admits that the number for 1973 is an interpolation), but the increase (4,911) of industrial workers is, again, rapid. Why doesn't an increase of industrial workers also increase estimates of the general population?

Puzzle 4: The more we consider these figures, we realize that the labor force, including the industrial workers, need not be living inside the city since their statistics do not necessarily come from the city census. So where do they come from? At the bottom of this table, there are footnotes that list such documents as the "1966 General Plan, Angelstown" and the "Illinois Bureau of Employment Security, December 1977." The labor statistics, then, come from these documents. To understand their data-gathering methods, we would have to retrieve those documents and scrutinize their sources. These constitute for us a potential labyrinth of reference.

Puzzle 5: Let me confuse matters more. During the late 1960s, as we will soon see, a large number of Mexicans and Puerto Ricans began arriving in Angelstown.[8] Many of the Mexicans, then and later, came illegally. The inability of census takers to find the undocumented is a notorious problem.[9] But the undocumented are only one aspect of a more generalized illegal world intent on protecting itself. During our research Edmundo, Dan, and I encountered a team of defrauders, numerous drug dealers, and several people purported to be assassins. Beyond these, however, were the rumors of others being operators of gambling rings and forgers. Several times, in fact, Edmundo and I talked of the world of appearances and how it masked over what we later learned. Literally, every grocery store owner was rumored to be involved in illegal services, and one of them was assassinated a few months after being interviewed by us. Any discourse of measurement faces enormous problems in gathering reliable information in communities that are scrambling to maintain themselves economically.

Puzzle 6: Subsequent statistical tables reveal that the city is projecting a population of 150,000 in the year 2000. (At this writing, 1996, the population is

50,000 inhabitants short.) Population projections are then multiplied by labor force and industrial force percentages for prior years until a projection is made concerning the numbers of workers and industrial workers for the year 2000. These numbers, then, are submitted to mathematical calculations in order to determine the necessary industrial acreage that will employ the projected numbers of workers. From these calculations, the city determines how much land to devote to industrial development as opposed to other business developments. The colonization of the open spaces on the map is, in part, guided by these discourses of measurement. In short, policy making emerges from these kinds of documents. However, each projected line of numbers represents another set of assumptions that ignores the thickness and unpredictability of reality. As the clean, numerical logic ascends step by step, the accumulating flaws in the structure create an ever widening fissure between difficult human material and the clarity and exactness of numbers that attempt to mold that material.

Let me pause here in order to modify what I appear to be saying. These documents and the discourses that fill them guide policy makers less than one imagines. For instance, Angelstown's "Comprehensive Plan, Industrial Land Use" was eventually revised, forgotten, and shelved alongside other documents like it (and well it should have been since its population estimate of 150,000 by the year 2000 will, more than likely, prove to be remarkably off.) In short, figures, no matter how exact, do not necessarily convince the common sense of policy makers. Hans-Georg Gadamer locates common sense as part of the lifeworld, which "proclaims itself distinct from the scientific world of things and objects discernible through the idea of methodological knowledge."[10] I call the lifeworld the site of rhetoric. Thus, the lifeworld is the site for those endless wrangles among city officials about the zoning of land and how much is to be zoned and which companies to attract and the wrangles between city and company officials and the deals that are struck and the deals that are lost and the readjustments that must occur before company X locates itself in Angelstown. The "Comprehensive Plan" with its pristine numbers and idealized logic was, on the one hand, an opening gambit, a rhetorical move that made use of the discourses of measurement in order to appear exact so as to structure ensuing arguments over land use.

On the other hand, the "Comprehensive Plan" did more than just lay out the bases for future arguments; it also *represented* the argument for economic development. In this representation, development was a given and, therefore, impossible to critique because it was so thoroughly enmeshed within the cultural topos that economic development is a major goal of city governments. It was also enmeshed in a social reality, which I will document later, of recent factory closings. In these kinds of situations, a social reality limits imaginative options so that policy makers are left only with the options (topoi) that a culture has already given them. These options, thus, acquire a kind of deep reality and go unargued. In short, in contemporary America the argument for economic development has become "naturalized," a common sense response, backed up by facts and figures, to urban crises. No other option seems reasonable, and so the "Comprehensive Plan" made its land use, population, and labor force projections from the assumption that only economic growth could solve social problems. However, by the late 1980s and early 1990s after the unprecedented growth in both population (approximately 25,000 in twenty years) and jobs (the city made itself attractive to insurance companies, a gambling casino, and other service industries), social problems only became more notorious in the poorer parts of the city. Indeed, the response to social problems, as we will see, began to shift toward more aggressive measures: zero-tolerance of crime, rezoning of housing in the poorer areas from multiple-family to single-family, and an assortment of other ordinances meant to improve the "image" of the city. In effect, the controlling of social problems was no longer in the hands of laissez-faire economic development in which the mere creation of jobs supposedly solves everything. City policy began increasingly to include an aggressive transformation of property values, which, in turn, would, it was hoped, dislodge the poorer populations and push them elsewhere.

I return to the map. Its most obvious characteristic is its division into wards. It may be helpful here to frame our understanding of a ward map in recent theories about the public sphere. Nancy Fraser, moving beyond the work of Jürgen Habermas, summarizes in exemplary fashion what the term "public sphere" designates. Fraser describes the public sphere as functioning at two levels: at one level, it designates an institutional mechanism by which the state becomes accountable to the citizenry; at another level, it designates "a specific kind of discursive interaction," "an ideal of unrestricted rational discussion of public matters."[11] We might understand a ward map, then, as an ironic document, for behind it one can see simultaneous attempts both to realize the public sphere as a plethora of voices that will contend with government but also as something to be shaped according to the images of democracy that reverberate inside the heads of those powerful enough to map. If a city grid consisting of straight streets crossing at ninety-degree angles, then, is an efficient way to manage the movement of people and goods, ward maps represent the management of the body politic, hence, public discussion.

Stories about the drawing and redrawing of ward and precinct boundaries in order to serve some individual's or some constituency's political interests abound in American politics. Wards are abstract communities whose identities are manufactured during political wrangles, wrangles that often depend on interpretations of census data. Angelstown contains its own stories about quickly shifting ward boundaries. During the 1980s and 1990s, the wards in Angelstown were configured and reconfigured numerous times. In 1988, for instance, ward 2, which is where most of our fieldwork occurred, had a bizarre design that tried to yoke together the mostly poor, minority communities of the near east side and some of the affluent subdivisions on the far east side that I described earlier as following the rhetoric of circuity. It was well known in the city that ward 2 candidates of that era had the almost impossible task of representing what, in effect, were two separate towns. Late in 1990, the mayor of Angelstown redrew the boundaries before the new census had come out, thus almost instigating a lawsuit. Insiders in the mayor's office saw the redrawing as an attempt to eliminate the schizophrenia of ward 2. In effect, ward 2 had its western boundaries slightly extended so that they crossed the river, and its eastern portions were divided so as to produce two new wards. The mayor hoped, it was said, that ward 2, now newly fashioned, might elect a Latino/a and, in its new neighboring ward, an African-American. In contrast to these poorer wards, the far east side now also had its own ward to help consolidate its wealthier identity. As one might imagine, the exact placement of the new boundaries was caught in the push and pull of political forces that persisted long after the election. The interviews I had with the mayor and that Dan Anderson had with one of the alderpersons verified the anger that had been stirred by this boundary dispute. During one of our most engaging afternoons, Dan and I heard it this way from one of the most savvy of Angelstown's Latino political leaders: "I was not there when he (the mayor) drew it. . . . I question the city . . . if you want to really make a minority district, why are you pushing it so far west side to include so many Whites? . . . What I'm saying is, if you really have a true interest in making a minority district, why are you splitting it like that? Why are you making so many divisions? And it was obvious that he . . . didn't want to be perceived as the individual who made the district for Hispanics."

As he spoke, he made the point that even the so-called African-American district could be won by a Latino because that area included a considerable number of "Hispanic home owners." And so it goes, the discourse over ward and precinct boundaries. In Angelstown, Latino leaders struggled for their place in the public sphere, but so did African-Americans, Whites, and, probably cutting across ethnicity and race, the monied versus the unmonied. In Angelstown, the public sphere was deeply fissured, and so the constant drawing and redrawing of ward and precinct boundaries reflected contentious desires that, on the one hand, wanted to give voice to some fissured segment and, on the other hand, to gag some other segment.

Is it possible to imagine in all this that a scrupulous drawer of a ward map could have fixed an eye on block by block census figures and told the hand to faithfully transcribe, making map reality jive with street reality, and allowed, finally, for the public sphere to bloom in all its variety? Such an eye and hand do not exist, for any unit as large as ward 2 could not enter the public sphere with any singular Latino voice. Puerto Ricans, *mexicanos, tejanos* (Mexican-Americans from Texas), younger Chicanos, the undocumented, *cheros*,[12] store owners, gang members, and more constituted a set of fissures that representative government could not pay heed to except by generalizing from the whole roiling mass of it until particularity itself dissolved into something far more bland called the Latino community of Angelstown. No matter what jigsaw pattern emerged on an Angelstown ward map, segments of the community would be heard and others would not. The Latino leader quoted above, for instance, admitted that he could not fathom gang membership, that it made his own *latinidad* look bad, that it stood in the way of creating the kind of city image that attracts investment. For him, street gangs did not offer "rational discursive interaction," and so their voice of anger, upheaval, and vatic challenge thrown like a gauntlet at the feet of authority could not be heard by most Latino leaders. Or witness the fact that the Latina candidate who ran against a White in ward 2 in 1991 lost, in part, because she alienated older Latino neighborhood leaders who didn't like her procedures or even the idea of a female candidate; and among the Whites, her "heavy Spanish accent" was unappealing, the sign of a foreigner. One of her campaign managers said there were other reasons as well, certain personal failings, but the point is that in these instances the public sphere presents itself more as a site in which the struggle to be heard is matched by the struggle to silence others, rather than a site for rational discursive interaction.

And silence speaks loudly when the silent become acculturated to silence; indifference settles in, for whatever reasons, and most do not vote. In ward 2, for instance, approximately 79 percent of the registered voters did not vote in the 1991 election. Of course, democratic participation in the public sphere is realizable through means other than voting, but, as we will see later in chapter 6, the public sphere can never be a place for equally contending "rational" voices when the society itself is so fissured that an accent, a gender, an appearance, or an action can by itself signal in the minds of some a discourse that should not be heard. But the problem may run even deeper than human bias. It may be structurally impossible to hear all contending voices when the sheer plethora of voices is too numerous. For instance, providing a general category such as "Hispanic" on census figures may appear to encourage democratic participation, and yet any generality subsumes a plethora of contentious voices and a whole range of distinctive characteristics. To a significant degree, these voices and characteristics must be sacrificed in order to be brought together under the umbrella of a generality.

The problem, then, behind this ward map and all the feuding over ward and precinct boundaries may go beyond the problems of how a city's power brokers control or liberate democratic participation in the public sphere. The deeper structural problem may be a tension between the particular and the general. As particulars multiply and become more complex, the ability of any general scheme to cast its net over the entirety becomes more and more difficult. If each particular represents an array of characteristics, it is only through the reduction of this array that any general scheme can be even imagined. As we apply these reductions to an ever larger number of particulars, the generality itself may become increasingly dislodged from whatever it meant to explain in the first place. The holes in this net may be wide indeed. The city kept shifting its ward boundaries, arguing over percentages of this or that group, cutting up the city into abstract units in order to manage the city more adequately. Despite the shortcomings of ward making, however, one needs to inquire whether or not a better system exists. If the problem is the management of large populations, can a net made of fabric other than exacting rationality and system making be cast over such an unwieldly monster? In short, Fraser rightly points out that differences of income, gender, language proficiency, and so on may be associated with social inequalities that muddy the possibility of equal and democratic participation in the public sphere, but to these social problems one might add an obdurate structural problem rooted in the very size of our social systems. Let us assume, then, that large populations are, indeed, unwieldly monsters, that in the management of such systems the small-scale and large-scale oppressions that result have ideological origins but they may have structural ones as well.

Thus far, my analysis has been admittedly speculative. I have suggested that place names have a rhetorical dimension that can be uncovered and that city grids and subdivision meanders represent different geometries that are rhetorically (some might say semiotically) opposed, hence, related. I have also discussed the colonization of formlessness, and suggested how the statistical tables of city planners represent idealized arguments that eventually enter the rhetorical and common-sense wrangles of the lifeworld. I have also made the point that the making of wards is a strangely abstract game that attempts to make cohesive an array of particular lives. I have lumped these speculations together and made the point that a map is an abstraction or representation, a kind of text that, like certain other texts, is both a lie and an important revelation.[12]

the lay of histories/the lay of texts

A map, then, is one kind of optical knowledge that comes into being after real space overwhelms the eye. We transform real space onto a "surface that can be dealt with," and in so doing we recover and extend the power of the eye. Our confidence grows. We have transformed matter: that which was large has found its smaller representation—but not its equivalent. This making of things material—a map as the material representation of space, or the transformation of thoughts and feelings into art objects—gives dominion to the eye and hand. But at the moment of dominion, I, at least, begin to feel a subtle estrangement.

What is before me now is another kind of optical knowledge, another text, another overview—in this case, of historical events. It is the first recorded history of Angelstown published in 1858 in the *Angelstown City Directory and Business Advertiser*. After 1858, versions of this same history appeared in subsequent directories and became a kind of canonized history. Later in the next century, when the city needed to celebrate a centennial or sesquicentennial or a newspaper article needed to talk about the city's founding, authors turned to it as a primary source. The author of the history is not firmly established, but on the title page of the document is the name of the publisher and compiler: Alasco D. Brigham. It is a good bet that Brigham, then, was also the author of the history. At any rate, I will refer to him as such throughout this text.

What is far less ambiguous was the purpose of the *Directory/Advertiser* and the role of the history contained therein. The whole document was meant to promote the city to its own inhabitants but particularly to eastern investors and settlers. Angelstown in 1858 was one more "western" city, and in order to insure a thriving economy, it had to create an attractive image that might compete with the images of all other western cities. To this end, the style of the history is often times folksy and risqué, naming the local famous and infamous, and recounting the stories that made them so. But something else is at work in the text, and in order to consider this other element I quote from the first three pages:[13]

History of Angelstown

I pick up a pebble on the sea shore. It is a conglomeration. It has a history—a history that might fill volumes and yet not be fully written. But it is older than man upon the earth, older than the beasts of the field, older than the Cedars of Lebanon, older than the sea on whose shore it is found. But how shall we fill pages with the history of a quarter of a century or less? 'Tis the history of man—swift-moving, path-finding man—whose life is a span, is of greater interest than the thousand ages that preceded him.

But his history is not engraven on the rocky table; rather is it printed in plastic wax, that take [sic] the impressions not so much of the events that transpire, as of the fancy or prejudices of the moulder's hand. Nothing is more uncertain than human history, [sic] it furnishes its closest student with an interminable range of controversy. We read history and suppose we read facts, but there is more of fancy perhaps. It was Raleigh, I believe, who once contemplated writing a history of the world. One day he saw a fisticuff fight between two men under his window; an hour after he saw two other men disputing about the history of the fight; he joined them, and tried to explain the mystery, but the three found themselves unequal to the task. Raleigh smiled as he reflected how presumptuous would be his attempt to write a history of the whole world, when three eyewitnesses could not agree on the data of a single scene, and abandoned his scheme of becoming a cosmopolite historian.

True, I am not about to attempt a history of the world, but it is the next thing to it—the history of the city in which I live. As Oliver Holmes says in his "Autocrat," there is a town in Massachusetts where they read a line from Pope thus:

"All are but parts of one stupendous Hull."

Data will, doubtless, sometimes be found to be incorrect, and be thought so, much oftener. Some will blame me for recording a disagreeable circumstance connected with their friends, others for not giving their enemies particular "jessie." I have sometimes almost wished the world might be as wise as the jolly Scotch Doctor, who prided himself on not having a single historical fact in his memory; —that the past might rest in peace, and never be called up to excite either fruitless discussion, sectional animosity, national pride, or mortification. But Bacon says "histories make men wise," and so, I suppose, we must believe it.

The most pleasing and inspiring book of man's history is that which tells of his exodus—of the daring adventurers, who in ancient times went out into the world to conquer empires and found dynasties, and still more of those who in modern times, no less daring, but with a nobler motive seek homes and independence in the howling wilderness, and become the pioneers of a civilization that contains the germ of indefinite expansion and progress. We read that this exodus commenced when the tongues were confounded at Babel. In the Babel of the New World, men and women of every nation, speech and kindred meet, and are bound together again by the various ties of patriotism, fraternity and kin. Thus the circle of human brotherhood has been completed. Let us now build a tower which shall stand forever. Let it be founded in the recognition of the rights of man as man, and let that tower be Liberty.

In early times, the camp of the marauding emigrant-conquerer, became the nucleus of settlements, and the future seat of learning, government, luxury and vice. In modern times a saw or grist-mill, or some quiet creek whose obstructed waters turns willingly the wheel for the modest mechanic, becomes the center of population and interest. It was so with our city.

In the autumn of 1833, a young man by the name of Joseph McCarty, a millwright by trade, about twenty-four years of age, left his native town, Elmira, N.Y., to carve out a fortune for himself in the Great West.

He descended the Ohio River, and spent a part, at least, of the winter in the South. In the Spring he ascended the Illinois river on a tour of "prospecting." He found the points he had thought of already occupied, and moved on up the valley of the Fern river, and in April 1834 arrived at the Indian village of Wau-bon-sie and his tribe, on the west bank of Fern river, just north of where Angelstown is now situated, and on what is called the McNamara farm. Here he found a swift river and an Island facilitating the building of a dam, and with Robert Faracre, a man he had hired in Ottawa, and John Barsley, a youth whom he had brought with him as an apprentice, he "drove stakes," by erecting a log cabin 14 by 16 feet. This was built near where the saw-mill is now situated, on the east side, where he claimed about 360 acres. He subsequently built one on the west side, where Dunning's block now stands, to hold his claim on that side, which was about 100 acres.

. . . About the same time a squatter had made a claim of some four hundred acres south of and adjoining McCarty's claim. He bought out this claim for his brother Samuel, a junior by two years, whom he expected soon, paying the squatter sixty dollars for it. It is now worth something more.

Having secured lands and tenements, the next thing in order was a dam . . .

How does one make sense of the relationship between the text above and the supposed events that it recorded? The overwhelming number of particulars occurring from 1833 to 1858 in a relatively small area on the banks of a small river were transformed into a booklet that the hand can hold and the eye read. What is before me, then, is another kind of optical knowledge, another text, another overview. Unlike the map, however, this text acknowledges the limits of its own action. It doubts its own possibility. Whereas with the map we had to uncover its degree of falsity without any hope that it *itself* might agree or disagree with us, with this text we have Brigham's own words to validate our analyses: "history is not engraven on the rocky table; rather is it printed in plastic wax, that take [*sic*] the impressions not so much of the events that transpire, as of the fancy or prejudices of the moulder's hand."

I imagine Brigham this way: a local historian/writer with real talent and, perhaps, some pretension, producing a text a few years before the Civil War in a "western" town whose obscurity rivaled, perhaps, his own in the world of letters of his time. The purpose of his text was the furthering of local commerce in the midst of western competition for eastern talent and investment. His goal was to create an image of his town that would maintain the investment that already existed and attract even more. Like Joseph McCarty before him and the whole train of city officials, publicists, and business people after him, he had to fix for his readers a sense of unusual prosperity and opportunity in a special place called Angelstown. Since his charm and skill were quite exceptional, his text became a synecdoche for the city. His language—charming, educated, witty, worldly, practical—*was* the city in miniature, and this city, now artfully textualized, could become for a reader an object of allure. Of course, first-hand knowledge of the city (or disbelieving cynicism) might free the reader of this textualized version, but lacking these we are easily suckered. With these possibilities in mind, let's dig into his text.

Perhaps the most dramatic tension is that between the Potawatomis and the early settlers. Later in Brigham's text, the Potawatomis are described as "simple-hearted children of the forest," whereas McCarty and his fellow settlers are daring moderns in the "howling wilderness," "pioneers of a civilization that contains the germ of indefinite expansion and progress." Indeed, if we examine the artful construction of Brigham's text, what is prominent is the long (six paragraphs) introduction/paean to civilized history. He begins with the innocuous pebble that cannot textualize itself and dismisses it so as to celebrate "pathfinding man," who can. The distinction is between unconsciousness and consciousness. As we will see, unconsciousness eventually becomes associated with those cultures that do not leave a record of themselves, while consciousness becomes associated with high culture, particularly Western civilization and its ability to create a historical record by which the present becomes consciously aware of its relationship to the past. Through the figures of Raleigh, Oliver Holmes, Pope, Bacon, and such biblical places as Babel, which melts into the founding of America (the Babel of the New World), Brigham notes high culture's ability to become conscious of its history. Moreover, in the worldview of Brigham's idealism, almost every moment of the civilized scene is a confirmation of destiny. (But let's not forget that he has other voices, more skeptical ones such as his nonchalant "I suppose" as a reply to Bacon's more pompous "histories make men wise.") He rounds off his high paean with his most simple and unaffected, therefore, seductive sentence—"It was so with our city"—and in so doing not only introduces his city's history but also suggests that every dam that harnesses the river, every nail put into a board carries those same flashes of civilization.

However, in order to find the moment of juxtaposed cultures—Potawatomis versus early settlers—and the turbulences that this moment represents in American history, I turn to Samuel McCarty's own words written in 1875, forty-one years after he helped begin the settlement with his brother Joseph:

> The old chief, Waubonsie, was a large and powerful man, six feet four inches, weighing about two hundred pounds and as straight as–an Indian. The most of their village was composed of movable or temporary wigwams, as the tribe was a wandering and unsettled people. They spent their summers here on the Fern River but would emigrate to the south to spend the winter on the Illinois or Kankakee, returning in the spring. The old chief's wigwam, being the capitol of the tribe, was built very substantially, apparently to stand for centuries, the posts and frames being of red cedar. The "palace" was built with a good deal of mechanical skill, although the mortices through the posts for the girders were chopped with their tomahawks, but in much better style than you would think possible with such a tool. The building was about 20 feet wide by 30 feet long. It was built by setting

the posts firmly in the ground, forming four bents, with girders over-
head and ridge pole. The principal rafter and cross-bearers were very
ingeniously put together to gain strength to withstand the heavy
gales of the prairie. There was a hall about ten feet wide running
through the building with a door at each end. The rafters and all of the
cross rafters were small straight poles, with the bark all pealed off,
which made them appear neat and comely.[14]

Mary Louise Pratt has elaborated the connections between travel accounts
and ethnographies.[15] McCarty's account shares some of the discursive practices
of both. We might call his account a kind of proto-ethnography or a description of "first contact." The discourse of measurement is quite noticeable: He
estimates the size of Waubonsie and his wigwam, and details characteristics of
the wigwam and its method of construction. Further, his discourse of measurement relies on the "to be" verb (eleven instances in this paragraph) to reinforce
the existence of his observations. It is interesting to consider here how nouns
under the conditions of the copula seem to lose their linguistic origin and move
toward a deeper identification with the objects being signified. In short, a noun
like "hall" is not taken as one choice from an array of nouns or other linguistic
possibilities, but as a reality now labeled. Although his purpose is to provide
"facts" (and we read him as doing so), subtle translations of what he "saw" are
embedded inside his text. For instance, some of the more noticeable translations consist of the wigwam becoming "the capitol of the tribe" and a "palace."
These are the translations of Native-American life into a nineteenth-century
American worldview. We might understand the quotation marks around "palace" as McCarty's self-recognition of his own translation processes, a wink to
the reader that he knows the difference between a wigwam and a palace but that
he also enjoys the hyperbole.

At a deeper conceptual level, however, the problem of ethnographic translation is even more pronounced. A conjecture, perhaps, but Brigham's and
McCarty's texts find a substantive difference between Native-Americans and
pioneers regarding the occupation of place. The "Indians" wander and are "un-
settled people," whereas the pioneers are, as their names suggests, "settlers" or
"squatters." However, even as McCarty and Brigham describe the Native-
Americans as wandering, they acknowledge the existence of Potawatomi
burial sites, seasonal returns to the same locations, and years later, after resettle-
ment to the west, the occasional return of a Potawatomi to view the old "hunt-
ing grounds."[16] These conditions suggest a viable concept of place, but
McCarty and Brigham cannot read it as viable because, for them, it does not

engage the engine of productivity. Only fixed habitation and the application of modernity can do that. The characterization of Indians as wanderers, then, would seem to be a potent invention through which settlers could imagine their own unique historical moment as carving from the "wilderness" fixed habitations so as to generate a nation and an economy and continue the trajectory of civilization.[17]

Despite my interpretation, however, we should not so quickly leave behind McCarty's image of the "palace" as a substantial place capable of permanent habitation. The "palace" was meant "apparently to stand for centuries" and was capable of withstanding "the heavy gales of the prairie" (another version of Brigham's "howling wilderness"?) because its posts were set "firmly in the ground." Are the Potawatomis, for McCarty, really wanderers or, like settlers, holders of a place? Again, this is conjectural, but McCarty's is a concept of place and habitation that is sentimentalized admiration. He can understand the "palace" because of his own experiences as a sawmill owner and a builder of log cabins. His "palace," then, is an artifact whose Native-American interpretation was translated into the language and worldview of settlement. He cannot recover the Potawatomi version of the "wigwam," and so he sees it in the ways that make sense to him. For McCarty, the "palace" and all other signifiers of a viable concept of place, then, are translated out of their locus of meaning into the meanings of settlers, and so we have representations: "Indians" as wanderers, "simple-hearted children of the forest," whose talents and ingenuity, though sometimes surprising, were never put to practical use and so remained outside the forces of cosmic destiny, which Brigham in his wonderful introduction calls civilization.

In considering the rhetoric of McCarty and Brigham as revealing a major contrast between wandering and settlement, I am on the frontiers of more mammoth themes (for instance, fluidity versus fixity), themes that relate significantly, as I hope to show, to maps and texts as practical tools that help to fix a place. Settlement (staking out the land) is not only furthered by mapping and texting but, more significantly, the processes of mapping and texting contain, as part of their beings, the desire to conquer and colonize. But even as we explore these possibilities, we must not forget that even an unknown writer, Brigham, can point shrewdly to the impossibility of satisfying such desires—even as he practices them. Let us time-machine Brigham, this unknown who had a job to do and did it with finesse, to our own era and introduce him to our theoretical wrangles over linguistic representation or historiography. He would understand and maybe even say something, but he would also leave early, saying, "I'll not philosophise but will be real."

In the winter of 1835–36, the McCarty brothers mapped the original grid of the city.[18] Prior to this, in 1834, Joseph McCarty claimed 360 acres east of the river and 100 west. How does the very concept of property and ownership come to be? How is it that Joseph McCarty "claims" land, yet south of him, according to Brigham's text, there is a "squatter" with 400 acres? Why is one a "squatter" and the other not? According to officials in the Angelstown Historical Society and Museum, one could be called a squatter if one settled the land prior to a government survey. What was land before it became the body of the nation, before it came under the rule of a legal system, before it was measured by survey instruments and recorded on pieces of paper that could now be stored with other "official" documents? The acts of mapping and texting here at the borders of the nation changed land from a kind of expansiveness to something reigned in and placed under control. Through such actions, the nation kept moving west, imposing a legal system and survey instruments upon lands that formerly had been treated less precisely. It is this move toward greater precision that sounds again one of the central metaphors of the discourses of measurement: the making of a shape where before there was a different shape. McCarty's squatter, then, was outside the shaping systems as were the Potawatomis who signed treaties that enabled the new shaping systems to sweep in. It is interesting that we know next to nothing about the squatter and his story and only a little more about Waubonsie. The actions of these figures were not the ones that enabled the founding of Angelstown, and thus they disappeared in the popular history. The old warrior Black Hawk, whose defeat opened up the territory to settlement, was also outside these new shaping systems. Yet, with an interpreter, whose help he requested, his life acquired shape, hence, greater permanence, in the forms of an "autobiography" and later a wealth of place names, monuments, and markers scattered in the valleys of the Fern and Mississippi rivers.

There is something, then, about the moment of founding—the maps, texts, and discourses of measurement that enable it—that needs to be carefully considered. Take, for instance, the array of physical actions (walking the land, laying roads, and building a dam, a sawmill, and log cabins) and juxtapose these with accompanying textual actions (the drawing up of claim forms, contracts, bills of sale, the making of maps and building designs, and the naming of streets). These twin actions, these actions of founding, are Siamese; they are parts of a formal system of laws, property rights, and economic practices that themselves were engineered by the discourses of measurement. Somewhere behind and within the thick nexus of this formal system is a notion of the individual that the formal system is meant to protect. And this notion of the individual may itself be, in part, the product of the discourses of measurement, for we can speculate here on a historical process in which human collectivity (society as single organism) gets carved into its individual components partly because an insistent discourse of measurement presumes to locate psychic and physical boundaries around the ego-filled individual rather than the collectivity. At any rate, I suggested earlier that, prior to the appearance of McCarty, the Potawatomis may have had a different concept of ownership that was not articulable through the discourses of exacting measurement, and so these other concepts remained voiceless to a formalizing system that was deaf to everything except itself.

At one moment there are islands in a river and nearby forests. At another moment, there is a man who turns these into personal property with nothing but the imprimatur of a text whose legitimacy rests on nothing except a formal system, which itself was legitimized, as Brigham tells us, on peculiar abstractions, a "tower" of "Liberty" to be "built on the rights of man as man." In one sense, all this sounds preposterous, that a formal system could be carried to the edge of a nation's borders and change the use and meaning of nature. A river is dammed, a sawmill is built, trees are cut, land is measured, boundaries are drawn, deeds are written—these are actions of founding, mapping, and texting in which the exterior world is reshaped to follow less its own impulse and to follow instead the impulses of ownership. At the very heart of founding, mapping, and texting, then, is the reshaping of matter. Maps reduce overwhelming space; histories reduce time to visible space. To repeat but with different words: In the case of a written text such as this one, the enormity (substitute Brigham's "howling wilderness") that the content points to becomes fenced by the edges of paper. Further, the written word itself is a transformation of elusive sound (more accurately, the perception of spoken sounds) into visible space. By converting enormous forces into objects under the control of the hand and eye, we create the illusion of management.

from then to now

I offer next, like Brigham, my own brief history of Angelstown (from the founding moment in 1834 until I started my ethnographic work in 1987) while doubting its possibility. As a text, it will be one of the discourses of measurement, the narrative kind, and like a map it will pretend to an overview that ultimately it does not have. I wish to probe a single geographic location that is immensely important to and even symbolic of Angelstown's many transformations. The location has had three major names: Big Woods, Roundhouse, and Transportation Center. Each of these names has appeared on maps that belonged to specific eras. For instance, the name Big Woods was associated with land clearing performed by pioneers, the Roundhouse with industrialization, and the Transportation Center with the new information or "network" economy invented by technocrats and dependent on the mobility of workers, goods, and services.

Each change of this same location summarizes the conditions of the city at important historical moments.[19] In its first incarnation, this location was part of Big Woods, a stretch of forest that ran a considerable distance along the river and, of course, preceded the arrival of pioneers. In the original plat of the city, drawn in the winter of 1835–36 by the McCartys, it was still off the map. In the language of this book, it had yet to be bent to the shaping wills of the pioneers. Because it was close to the river and below a sizeable hill and because a stream flowed nearby before emptying into the river, it is quite reasonable to imagine it as a marshy area or at least as part of the river's floodplain. Whatever its conditions, it was caught in the ebb and flow of natural change, relatively free of human manipulation, although it is quite possible that the Potawatomis may have had some specific use for it since it lay almost directly across the river from their "palace."

Of its second incarnation, not much is known. Because the city was growing fast, the location must have been surveyed, mapped, texted (on a bill of sale, if nothing else), bought, and sold several times. At this point, I imagine it entering the general network of pioneer commerce and becoming productive. It became measured and confined, a means for making a profit.

In its third incarnation, this location became distinctly fixed in the history of Angelstown. It acquired a moment of origin, 1855, and it became an important site for a national company, the Chicago, Burlington, and Quincy Railroad. In this incarnation, it was known as the Roundhouse. It was responsible for the manufacture and repair of railroad engines, and it operated in conjunction with a series of "car shops" that made this location the largest employer in Angelstown during the nineteenth and well into the twentieth centuries.

Made of a combination of limestone blocks and fired bricks, the Roundhouse and its adjacent buildings are of particular interest. The entire transformation that I've been discussing, the conversion of nature into industrial productivity, the act of quarrying a raw material, the effort of an exacting consciousness playing upon dumb substance, is contained in the limestone building blocks and so in the very structure of the Roundhouse and its attendant shops. Might we call the act of quarrying a kind of writing on the body of limestone? Incision, measurement, separation, refining, and reassembling are actions that reshape matter into forms that obey the wills of owners, architects, and engineers. I am making a link, or at least a metaphor, then, between owners and managers acting upon limestone and authors acting upon texts. Prior to these actions of incision, measurement, separation, and refining, there was the sheer mass of unquarried limestone, and this mass is the metaphor for an intuition that has yet to be texted in analytic fashion or a mass of land that has yet to be surveyed and mapped. I point to the regularities of the limestone blocks and the rules of standardization that enabled efficient construction. Standardization is a molding, a shaping, the placement of a nearly arbitrary order upon phenomena.[20]

And let us not forget the circulation of written texts that enabled the construction of the Roundhouse. There were the deeds of ownership, the contracts between quarry owners and railroad officials, the laws that controlled these negotiations, the documents that binded workers to employers, the keeping of accounts, the blueprints of the future Roundhouse, the work orders, the work reports, and so on. These texts, of course, were merely the visible surface of a huge substratum consisting of official and unofficial conversations in which commercial arrangements were first broached and, perhaps, finalized. The real work of life was probably accomplished in this oral substratum, and although the sorts of texts described may be mere fragments emerging from the substratum, their power to regulate, report on, and sometimes create the physical actions of people was significant. The texting of things became an entry into officialdom. (Let us think again of that clot of terms and phrases—paper money, paperwork, legal papers, paper pusher, paper trail, putting it down on paper—through which modern societies have come to accept the use of print for the making of an official world that bureacratically administers daily life and the strangeness of such a world when compared to the "wandering" Potawatomis who regulated daily life differently in this same locale only a few decades prior to the building of the Roundhouse.)

But the Roundhouse is more than an object whose limestone can be read as a symbol of an era. Inside its structure, work occurred. Since the railroad was the city's major employer during the nineteenth century, the Roundhouse and the other Burlington shops were where many of the city's immigrants encountered each other on a regular basis.[21] Germans, Swedes, Norwegians, Greeks, Luxemburgers, Lithuanians, Poles, Russians, Dutch, French Canadians, Irish, Hungarians, Romanians, and Italians arrived during various immigration waves. Table 2.2 shows the percentage of immigrants living in Angelstown during the latter decades of the nineteenth century.

Table 2.2

Angelstown Immigrant Population

	City population	% of foreign born
1870	11,162	28%
1880	11,873	22%
1890	19,688	24%*

*The 1890 figures do not separate foreign born from foreign stock.[22]

Perhaps more significant than demographic charts for catching a glimpse of immigrant life, however, is a reading of specific events. The formation of distinct communities via the publication of newspapers and the building of parishes is a possible starting point. The Germans, in particular, identified themselves as a community by publishing their own newspaper in 1868 and continuing it well into the twentieth century. They also formed their own parish in 1861:

> Previous to the year 1861 the Catholics of Angelstown and vicinity were united in a single congregation, irrespective of language. Due to the steadily increasing number of German immigrants a need was felt for a separate parish where the Germans could hear their own language. These settlers came principally from the Rhine province and Westphalia in Germany and from the Grand Duchy of Luxemburg. They all spoke German, and until such a time when they could become familiar with the American language it was desirable and necesary [sic] to have a separate church. Accordingly steps were taken for the founding of a German parish. This was brought about on February 16, 1861, under the direction of the Rev. Joseph Mueller . . . of St Michael's church in Chicago.[23]

It should be clear that during the latter half of the nineteenth century and the first decades of the twentieth, Angelstown had a significant immigrant population. As the city's major employer, the Burlington shops including the Roundhouse were sites for the mixing of different peoples and languages. Both inside and outside these buildings, centrifugal forces of ethnic tension were also at work. During the first decades of the twentieth century, for instance, the newly arrived Romanians also developed their own parish and distinctive

neighborhoods. And following the Romanians, the Mexicans came to Angelstown in the late teens and early twenties and also worked in large numbers
for the Burlington. In fact, the earliest documented account that I have been
able to locate of the Mexican presence in Angelstown is framed within the centrifugal forces of ethnic tension inside the Burlington shops:

> John Luckney, an employe [*sic*] of the Burlington shops, says that he
> has had much experience working among Mexicans and that when he
> thinks one of these fellows is trying to get his knife out to carve him
> with, it has always been his policy to get the other fellow first. Last
> Tuesday Luckney came in contact with a Mexican named Valenso Ma-
> reno while they were at work in the Burlington shops. They had some
> words and according to Luckney, the Mexican made a move as tho
> [*sic*] to pull a knife, also telling Luckney that he was going to carve him
> deep. Luckney beat Mareno to it and hit him over the head with an iron
> bar. This ended the battle until Thursday when the Mexican had Luck-
> ney arrested on a charge of assault and battery.[24]

What interests me in these accounts of the founding of a German parish and of
the Luckney/Mareno fight is the tension between order and disorder, which is
also the tension, in this case, between a text (an example of order) and the reality (an example of messiness) that the text purports to embrace. In the text that
describes the founding of St. Nicholas, so much is hidden by the phrase "a need
was felt . . . " By having such a single "need," the German immigrants become
a coherent community. What is lost are the probable disagreements among the
immigrants, the wrangles over how to finance such a project, the resentments
on the part of the other Catholics against the immigrants, the perspectives of
church officials, the possibility that some city leaders considered ethnic fis-
sioning a threat to the workplaces, schools, and businesses of Angelstown. And
in the Luckney versus Mareno account, so much is hidden by "They had some
words." The actual argument itself, the real gestures and threats, the possible
misinterpretations of words and gestures, the personal histories of two men,
and perhaps, their proclivites to violence, in short, the actual scene of conflict
disappears behind the orderly syntax of printed words. Moreover, the account
seems to be written from the perspective of Luckney. It is Luckney who "says,"
and the "according to" is Luckney's. The newspaper's account is largely Luckney's ordering of the episode. In both accounts, reality is kept at a distance, and
yet its semblances, via print, persist over time, enabling and confusing the interpreter. These accounts, then, have something in common with the texts

mentioned earlier that enabled the construction of the Roundhouse. All of these texts, which are varieties of the discourses of measurement, attempt an ordering, an understanding, a fixing of protean and complex conditions.

But I return to history making, to Valenso Mareno (Moreno?) whose personal history I cannot recover. What was the backdrop, invisible in the newspaper accounts of the time, from which Mareno/Moreno (?) steps forth because of a moment of violence recorded in print? He was, in fact, part of a significant wave of Mexicans arriving in the Midwest. This first wave occurred in the first two decades of the twentieth century and was associated largely with railroad work. Many of the workers were single men, but some came with families or brought families north after settling in Chicago or Angelstown or a variety of small towns in Illinois, Kansas, Iowa, and elsewhere. These laborers were responding to the social disruptions caused by the Mexican Revolution and taking advantage of the rail lines that not long before had begun linking southwestern United States to northern Mexico.[25] Most importantly, however, railroad representatives, operating out of such border towns as Laredo, Texas, aggressively recruited Mexican laborers, hauling them for free to work in the railroad industry.

In Angelstown in 1923, three years after the Luckney/Mareno (Moreno?) fight, the railroad company began housing a Mexican community whose numbers fluctuated, ranging anywhere from thirty-five to fifty families, in boxcars on the eastern fringes of the city. Nearby, the railroad maintained a scrap operation that reclaimed what was still useable from old railroad engines and railcars. Boxcar communities associated with various kinds of railroad work were not uncommon in many parts of the Midwest. The Mexicans of Angelstown called their boxcar community *El Campo* and the place where these men worked *El Scrape*. What I wish to focus on, however, from the ten years or so during which this community existed, are the semblances of a public life that others might call emergent forms of social organization. What emerged in *El Campo* did not seem to emerge elsewhere among the other Mexicans living in Angelstown, and one reason for this difference seems to have been that *El Campo* represented a concentration of Mexican life in a defined space. For instance, shortly after its founding, the community, using lumber and nails provided by the company, built a small chapel with steeple. Catholic priests (for a while, a brother of one of the residents of *El Campo* officiated) came to this chapel to deliver mass and communion classes, both of which were sometimes attended by Mexicans from the city proper.

The residents of *El Campo* also established a *mutualista* or self-help society that acted primarily as a burial society offering a financial cushion whenever necessary. The mutualista had a constitution, elected officers, and regular meetings. Sometimes it sent money to the Mexican needy through the channels of the Mexican Catholic Church, and oftentimes it channeled political, social, and economic information from Mexico back to the residents of *El Campo*. The residents also built a small social hall where the women sometimes organized *jamaicas* or bazaars with food, music, and dancing. National and religious celebrations also occurred here. All in all, *El Campo* seems to have been a hub for almost all Mexicans living in Angelstown, a place that one went to for weddings and other social events. *El Campo*, then, might be comparable, although on a smaller scale, to the kinds of community consolidation that led to the Germans building their own church and a few decades later to the Romanians building theirs.

Pertinent to my thesis of ethnic tension are a series of events surrounding a "night school" held in a school district building and sponsored, in part, by the Angelstown Chamber of Commerce, the Kiwanis Club, the Woman's Relief Corps, the Rotary Club, the Daughters of Veterans, the Drama League, the Daughters of the American Revolution, the Lions Club, the Catholic Daughters of America, and the Community Chest.[26] As might be imagined, Angelstown's night school was part of a national effort promoted by the Department of Labor to educate aliens for citizenship. Beginning in 1914, the majority of night school enrollees were Germans and Romanians. For those years prior to 1920, total enrollees were typically below 100. However, during the first year, 1914, there were 325 students, and 1919 had 199. Throughout the existence of the night school, attendance was notably spotty and almost totally male. During the 1924–25 school year, however, 27 Mexicans enrolled, the third highest number after Germans (81) and Romanians (66). During the next school year, 123 Mexicans attended, which more than doubled the attendance of the next nationality. Such high numbers were partly due to a bus sent by the night school to *El Campo*. During the next school year, 1926–27, however, school board reports indicate the emergence of a significant disagreement between the Mexicans and those groups who wanted to Americanize them. The board of education report from 1928 outlines the problem quite clearly:

> While it is highly desirable that all residents of the state should be familiar with the language of the country, it may be questioned whether the community is warranted in expending its resources for such as are unwilling to become citizens of the state. . . . The Federal

Government will provide text-books only for those persons who have
received their first papers. The Mexicans are glad to come to Night
[*sic*] school but do not care to sever their allegiance with Mexico, and
so must buy their own text-books.

What is the occulted position behind the claim that a group of people "do
not care to sever their allegiance" to their native country? And is it fair on my
part to sense annoyance in this claim, a kind of befuddled "how could they"? If
annoyance is, indeed, there, this is the place where the critic can begin searching for the occulted position, that speck of darkness or unawareness that the
writer of the report (and, by extension, a significant number of mainstreamed
Americans—those sincere Rotarians and daughters of the revolution, and so
on—who took as their duty the difficult task of Americanizing their alien
neighbors) cannot illuminate. I wish to argue that much of our argumentive
discourse struggles to establish itself as real. In this case, the supposed "real" is
that the Mexicans cared too much about remaining Mexican and not enough
about becoming American even as they earned American wages. In order to illuminate what remained occulted to the Americans, however, we might turn to
the Mexicans themselves, their own arguments and explanations. For instance,
an elderly man who grew up as a child within this first Mexican community explained it this way: "The majority of Mexicans were gonna go back. Ninety-
five percent were gonna go back and why bother with any papers." And an even
more elderly woman, the former wife of one of the railroad workers, explained
in Spanish, "Yes, there were night schools back then. My husband never went.
It just didn't interest him. For example, there were jobs where English was important, but then there were jobs where English didn't matter. Say, for example,
those who worked on the tracks, why would they care to learn to speak English?
It was all hard work." Many years after the night school closed, this same husband became a citizen, but his motives were pragmatic—to make sure that he
received his pension—and had little to do with the ideals promoted by the
Americans and with the night school efforts of the federal government to educate the aliens into the English language and, finally, citizenship.

If these commentaries reflected community-wide practices and beliefs—
and I think they did—they suggest that the Americans did not fully grasp that
the Mexicans were not authentic immigrants. Indeed, in so far as the night
school interpreted them as immigrants it occulted from itself what the Mexicans knew experientially, if not consciously, namely, that they were laborers following the possibilities of cash. They were nomadic, migratory, opportunistic,
and such notions as residency and citizenship (the metaphor of "papers" again

as fixing devices) may have been appropriate for the Germans and Romanians but a misinterpretation when applied to Mexicans, an interpretation that was bound to lead to trouble and, finally, to befuddlement and annoyance on the part of the Americans. The Americans did not seem to fully fathom what was obvious to the Mexicans: Mexico was only a day or so away by train. Mexico was available for short and long returns and easy retirement. Moreover, the trip was free if one worked for the Burlington—and almost all did. The term "immigrant," then, was a mistake, an occulting term that may have been a "realistic" description by which the Americans explained the presence of their Mexican neighbors, but when the term attempted to enact social policy, the Mexicans resisted its pigeonhole. Apparently, for many Mexicans, America was more a source of cash than it was a place to commit oneself to.

In 1934, *El Campo* was literally dismembered. The boxcars were cut up, and some of the lumber went with its residents to build actual homes in Angelstown. The first wave of "immigration" was, for all practices, over, cut short by the depression and to a lesser extent by repatriation. The children of those who stayed gradually became Americanized, even if their difference remained, more or less, intact.

The second wave of Latinos arrived in force after World War II. This wave was more complicated in so far as it included Mexicans and Puerto Ricans. The expansion of the industrial economy during the 1950s and 1960s and communication among family members and friends already living in Angelstown with those in Mexico or Puerto Rico or Chicago created a network by which new arrivals could find jobs and housing. Indeed, as we will see, the city passed during the 1950s special ordinances allowing single family housing to become multiple family housing, thus increasing local densities, at the behest of local manufacturers who wanted more workers. The working-class populations that arrived seemed to have been southern Whites, African-Americans from Chicago and elsewhere, and, of course, Latinos. As Angelstown's Latino population grew, new and more elaborate forms of social organization appeared. Mexican grocery stores began to appear as did the Latin American Club, Club Guadalupano, League of United Latin American Citizens (LULAC), the Puerto Rican Club, and Centro Hispano Americano (a Jesuit-sponsored political organization that tried to unite a fragmented Latino community and open up factories for Latino/a workers). Moreover, at this same time *Fiestas Patrias* celebrations and Mexican dances held on a regular basis at a rented ice rink helped to reinforce Mexican cultural identity.

If this second wave of Latinos arrived slowly but surely throughout the 1950s and early 1960s, this pattern began to change starting in the late 1960s and

early 1970s, when the pattern became one of quick acceleration. That the face
of Angelstown was, at this time, changing was noted not only in census figures
but also during oral history interviews with long-term Latino residents, school
district officials, and city officials (see table 2.3).[27]

Table 2.3
Latino Growth in Angelstown since 1960

Census	Total population	Latino population	Latino percent of total
1960	63,715	4,465*	7.00%
1970	74,437	5,412	7.27%
1980	81,293	14,482	17.80%
1990	99,581	22,864	22.96%

*The 1960 census does not report a total for Spanish origin. I derived this number by
adding the total of Mexican and Puerto Rican residents plus the number in the "Other
and Not Reported" category. The result is the largest possible number of Latinos for this
census. I cannot explain the jump of more than 9000 during the 1970–1980 period
when total population growth for the same period was less than 7000; possibly it indicates a miscount by census takers.

This third wave which began in the late 1960s has continued to the present
causing surprise and some consternation among the mainstream citizenry and
even among some Latinos who arrived during prior waves. Some who arrived as
small children in the first wave, for instance, often have complained about the
new arrivals and how they do not encourage the speaking of English among
their children. On the near east side of Angelstown, which is where most of the
Latinos have settled, the changes have been most dramatic. As I will discuss
later, a few elementary school buildings located in this area are now teaching an
almost 100 percent Latino student body. And the St. Nicholas parish which was
first constructed by the local German population has become in the 1990s
largely Latino. In the entrance of that church a memorial lists the names of parish members who became nuns and priests starting in the nineteenth century.
The names are, indeed, almost all German, but the masses are now largely in
Spanish, and the parish's name has been changed to Oscar Romero. The Burlington shops may no longer exist, but the near east side of Angelstown, where
the parish is located and where many of the Burlington workers used to live,

continues to offer the cheaper housing that first attracted the Germans, Romanians, and other immigrant groups. The near east side, then, continues certain socioeconomic traditions: It houses the working class, the unemployed, the linguistically and ethnically different.

Not all of the Burlington shops, however, have disappeared. The Roundhouse and a connecting building have been saved, indeed, transformed. It is now the Transportation Center, and with this name, following Big Woods and Roundhouse, this site enters its third incarnation. Steam and diesel train engines are no longer manufactured here. Rather, these buildings are a hub for the movement of people. Commuter trains carry people to and from Chicago and points between, while buses, also arriving here, carry others to areas closer by. I cannot help but read this transformation of the Roundhouse to the Transportation Center as a metaphor of an attempted transformation of the city's industrial base.

During the 1960s, Angelstown's industrial base weakened—as it did in many other parts of the Midwest. The closing of the remaining Burlington shops in 1974 is a particularly significant moment.[28] It meant the end of the railroad industry, which for so long had been a cornerstone of Angelstown's economy. More or less at this same moment many of Angelstown's downtown businesses started to leave partly because of competition from a nearby mall, or, as a city planner described it, "a retail machine." Despite a deteriorating and changing economy, however, Latinos continued to arrive in quickly expanding numbers. These three converging forces explain much about the stresses to which Anglestown has had to adapt. On the one hand, the kind of work that the nineteenth- or early twentieth-century immigrant might have entered became less reliable; on the other hand, the flow of the ethnically different did not stop. There were still jobs to be had—if not in Angelstown itself then nearby— and even if they were low paying, they still offered more wages than could be had in Mexico or Puerto Rico. In all my interviews, I have yet to find someone who would choose the wages of their native home to the wages found in Angelstown or the Chicago area. The 1970s and 1980s, then, were characterized by a weakened economy but expanding Latino communities.

In the late 1980s, when I began my fieldwork, a fast-moving economic miracle from the East had finally arrived in Angelstown. The city became, at last, the western edge of a high-tech corridor that had been moving steadily west through a series of Chicago suburbs that lined a major artery. A new sort of economic base began to emerge and with it a new kind of Angelstown citizen. Many of these newer arrivals, as I described earlier in this chapter, have moved to the winding subdivisions surrounding the astonishingly successful mall complex described by the city planner. This "new"Angelstown, better known as the far east side, has remained safely distanced from the near east side by a mile or two of undeveloped land. Its identification with "old" Angelstown has been weak at best, and sometimes residents of the far east side have disparaged Angelstown, the look of it, its street gang wars, and its large numbers of ethnically different people. During a recent city election, for instance, 37.4 percent of "old" Angelstown voted compared to 13.3 percent of "new" Angelstown. And during a recent heated city meeting that occurred in the subdivision area, one of the newcomers complained, "I'm tired of people telling me I have to be an Angelstownian. When I say I live in Angelstown, people say, 'Oh . . . ,' but then I say I live near the shopping center, and they say, 'Oh, that's cool. We don't want the people of Angelstown coming out here.' "[29] Yet, it has been this very group that city leaders have tried to attract, for this group symbolizes economic recovery. How to make the city attractive, then, to new sorts of homeowners and consumers—those who might restore old homes and raise property values—how to restore the central business district and refurbish the corridors linking this business district to outlying subdivisions? These have become major questions for city leaders.

The Transportation Center, then, is one project emerging from the rhetoric of revitalization. The building has been remade with these newer citizens in mind—and in their image. Inside, one finds pastel colors, a proliferation of wood trim, men and women in business suits, and commuter-related services (a laundry drop-off, a newspaper vendor, a fast-food establishment), and these are parts of a whole that might be described as the city's desire to create an upscale image. The insides of the building, then, have been converted into contemporary colors and ambience while the outside, similarly, has had its limestone sandblasted. The past here is a shell that houses the contemporary, but since the contemporary aesthetic is fond of the past and how it has conquered it, there is in the center of the building an arrangement of pictures of railroad engines and brute working conditions. The city and its history are somehow all here, both in this building and in this moment of our text. First, there are the pictures that capture an era of robust industrialization symbolized by the railroad industry, which itself was built on the shoulders of a pioneer economy and which was started about the same moment that Alonzo Brigham wrote his pioneer history in order to attract even more economic development for an economy that had expanded beyond the exploitation of Big Woods. Second, there is the shell, the Transportation Center itself, that might be read as an appropriation of the past.

How does the past exist in and on this building? In one sense, the past has been sandblasted off the walls, tamed, sentimentalized, and memorialized in pictures. It has also become heroic. The limestone shell monumentalizes the past, and the pictures in the center of the building, because they hold reality at a safe distance, can make industrial working conditions heroic. Indeed, immediately outside the Transportation Center is a piece of celebratory sculpture, a brawny railroad worker titled "The Journeyman." This is the gumption and strength that built muscular machines, and these machines helped to bless a nation with economic prosperity—or so goes, perhaps, the rhetoric of these images. This sort of heroism may mask violence or even use violence to further the heroic. By viewing these scenes as heroic, however, we pay tribute to the foundations of our contemporary economy and, thereby, valorize ourselves. These images, then, are both documentary and rhetorical. Through them, I think, we find an economy whose brutishness has been transcended. The contemporary information or "network" economy may look anemic compared to the physical muscle that gave us nineteenth-century industrialization; nevertheless, the information economy offers the powerful argument of success, of expanded comforts, and this argument allows us to continue the ascension of civilization very much in keeping with Alonzo Brigham's intentions described earlier. We are asked to renew the urge of civilization even though some in the bustling crowd may hold the stealthy desire to abandon ship, feeling darkly that something has gone wrong.

If the commuters who enter and exit the Transportation Center daily should peek over the large railroad levee directly east of them, they might glimpse something of what calls up these feelings of estrangement and fear, for the other side of the levee demarcates the start of a territory patrolled by the Almighty Latin Kings Nation. The railroad levee is a kind of unintentional, symbolic border, an obstacle separating and yet linking two sorts of peoples. Hidden by the levee is the fieldsite where most of the stories in this book began. In fact, the apartment where I slept bordered the other side of the levee, and the freight trains at night would screech slowly and endlessly as they made a big turn before heading to points further west or on the straight shot east to Chicago. Just a few blocks further east of that apartment is the Oscar Romero Catholic Church, formerly the St. Nicholas church begun in 1861 by the Germans.

The Transportation Center, then, in its most recent incarnation holds, even if only vestigially, all prior incarnations. More importantly, it summarizes the current scene in which city leaders have attempted to revitalize decayed conditions by seizing the glamor of a new sort of economy while at the same time struggling with the social problems of a largely alien and sometimes alienated group. The fieldsite of this book, then, is juxtaposed to the Transportation Center but literally hidden from its view by a railroad levee, and this juxtaposition of two groups separated by a symbolic barrier summarizes a range of human tensions and desires—the desire, for instance, to keep at bay that which is ugly, dirty, and threatening, on the one hand, while, on the other, the desire to acquire power and respect under social conditions that have not found the formulae for distributing adequately these human needs.

3

LOOKING FOR

DON ANGEL

Take a passport, a green card, or a driver's license: each identifies its holder from without—much as a posted sign in a museum or in a zoo identifies rocks or animals. As long as some men and women cannot even decipher, let alone attempt to interpret the writings whereby society defines them, their documented identitites must remain essentially foreign to both the public and the private conduct of their lives.... Indeed, the way in which a literate bureaucracy can impose on the unlettered the pseudoobjective identity of printed documents almost recalls the lethal role assigned to writing in Franz Kafka's "Penal Colony."
—Paul Hernadi, "Doing, Making, Meaning"

Mexican immigrants in Angelstown used such phrases as *arreglar sus papeles*, "to fix your papers," or *tengo que arreglar mis papeles*, "I need to put my papers into order," to indicate the complex procedure of making oneself legal in the United States, including the procedures of becoming a citizen. There are no surprises here: built into these phrases were strong associations between officialdom and paperwork, suggesting that authentication for bureaucratic purposes occurred through the written word. When I first heard these expressions, I was particularly attracted to *arreglar* in its meaning of "putting into order" because it reminded me that writing itself (as a synecdoche for *papeles*) is also an ordering. The Spanish phrases seemed redundant in their emphasis upon order, even abundant with the concept of order, for, additionally, there is also the very purpose of legalization papers, namely, the maintenance of order among the inhabitants of a state. These phrases used by Mexican immigrants were similar to English phrases that label immigrants. For instance, it is said in English that an immigrant is documented or undocumented, legal or illegal, has papers or does not have them, has residence papers, a green card, or a work permit or does not have them. Across two languages, then, one can spy a semantic domain in which state order, officialdom, and paperwork are thickly associated. *Suggestion: Being a member of a state is not the same as being a member of a community, a people, or a tribe. Membership in one of the latter does not necessarily entail a writing act that declares a relationship between the individual and the abstraction the individual belongs to. In contrast, the state cannot exist without these recorded relationships. The management of individuals via the state, then, is a major function to which writing and other recording devices have been put.*

But let me stop for a moment to consider how the power of a "literate bureaucracy" fails to impose on anyone a "pseudoobjective identity"—something Paul Hernadi did not note in the quotation given above. Simply put: A passport, a green card, and a driver's license can all be forged, and the act of forging is a claiming of power. Even as the literate bureaucracy attempts to control via printed documents, the "controlled" respond with their own devices. From this perspective, reality appears as an excess; hence, its textualization by a bureaucracy can only be approximate. The result is that the supposed controllers have less control than they imagine and, in some cases, are being controlled. Hernadi's quotation pointed lucidly to the intentions of a certain genre that might be called legal documents, but, as real life often reveals, intentions are sometimes not realized. In this chapter, I first consider the rhetoric of the "legal documents" genre and explore some of its cultural meanings and intentions and, likewise, consider the forgings of legal documents as a profound manipulation of appearances whose goal is freedom from the forces of control. After that, I shift my analysis toward some specific oral discourse genres whose appearances, at least to the uninitiated, are also deceiving. My entire analysis is directed toward an understanding of Don Angel, a man whose life has been both banal and transgressive and, for me at least, deeply moving. If sometimes a bit irritable, he was also generous in a quirky sort of way, and because of that latter characteristic, he opened his small apartment to my research assistant, Edmundo, and me. Quite often until late at night, we would listen to his stories and theories and his recalling of the events of the day, and during and after those talks and using his cramped quarters as a base, I began to imagine the shape of this book.

In Don Angel's apartment, I, typically, slept on the floor atop a variety of chair cushions in the small room that contained his bed and served as a living room. Edmundo slept on the floor in the next room where a variety of Don Angel's roommates also kept temporary quarters. There was no door to close between these rooms and no door to close off the kitchen, and so conversations floated easily among the four or five of us, depending on how many roommates he had. I spent much of my time searching for Don Angel in, what I consider now to have been, a vain attempt to comprehend him. That which I knew of him was, in part, a construction that he, Edmundo, and I had invented. For instance, he was never called Don Angel until Edmundo dubbed him such during a *relajo*, "joke," very early in our first stay in the summer of 1990. *Don* signals dignity and respect to a male of a certain age and is typically used before the first name. Suddenly, Angel became Don Angel, and the title stuck and was picked up by his landlord, landlord's children, and roommates. To most, however, he was simply Angel, and some may have known his occupations as janitor, dishwasher, gardener, and, later, as nursery worker. The young people in the neighborhood referred to him as *chero*, which was short for *ranchero* (literally "rancher" but, in fact, meaning "country bumpkin" or "hick"). An ex–parish priest knew him literally as an angel, and this description referred to his devout Catholicism and deep strain of goodness. His landlords and roommates thought of him as *demasiado delicado*, "too fastidious, easy to irritate." Edmundo and I typically thought of him as a source of *curanderismo* (the practice of folk medicine and healing) and a master of *albures* (a verbal art, almost a duel, in which a poker-faced conversation is maintained during considerable sexual punning).

Don Angel had lived and worked in the United States under five different names: Esteio Aurea D., Daniel J., Raymundo M., Banincio P., and currently his actual name, Angel L., although this last name too had been used on otherwise forged documents. Don Angel gave me permission to examine and display here two kinds of illegal documents: identification cards and birth records. I searched these in order to construct a unifying rhetoric for the genre of legal documents. How did these documents represent reality? If there was a consistent rhetoric, can one see in their numbers and words a cultural intention in which the management of people is accomplished through the specification or fixing of the individual, and is this notion of specification or fixing another instance of the discourses of measurement? The identification cards typically contained the following:

1

The name of the institution that needed to identify the individual (Social Security Administration, Immigration and Naturalization Service, the Illinois Secretary of State's Office, a local bank, an employer).

2

The institution's distinctive logo or sometimes its seal.

3

An identifying number for the individual.

4

Date of issue and expiration date.

5

The address of the individual.

6

The date and place of birth.

7

Physical characteristics (height, sex, weight, color of hair, color of eyes, "scar right eyebrow").

8

A photograph of the individual.

9

The signature of the identified individual and sometimes the signature or name of the authorizing agent.

10

Instructions on what to do if the card was lost or if one should relocate.

11

Regulations and explanations for the use of the card and a mentioning of the laws and so on that authorized these cards.

Similarly, the birth certificates contained the following:

1

The name of the insitution that produced such certificates (Los Angeles County, California; Crockett County, Texas).

2

The institution's identifying seal.

3

Identifying numbers of the certificates.

4

Date of filing.

5

The name and sex of child and whether it was a twin.

6

The place and time of birth.

7

The identification of parents according to age, occupation, address, and color or race.

8

Signatures of authorizing agents, including those of the physician, registrar, and person releasing the document and the date of its release.

I will begin at the beginning, at the moment of birth when one is recorded/inscribed in a bureaucratic culture. This action sets up future inscriptions in which paper and print—and now a computer's memory—help to fix at least a part of us. How have these cultural practices come to be? When did these artifacts called documents of identification and birth certificates begin and how have they evolved? There is a history here, for it is hard to imagine them existing in far more traditional cultures accustomed to face-to-face interactions. If I had the space, I would explore these histories, find out the origins of these documents, who the record keepers were, and their motives.[1] What is more central to my project, however, is to examine rhetorically the artifacts themselves and to see them as emblems of the current scene.

I believe these documents may be taken as signs of distance. They were inventions that came into being precisely because of a lack of face-to-face interactions. I wish to consider momentarily the implications of distance. How do a people bridge distance in cultures that have grown so large that knowledge of the Other is not often the norm? What sorts of actions establish relationship across distance? These cards and papers were parts of a genre, which itself may be part of a more complex system of rituals (including inquiries at a cocktail party, for instance) that attempt to bridge distance. Documents of identification, in particular, might be taken as contracts or signs of relationship between individuals and the institutions the individuals circulate through. In order to establish the relationship, however, the institution, out of self-protection, must be guaranteed that the individual seeking relationship is, indeed, the person claimed. It is at this moment, then, that all sorts of verifications are requested, verifications, which after being established, will ground future interactions. If these individuals are not the ones named, the institution itself may lose something of what it owns or controls and do harm not only to itself but to others who must also deal with the institution. From this perspective, then, one can understand the complexity of the verification process as a system of redundant identifications in which, for instance, pictures of the person are juxtaposed to a list of physical characteristics. One set of identifications mirrors another set and both are meant to be mirrors of the real person being verified by an agent of the institution.

In all these redundant self-protections, I sense degrees of fear and hostility or at least suspicion.[2] In order for institutions to protect themselves, they must be able to pinpoint weight, height, color of eyes and hair, age, and "scar right eyebrow." Here is a display of specific details whose ultimate goal is the separation of one individual from the masses. The use of numbers is a handy means by which to realize this goal because numbers offer a coding scheme remarkably brief and exact. Only one individual can have a particular number. In addition, the need to protect one's institution also explains the use of signatures. For instance, for the most part, these documents preferred print over handwriting, which is the choice of machine over hand. This choice means that there is a strong need for the signatures of authorizing agents and the person being identified because a signature is believed to be the person in microcosm and not repeatable. (Is there an irony here that a civilization in search of the rights of the individual should also search out the devices by which to precisely designate its individuals so as to better manage them?) These cards, then, are products of a lack of trust that plays itself out as a momentary curtailment of freedom at the moment of verification. Perhaps the hostility is even embedded deeply inside the identifying card. For instance, the cards and birth certificates are typically a surface of cubicled spaces, each space labeled with a request for a particular bit of information. Once filled out, these documents are themselves cubicles, often wallet size, framing in orderly fashion a set of particulars from a person's life. Metaphorically speaking, the individual—more accurately, specifics of the individual—become objects framed by the institution. The institution supplies the documents, records the information, and its authorizing agents certify the individual. It is clear that power resides with the institution, and through these shallow but efficient representations of people, the institution protects itself. These documents, then, are objectifications that reduce to manageable proportions the excess of what it means to be an individual, and this process is similar to a map or a text managing the excesses of reality.

Of course, all these conditions are not necessarily negative. For another group of people—for instance, those who have access to the managers of institutions—trust becomes more of a possibility so that these people need not present their identification cards to an insitution. However, I write from another perspective, one that acknowledges power differentials and sees the world from the eyes of the managed. To create this perspective, I choose phrases such as "cubicled spaces" to suggest the cells of a prison. It is from this perspective of accumulated resentment and hostility that we can understand the actions of institutions as curtailing self-interests. As Don Angel sarcastically said one day—in Spanish, of course—"The Americans must be very smart because they know how not to work and how to make others work for them." But even among these resentments, there was an important ambiguity. Don Angel had, indeed, fixed his *papeles*, "papers," and no longer depended on illegal documents, which meant that soon he could remove his savings from the bank, collect all the social security that, under various names, he had earned in the United States, and retire to his home in Mexico that he had built with American wages. How many institutions, then, have helped to create his future pleasure? Simultaneously, how many institutions were thwarted in order to secure this pleasure? Any portrait of institutional life needs at least two versions: one that acknowledges the curtailment of self-interest but also the furthering of self-interest. Further, it is difficult to imagine a modern society organized in ways that might eliminate the onerous actions entailed in the recording and verifying of individuals. These actions cannot be easily determined as just or unjust. Perhaps we need to view the management of people and the devices used for management as cultural responses to the problems and successes of modernity: an explosive growth in population, the erosion of face-to-face interactions, an intensified concept of ownership, and so on. *Suggestion: The conditions that have emerged are not in a cause and effect relationship to the management strategies now in place; hence, this constant critique: In protecting the institution in the name of "all," what actions become justified?*

Don Angel's false documents were a display of identities allowing his person to escape observation. They increased the bureaucratic clutter. They parodied and manipulated bureaucratic discourse and its forms of representation so that he could hide behind the array. Because I am pursuing the rhetoric of these documents, I am attracted to those moments of language when the document, in its moment of most truth-telling, speaks a lie. The key phrases, then, in Don Angel's documents were: "This is a true certified copy of the record if it bears the seal of the County Recorder . . . "; "I do hereby certify that the above and foregoing is a full, true, and correct photocopy . . . "; "I hereby certify that the information is true of my knowledge"; "I hereby certify that I attended the birth"; and "This is to certify that . . . "

These phrases seem to be awash in a mystique of certainties, or at least apparent certainties. If, as I have been arguing, identification documents and birth certificates are essentially representational, then some deep clue about their representational functions ought to be built into their language. I start with the word "certify" that occurred so frequently in these documents. It comes from the Latin *certus*, which means "certain," and *ficare*, which means "to make," in short, "to make certain." In addition, deictics, or pointing words, also occurred ("this," "the above and foregoing"). The objects being pointed to were, of course, the documents themselves. *To be* verbs also occurred, and these emphasize states of existence or reality. Here in this preliminary analysis, I note an abundance of truth conditions: deictics point to the documents they are written on, and the very existence of these documents "make" a certainty. In describing the evolution of official discourse, Clanchy has said, "Writing shifted the emphasis in testing truth from speech to documents . . . "[3] In this sense, the document as symbol of official discourse circulates almost independently of the human body. I wish to further claim that Don Angel's documents were nearly freestanding in the sense that they attempt to represent the truth, and depending on the accuracy of representation, they become the truth with the power of initiating very significant actions. For instance, as long as the documents remained credible, they had an enduring authority to determine, among other things, deportation or the continuation of residence.[4] And one might momentarily consider the parentage of this authority, the long lineage of laws and court decisions whose ultimate parent is the constitution, which, so to speak, is the voice of something transcendent, the "Natural Rights of Man." And the constitution, as a vessel, perhaps, of transcendence, reminds one of biblical texts as vessels of another transcendent authority, the voice of God. Something of all this at some level is embedded inside these documents, and this begins to explain a language that tries to free itself of contingent conditions. Even those contingent conditions that are admitted—" . . . *if* it bears the seal . . . " and " . . . is true *of my knowledge*" (emphases mine)— act as a kind of enthymeme declaring the truth of the documents if the conditions themselves are true.

Don Angel's false documents and certificates, then, were a leveling of the ability to represent truth. They spoke lies by impeccably mimicking the form of truth. These documents were artful dodges that mimicked the discourses of

on a single sheet of paper

identity is not found on any sheet of paper

power, and behind that cloud of interference, the real Don Angel escaped. These documents, then, were also a leveling of state power. In that space between the individual and the state, Don Angel inserted his own set of representations and, thereby, began to control that space himself (after the payment of money, of course, to professional forgers—1,000 pesos for the documents of Raymundo M., 100 dollars for those of Angel Galvan-L.). However, getting control cost more than money. One had to always be alert and nervous, for the state, at different times, almost discovered him. For instance, when the Social Security Administration started inquiring into Raymundo M., he switched to Daniel J. Again, the artful dodge.

But in juxtaposing a leveling both of the representations of truth and state power, I have, unexpectedly, arrived at a place not imagined when this chapter began. *Suggestion: State power depends on representing itself as embedded in a communally shared truth. If the state cannot do this, how can it maintain authority? The laws and documents issued by a state must have that germ of shared truth inside them, and if they do not, they will be disobeyed or altered. A state, then, must weave itself with some sort of truth and constantly project that tight synthesis rhetorically. The task is a fragile one, always on the verge of being undermined by egocentric self-interest, natural and human circumstance, and, more insidiously, by a kind of exhaustion of images in which the original truth vision becomes worn out like a too often projected movie that has lost color.*

And this brings me, again, to Don Angel's false documents. They and other instances of illegal immigration suggested that the truth was not communally shared. For instance, representatives of Don Angel's employers were the ones who sometimes procured the false documents. In short, citizens of the state saw advantages in breaking the laws of the state. Therefore, Don Angel's manipulations of the system occurred in the context of a law that, in the eyes of those who broke it, seemed frayed and soiled because it was not woven with their individual truths. It is curious, then, to consider these false documents in the larger context of state power. State power and communally shared truths are presented as woven together, and yet that project has fallen short because individual truths and needs—Don Angel's, for instance, and those of his employers—are so multidimensional that the law cannot free itself of contestation and, finally, violation. In short, the unidimensionality of a law or regulation cannot help but straitjacket the multidimensionality of human need and, even more so, the almost chaotic abundance of human desire.

the truth only applies to certain people

I have skimmed the various representations that Don Angel has made of himself in order to benefit from institutions that would otherwise not have been at his disposal. In doing so, I have argued that these were merely the superficial identities that he used at various times to outwit the authorities. Behind this play of identities, I knew that he was locatable, but, at a deeper level, I was not fully convinced that he was locatable, partly because he projected himself through a variety of discourses, some of which were strange to me. I use "discourse" as a trope here because language is so central to this text. Hence, other potential tropes, such as "consciousness" or "self," are rejected in favor of the trope of discourse, but I am quite unsure about the benefits and shortcomings, the truths and lies, that these three tropes and others offer. Whatever trope seems most appropriate—discourses, consciousnesses, selves—the central point is that they are layered, and the word "layered" would seem to be another trope, for I am doubtful that these characteristics, whatever they are, actually exist in layers. Furthermore, the "layered" "discourse styles" that I wish to describe are three, and the word "three" is certainly a popular trope, for academic discourse seems to be fond of analysis that reveals three or four categories. In raising the issue of tropological thinking in academic discourse, I, again, raise the problem of representation.[5] Hence, to what extent are the next few pages of analysis another false, or partly false, document?

Don Angel, who was born in 1934, was deeply connected to those he called *los viejitos*," the old ones.'[6] The *viejitos* and the world in which he grew up in the Mexican state of Aguascalientes have all but disappeared. He considered himself one of the few who remembered their folk beliefs, stories, *tratamientos*, "cures," and the way of life that once existed in his *tierra*, "homeland." The *viejitos* that he knew growing up were far more knowledgeable than he, and he believed, therefore, that he represented them poorly. They symbolized a kind of wisdom, propriety, and dignity, and what pained him was that the youth of today, both in the United States and in Mexico, lacked *los conocimientos de los viejitos*, "the knowledge of the old ones." The world of the *viejitos* held much emotional significance for Don Angel but also ambiguity. On the one hand, he was deeply attached to their world, for it represented a wisdom that the contemporary world lacked; on the other hand, he knew that the world of the *viejitos* had been conquered by modernity, and in so far as it still inscribed itself in his speech and gestures, he recognized his own marginalization both in Mexico and the United States. Indeed, his own modernity and pious Catholicism contributed to that marginalization, for he saw the world of the *viejitos* as deeply layered with superstition and even the devil. In a sense, then, he was a conquered man who contributed to his own conquering; nevertheless, he had inherited from the *viejitos* a certain amount of expertise in *curanderismo*, "folk healing," and he sensed its worth despite its subjugation in the face of modern

[handwritten margin note: Heavy Influence]

medicine. I call the first discourse style, then, that of *los viejitos*, and I consider its roots almost untrackable because it was a product of Spanish colonialism and indigenous characteristics.

Two of the major *viejitos* in his life were his grandmother and grandfather. His grandfather in particular was known in his community as *el tuliz* (I can only guess at the spelling). *Tuliz* is a word that Edumundo and I have not been able to verify in dictionaries of Náhuatl, the language of the Aztecs that was spoken by a number of indigenous peoples in Mexico and has contributed to modern Mexican Spanish such words as *chapopote*, "tar," *zacate*, "grass" or "grain," and *chocolate*, "chocolate."[7] *Tuliz*, then, may have been an indigenous word whose origins were not Náhuatl. Don Angel described the word as belonging to the *dialecto*, "dialect," of his region. In labeling this word and others as belonging to a *dialecto*, Don Angel acknowledged that these words did not belong to standard Mexican Spanish. Indeed, these words may have been survivors of some indigenous *lenguaje*, "language," that became temporarily fused to Spanish to make a particular Mexican variety, in short, a *dialecto*. At any rate, according to Don Angel, a *tuliz* referred to (1) a particular bird from his region and (2) a person who could both hypnotize others with his eyes and had the power to take on the shapes of animals or to disappear. So, *el tuliz* named his grandfather, but, from his grandmother and mother, he learned *curanderismo*, and acquired his knowledge of medicinal herbs.

As Edmundo and I transcribed and translated our three-way conversations that ranged quickly and widely across innumerable topics, it became fairly easy to isolate the sections of *viejito* discourse in which, for instance, the figure of *el tuliz*, or the lifeways of *los viejitos*, or Don Angel's partial knowledge of *curanderismo* were mentioned. However, I need to make a sharp distinction between *viejito* discourse and his version of it, for it is my strong belief that his was not the talk of an actual *viejito* but, rather, a set of traces of *viejito* talk. Nevertheless, these traces were highly pronounced and connected, as I will soon argue, with the semiotics of his body, for the community read him, even at great physical distances, as different, namely, as a throwback.

But let me emphasize further and more deeply: what Edmundo and I found in the tape recordings and transcripts were traces, *only traces*. In short, a set of *viejito* traces became visible because they themselves were part of a set of inscriptions—or *traces*—of actual, complex moments when Don Angel, Edmundo, and I engaged each other and attempted to make sense of each other's lives. Those moments are now lost, but what survives are a set of objectifications (tape recordings and transcripts of tape recordings) that mark such things as speakers, pauses, words, and sounds. But these markings are impoverished, for they are unable to mark the richness of fleeting life and its densities. Nevertheless, these objectifications enable the creation in writing of a distinctive lifeworld. The transcripts, in particular, offer a visible surface upon which to reflect, and it is this combination of both the visible surfaces and reflections upon those surfaces that I am calling the creation in writing of a lifeworld. These transcriptions, then, resemble the map as well as Brigham's history analyzed in chapter two. As objectified surfaces or representations, the opportunity they offer for reflection is extraordinary. *Suggestion: The hiding of something in order to bring something else to light, in short, the act of objectifying, is a significant ingredient in the illusion of mastery.* I think it is important to continually emphasize this notion of analysis creating a lifeworld that is born from but not identical to that which is analyzed. We might say that there should exist a kind of umbilical connection between the original ethnographic moment and its systematic analysis, and that it is through the maintenance of such a connection, despite the provisionality of a researcher's conclusions, that the researcher creates the ethos of someone worth hearing.[8]

In my analysis of his traces of *viejito* discourse, I will examine first a few extralinguistic and stylistic markers before moving on to an examination of content. For simplicity's sake, I call these stylistic markers the semiotics of Don Angel's body, for my interest here is in his gestures, his walk, the look in his eyes, his clothes, his tough fingernails—which he forced me to press one day in order to prove that years of plunging them into dirt had hardened them and that my fingernails couldn't take an equal pressure, and he was right.

What then was his gestural style that marked his body as semiotically different? Where did the style come from? How did he learn it? I cannot fully answer these questions because in Angelstown Don Angel was unique. Cut off from other examples of the style, Don Angel became, so to speak, ultravisible. But because there were no others like him, I have no way of fully understanding the style. Nevertheless, my strong suspicion is that his gestural style maintained strong traces of the *viejitos*, and, more emphatically, that his gestural style was more authentically *viejito* than the content of his discourse. At any rate, his gestural style seemed to occur frequently and prominently in the context of things *viejito*, such as when describing planting and harvesting. I quote from lightly edited fieldnotes made on 1 July, 1990:

> One of the more interesting things here is the physical demonstration of actions as he (Don Angel) talks. For instance, when talking about picking cotton, or corn. He demonstrates physically how it is done. He takes about ten feet to show how one moves down the row. . . .

He indicates that when one is picking cotton, the arms need to hang
loose. They shouldn't be resting on the area above the knee. The body
should be relaxed. Periodically one should stand up and just stretch
briefly. Anyway, he shows how it is done and doesn't provide too
much verbal detail in order to explain. For cucumbers he shows how
they are cut with the special knife that is used.

His gestural style, then, was, in part, a representation or a set of stylized actions that approximated the real actions as he remembered them. In other
words, he mimicked the picking of cotton or the cutting of cucumbers or the
standing up and stretching. What my fieldnotes did not capture, however, were
the sounds associated with the gestures: for instance, the "cha, cha cha" indi-
cating the chopping of corn or "ta, ta, ta" as he imitated the hammering of a
small nail.[9]

This same mimicking characterized one of the most significant conversations that Edmundo and I ever had with Don Angel. At the time, he was trying
to explain some rather mysterious divining practices of *los viejitos* that he recalled from his youth in Aguascalientes. One divining practice entailed praying
over a lit candle made of grease and asking the flame to indicate the direction
where a lost animal might be found. Another divining practice entailed a particular kind of *cedazo*, "sieve," pierced by an open pair of scissors. One person
would hold one handle and another person would hold the other, and they
would watch and interpret any movement of the sieve: *Y entonces ya le dicen,
díme si es cierto que fulano se llevó mi cochina, entonces el cedazo hacía esto, que sí,
ehh?* "And then they say, tell me if it is true that so and so took my pig, then the
sieve would do this, ehh?" In the first example, Don Angel mimicked the moving flame with his finger and during the second example he showed us the
moving sieve by using a towel. My point is that physical and oral representations of objects, actions, and events were very much a part of his vocabulary.
They did some of his "talking," and interestingly they were often associated
with the most dramatic moments of his discourse. For instance, in the earlier
example where he talked about harvesting cotton, cucumbers, and corn, the actions and sounds of harvesting, more effectively shown than verbally described,
were the essence of his explanations. Similarly, Don Angel's finger as moving flame and the towel as sieve dramatically crystallized the mystery of supernatural beliefs during the recounting of divining practices. His movements attempted to recreate the most dramatic moments in which participants were in
the midst of invisible forces. Don Angel's gestures and sounds, then, even more
than his words, ushered us into the pivotal moments of his narratives. It should

be clear that this documentation of Don Angel's gestures points to the notion of performance, for the term "performance" allows one to consider gestures and words as exchanges between two channels and the possible meanings that these exchanges imply. Although my final conclusion is a bit too neat and tidy, it was as if during his *viejito* performance style, words often gave way to gestures and sounds during the high points of a narrative in order to more completely and dramatically represent what was being communicated.

Other examples of his performative style included those moments when he theatrically invented characters who moved through the scenes of his discourse. At these moments, Don Angel abandoned the explanatory mode for a kind of embodied theatrics; he abandoned telling for showing. For instance, during the same evening when he described some of the divining practices of *los viejitos*, he also talked of petitioners praying to the image of Saint Anthony and, as part of the ritual, turning the image upside down. At certain moments, he posed as a stereotypical praying person, and his voice acquired the contours of someone pleading before the image of the saint: *Hay señor San Antoñito que me se haga con fulano, te llevo un . . .*, "Oh St. Anthony, let so and so become my boyfriend (girlfriend), I will take you a . . . " Shortly after this theatrical invention, he imitated the prayers addressed to an *ánima*, "soul" or "spirit," who was supposed to reply via a burning wick: *¿Qué dónde andaba? . . . ¿Por dónde andaba el animal?* "Where might it be? Where might the animal be?" Later in the same passage, he again shifted quickly from the explanatory to the theatrical: *Entonces ya la gente decía, no pos sabes que pa' tal parte, vete a buscarlo . . .* "Then the people would say, no well you know that certain way, go search for it." Moreover, in the scene with the sieve, there were two moments when he adopted, again, the voice of a petitioner: *Dime si es cierto que fulano se robó, ehh? Ahh, mi gallina, o se robó mi cochino, o se robó mi plato*, "Tell me if it is true that so and so stole my chicken, or stole my pig, or stole my plate"; *Dime si es cierto que fulano se llevó mi cochino*, "Tell me if it is true that so and so took my pig." The voice changes were oral quotation marks, and, indeed, when Edmundo first transcribed these sections, he automatically placed quotation marks at these points long before he and I had noticed Don Angel's performative style. However, there were numerous moments when Don Angel could have become theatrical but did not. Only on a few occasions, mostly during those moments of supernatural fervor, did he switch from explanation to animation of his words by theatrically creating with his voice and body the presences of others. The repertoire of Don Angel, then, included at least three ways by which to animate words: gestures, sounds, and the creation of others through voice, pitch, and bodily changes.

On the one hand, this repertoire removed from the context of his person is not particularly unusual. The use of gestures, imitative sounds, and theatrical inventions of others is commonplace among individuals from a wide variety of backgrounds. Moreover, I never made a video of what I am calling his *viejito* performance style, and so I am left with only descriptive words—a telling, not a showing—to convey his special semiotic and his special ways of communicating. On the other hand, his person, I still believe, was fraught with special meaning in the context of Angelstown. Hence, I am compelled to elaborate the following argument.

Don Angel's *viejito* repertoire, it seems to me, implied a relationship to words that is distinguishable from the ideology of wording that is common in mainstream life to the extent that such life has been shaped by schooling. In this sense, there is much in schooling that encourages logos at the expense of the theatrical, distance at the expense of involvement. I am reminded of my own markings of student papers or my own student papers marked by teachers: "exact word?" "shift in diction," "redundant," "too wordy, tighten up," "clarify!" "verb tense shift," "awkward," "dangling modifier," "your thinking is not coherent here," "is this logical?" "verb agreement problem," "what?" and so on. During such practices the word, phrase, sentence, paragraph, and discourse become objects of consciousness and begin to create what I am calling here an ideology of wording whose ultimate goal is the mastery of both discourse and the lifeworld that the discourse points to. An aspect of the ideology of wording is that the theatrical becomes a set of effects, important in their own right and in certain contexts but potentially deceptive in knowledge-making contexts. Indeed, much of Don Angel's knowledge—*curanderismo*, stories of the supernatural, and divining practices—were so far off the professional logos map as to be considered merely theatrical. In this sense, Don Angel's narrative style reinforced the marginalization of his narrative content from the professional and mainstream styles of the modern world.

On occasion, however, Don Angel explicitly restrained his own theatrics. Sometimes in the midst of a probing conversation, he would remark, *Bueno, es que no quiero exagerar mucho*, "Well, I don't want to exaggerate much." Don Angel was a fastidious, exact person, as fastidious about the cleaning of his house as he was exact about his words. Fastidiousness in all aspects of his life—personal hygiene, cooking, gardening, conversing—was one reason why some criticized him for being *demasiado delicado*, "overly fussy." He enjoyed the presence of Edmundo and me, in part, because our questions forced him to think about ideas, history, and words, and many of his debates with us concerned the origins of particular words or the appropriateness of a word in a given context or the exactness of a word for an idea or thing. His desire to not exaggerate much, I take it, was linked to his preoccupation with wording and, ultimately, his general fussiness. Because of Edmundo's and my own education and because of his lack of one (he attended school for only one year in Mexico and learned how to read and write Spanish outside of school), however, he mostly assumed that our knowledge would be more exact and definitive. In his mind, schooling and wording were inextricably mixed, and, as I explained earlier, I would agree. Hence, I would argue that Don Angel's version of *viejito* discourse—or rather his trace of it—was not incompatible with an ideology of wording, that to a certain extent they shared a common ground. The difference, perhaps, was that the ideology never sharpened its tools on his body and mind, which is a metaphorical (theatrical?) way of saying that he was never institutionalized by the ideology. In short, he acquired his interest in wording by following his own curiosity, which was itself partially formed in marginalized conditions that made the trappings of power, education being one, seductive. In not becoming institutionalized by the ideology, he became the cheap labor through which institutions maintain themselves. He was a gardener for St. Nicholas and for a doctor who lived on Angelstown's west side, a janitor in an insurance building, a dishwasher at a restaurant chain, a nursery worker (after being fired from his janitor's job for taking long naps), and in the past a *bracero*, "laborer," particularly farm laborer. (The *bracero* program, particularly during the 1950s, was part of a formal arrangement by which the United States received cheap labor from Mexico. I remember it well particularly during cotton-picking time before the advent of the mechanical cotton picker on the farm where I grew up in South Texas.)

I wish to impose, then, another meaning upon Don Angel's cynical statement that the Americans must be very smart because they always get others to work for them. I would suggest that the statement implied that life has become overdetermined by work and wages, in short, by one's niche in a cash economy. Part of this overdetermination includes how power has become a presence inhabiting body and mind. My point is an important one: Yes, I am saying that styles of power become molded to ways of holding the body and gesturing, to styles of discourse, and to ranges of thought—and all this might be called a style of being. Institutions—schools, businesses, corporations, and so on—as the centers for the circulation of cash, or the preparation of those who will circulate the cash, are the locations where bodies and minds are most distinctly inhabited by the presences of power. I use the plural "presences" because people express innovative versions rather than a singular "presence." And these innovations are parts of a thick semiotic that includes those objects, those technological innovations—computers and so on—which are the inventions of this sort of economy and further the work of institutions. In describing the semiotics of power as thickly constructed, as including, for instance, the animate and inanimate, we must note the strength of its magnetism, its inescapable gravity that pulls the individual imagination into its orbit. Even Don Angel, whose very peripheralness has allowed me to articulate more clearly the source of the gravity, was very much in its orbit. This economy was the source of his wages, the source of the objects and food that he bought, his future retirement, some of his sarcastic humor, and his understanding that he worked for others and was not smart. But he was also more than what this source could predict and manage, and recovering some of that unpredictability is one of the goals behind this chapter.

But let me continue arguing my point: A continuing theme in this text has been and will be the tension between the modern and the outmoded and how these were signaled in Angelstown through distinct semiotic systems, and how this tension occasionally became linked to another tension, order versus disorder. For most in the neighborhood, Don Angel was outmoded, and this was why the young people of the neighborhood read the dense semiotic of his person as *chero*. Through this insult, he was placed at a safe distance, for his antique image was a part of their own *latinidad,* and the word *chero,* in part, rescued them from their fear, helping them to escape in the direction of the modern.[10] An example: One fourth of July, Don Angel, a little drunk, which was not unusual for him, dressed up in his handmade *matachin* regalia and began to perform *matachin* dances on the sidewalk outside his apartment.[11] He became the talk of the landlord's teenagers. Once again he had displayed *cheroness*, and one of the most embarrassing and strange versions of it yet seen. In locating his performative style, then, as one more aspect of his *chero* semiotic, I am locating another outmoded detail to be arrayed alongside his walk, his Native-American features, his stories of *curanderismo* and *brujería,* "witchcraft." I am trying to understand what made these outmoded in the eyes of so many, and why the word *chero* implied a contrasting opposite that was associated with such terms as "with it," "contemporary," or, my preference, "modern."

Another example: Once a year, Oscar Romero Church, the local Catholic parish formerly known as St. Nicholas, held a fund-raising festival. At one level, the festivals seemed to be a collection of fragments that lacked cultural continuity. Here were *tejanos* (Mexican-Americans from Texas), Mexican immigrants from a variety of Mexican states and from urban and rural settings, Mexican-Americans locally born, Puerto Ricans, Black Puerto Ricans, a few African-Americans, very few whites of German or Romanian ancestry, and, of course, mixtures of any of these. At first glance, it was hard to find the communal in all this. For instance, Don Angel was an anomaly, the only person, to the best of my knowledge, who knew the *matachin* dances, spoke of the *viejitos*, or relied so distinctly on the performative style that I've been describing. My sense was that his semiotic contained strands of ancient histories, cultures, and discourses, but his uprooted condition meant that following each strand would lead to a dead end, for there were no other *viejitos*, or *matachin* dancers in the neighborhood to think about, to compare, to ask questions of. In this sense, Don Angel was a powerful symbol of the fragmentation throughout these neighborhoods. In short, these neighborhoods did not so much represent coherent discourse styles; rather, they represented discourses that entered each other and thereby contested stability. And this suggested that a deep jostling was at work, one that created new categories and alliances. In this sense, the word *chero* was profound, for it created stability by locating the outmoded. The young—whether Puerto Rican, of Mexican origin, or whatever—and many of the adults as well had cultivated another set of gestures; hence, both groups could distinguish themselves from the *chero*. The gestures cultivated by the young were often associated with the "hood," hip hop music, and street gangs. It too was part of a thick, highly performative semiotic, but it was very distinguishable from Don Angel's. At such festivals, the young people—some gang members, others merely part of the street culture—crossed paths with Don Angel and other *cheros* of the more urban variety. Everyone read each other immediately and accurately. Meanwhile, there were other young people, for instance, the eldest son of Don Angel's landlord or the dancers associated with a local, teenaged, Mexican folk dance troop. Many of these young people were attending college or aspired to attending college. Their semiotic was also staged for everyone to read and seemed more aligned to the semiotic associated with professional training or professional aspiration. In short, Don Angel's semiotic and the semiotic associated with youth street culture were sharply distinguishable, and yet both distinguished themselves as being outside the circle of conventional power and its own distinctive semiotic that seemed associated with (and I am speculating here, of course) the taming of the body, the rationalizing mind, and the ideology of wording.

Thus far I have been considering stylistic aspects of Don Angel's traces of *viejito* discourse. I will now consider the worldview or content that emerged through Don Angel's words. The worldview referred clearly to beliefs from the past and, moreover, to a past that was quickly fading. He constantly asserted that words, beliefs, and rituals had eroded from his memory and from the wider Mexican society. For instance, one evening Don Angel described how *los vie-*

jitos used large heated stones called *temanastes* to facilitate childbirth if a woman was having trouble giving birth: *Eso del temanaste . . . bueno ahorita los nuevos ni saben qué cosa es eso*, "About the *temanaste*, well now the younger ones don't even know what that is." And quite often in trying to recall incantations and prayers used by *los viejitos*, Don Angel could not remember how they went: *Pos decían otras palabras y ya no me acuerdo*, "They [*viejitos*] said other words and now I don't remember"; *Entonces le rezaban, pero yo . . . no sé qué le rezarían*, "Then they prayed to it, but I don't know what they prayed." The *viejitos* were not a part of contemporary life but images from a memory that was fading. And the slow erosion of these images from Don Angel's life was matched by a similar erosion of these images along another plane, that of Mexican culture itself, for what use do such rituals and beliefs have in a modernizing Mexico? Under such conditions, what about the force of nostalgia and its power to create a *viejito* world of wisdom and propriety? Indeed, something of this creative idealizing was at work, I believe, in Don Angel's imagining of the past. In my interpretive scheme, then, the more Don Angel could construct his own identification with a *viejito* world of integrity—their *tulizes* and *temanastes*, and all that they signified—the firmer his foothold in his more sterile present.

Much of the *viejito* past described by Don Angel was a mix of Catholic (Spanish colonialism) and indigenous practices and beliefs. However, knowing where one began and the other ended was more than I could determine. As explained earlier, the *matachin* dances were a good example of this mix, and the prayers to St. Anthony and the turning of his image upside down were probably another. But how does one trace another one of his *viejito* practices, which he described to us one evening, namely, the use of a *reata*, "rope," to encircle a camp so as to protect oneself magically from wild animals, or the use of candle flames and sieves as divining instruments for locating lost animals and objects? In these examples and others, how extensively have Catholic and indigenous systems grafted themselves together? These are details that I have been unable to track, but the fact that this mixture existed vividly in Don Angel is what gave him breadth and dimension in comparison to others in his neighborhood, for no one else could speak of *viejito* ways as if they were literally a part of his body.

What was salient among *viejito* ways, then, was a kind of dimensioned world in which real action is linked to supernatural action. A divining practice can only work if it is believed that a real candle flame or sieve and real words (prayers) spoken to them are linked, somehow, to lost animals and, similarly, that a rope placed around a camp can prevent wild animals from intruding. Modernity—not the whole of it, since it itself is too divergent, but that part of it influenced by the skepticism of science—does not have a theory that allows

objects, animals, words, people, and souls of the dead to somehow be in communion. When Don Angel said, *Esos cuentos sí . . . los vi yo, y sí . . . eran ciertos,
sí,* "Those stories, yes I saw [witnessed] them and yes they were true, yes,"[12] he
was answering the possible skepticism of another *viejito,* or Edmundo's and my
own skepticism, or that of the church, but more deeply he was answering the
skepticism of modernity. What biological or physical theory of communication might there be for linking the varieties of material existence or for linking
the present to the future? Prior theories of such communication were displaced
by modernity as superstitious. As a result, such theories—or sets of practices
based on such theories—exist in the contemporary world as less than powerful
counters to the authority of the church and even more so to the authority of
modernity. In the context of modernity, such theories have been rendered almost invisible in much the same way that Don Angel himself, as a dishwasher,
janitor, and nursery worker, has been rendered almost invisible, working in the
background of the institutions that need his cheap labor. In this sense, Don Angel was a metonym for one of the deeper ironies of modernity: despite modernity's arguments for democratic equality and human rights, it created a cleavage as it swept and colonized non-European cultures so that those who bear
modernity in their bodies and minds are separated from those who do not, and
this separation has manifested itself as a differential in work, wages, and
power.[13] Hence, Don Angel's body and mind have been only partially converted to modernity.

But I wish to place special emphasis on his partial conversion, on his acceptance (indeed, has he had any other choice?) of the melding of truth and power
as configured by modernity. For instance, he did not necessarily believe all the
occult practices that he had heard about, and when he spoke of the *Indios* who
built the temples of Central Mexico, he did not necessarily accept what he
knew of their truth system (the gods of rain, sun, and moon, for instance) but
preferred the truths of church and science. In short, his disappearing knowledge—words, rituals, and beliefs—placed him on a continuum of historic
changes so that his own *viejito* version could not be more than a trace, and the
viejitos themselves only a trace of those who might be called *los antiguos,* 'the ancient ones.'

I have been describing metaphorically Don Angel's traces of *viejito* discourse as
a kind of layer, a bottom layer, perhaps, upon which all other discourses rested.
It is important to emphasize again that my division of Don Angel into layered
discourses is a contrivance enabling me to explore areas of style and content

[handwritten margin note:] A → very true for Chicano experience

that caught my attention. Don Angel himself did not divide his discourses this way. Nevertheless, he knew that he was different, and this difference is what I am calling his traces of *viejito* discourse. In my interpretive scheme, they "inhabited" his body in the sense that he walked and talked in a somewhat old-fashioned manner, that of the rural Mexican peasant, and this is why many in the neighborhood called him *chero.* part 1   part 2

Don Angel's second discourse style, which I am calling *mexicano*, integrated Don Angel into the rest of the community. For instance, most of the adults I knew, including Don Angel, who had arrived in Angelstown from Mexico in the last several decades called themselves *mexicanos*. In this sense, Don Angel was part of a broadly shared identity related to contemporary Mexico. Because the term *mexicano*, then, was a communal marker, I have chosen it to label the discourse style through which Don Angel performed his everyday living. I cannot analyze even a fraction of Don Angel's *mexicano* talk. However, moments of humor, for reasons that will become evident, are a good starting place for analyzing Don Angel's *mexicanidad*. Let me start, then, by turning to a distinctive *mexicano* genre of joke-telling called the *albur*, which Don Angel was quite skilled at.

In Mexico, the *albur* is a fully recognized verbal art form. It has a singular identity in the stream of daily discourse so that those who play a game of *albures* can point to its boundaries when it occurs and point to those who are particularly skilled at it. Because it is so identifiable, one can purchase books in Mexico that provide *albures*. There are even male movie stars whose careers are based on the mastery of *albures*, and one can rent some of these movies in Angelstown. The *albur*, then, is a fully institutionalized Mexican verbal art form that, although limited mostly to males, is a distinctive part of Mexican identity.

The *albur* is essentially a lewd pun, and to play a game of *albures* requires speakers to keep punning off of each other's conversation until someone gets the last word. To get the last word, particularly with a straight face throughout, is to win, which itself is conceptualized lewdly, equivalent to having fucked the other. To play *albures*, then, is to join a male game in which the participants search through phrases, words, and syllables for every possible way to suggest the penis, sperm, feces, anus, and sexual entry and exit into women, objects, animals, and particularly each other. Although playing *albures* is primarily an intense male game, the sense of words having *dos sentidos* or *doble sentido*, "two meanings," one typically sexual, is understood by men and women. One female acquaintance of mine, for instance, described a *compañera*, "female friend," at the factory where they both worked who often used words with *do-*

ble sentido. My acquaintance, who described herself as more naive about the sexual level of these word games, said that she had to protect herself from her friend or get caught by the puns.[14]

Here is the best way to explain an *albur:* Imagine a language game among English speaking males in which, ideally, a conversation proceeded conventionally but with certain words maintaining another level of sexual meaning. In such a game, words such as "firm," "firm/ament," "af/firm/ing," and prepositions such as "in," "within," and "inside" and hundreds of other words would be especially coded with sexual dimension. For instance, certain words might imply the speaker's erection ("firm") while other words might imply the assholes, mouths, or whatever of the speaker's companions. Language skill, particularly verbal wit, would be associated with the penis and synonymous with power. This sort of hypothetical game provides English speakers a sense of how a game of *albures* functions. True, such a game needs to be described as sexist, and one might also point to the human degradation implicit in such a game and ask questions about the social conditions that would compel the need for sexism and other forms of degradation.[15]

My own interpretation of a game of *albures* will, more than likely, appear to duck the game's sexist dimensions. Even though I believe that such a game is sexist in so far as the penis becomes imbued with power and those who lose are, so to speak, "penetrated" and made submissive, such an interpretation runs the danger of ignoring the linguistic structures of such a game that, as I will argue, are related to the economic and political structures framing many of these games in Angelstown.

Don Angel said that he learned to play *albures* from those he worked with after leaving the region where he was born and raised. He did not learn this form of wordplay from the *viejitos,* but heard and played it often with other *braceros,* "laborers," particularly Mexican farm laborers who were part of a contractual link between the United States and Mexico around the middle of this century. His statements have helped me to justify separating his *viejito* discourse from his *mexicano* discourse, for the *albur,* according to his own description, was a discourse style and content that he learned during the process of experiencing the wider world of the *mexicano.* When he first heard a game of *albures,* he was surprised, wondering why the men were not coming to blows. According to Don Angel, then, to know the lewd sexual play of an *albur* was to distinguish it from a *grosería,* "indecency," that might be taken as a sexual advance. As a result, Don Angel played *albures* only with those with whom he felt comfortable. For him, playing *albures* was entertaining and a sign of cleverness, a way of gaining respect in an art form that was intricate and required such quickness that few, particularly in the context of Angelstown, could compete in the game or even understand it. Indeed, one Sunday afternoon in the backyard of Don Angel's apartment, Edmundo and I joined three men born and raised in Mexico in a game of *albures*. All of the men were at least thirty years of age, and, although there was nothing that might have prevented a younger male from playing, it is doubtful that those born and raised in the United States, such as the sons of one of the men, could have played at the required skill level. In short, English-dominant speakers of Spanish would have been shut out. Indeed, I only followed from the sidelines. It is important to consider the possibility that a game of *albures* in Angelstown was a pocket of *mexicano* talk and identity that excluded the English-speaking world, including the *chicano*.[16] In my interpretive scheme, then, a game of *albures* entailed intense political dimensions. In its inclusions and exclusions, it was a moment of seizing symbolic power, for power here was linguistically, not socioeconomically, construed. In these moments, a man like Don Angel, who was skilled at the game but close to the bottom of the hierarchy of the American economic system, entertained himself and others. More importantly, he acquired respect from others for his improvisations on *mexicano* cultural material, material that was associated with labor and otherwise minimally respected—and sometimes disparaged—by those more in charge of the economic system.

Let me set the scene, then, of that particular Sunday afternoon: A younger friend of Don Angel's, a man whom I will call Tomás, had dropped by to visit with Don Angel. Edmundo, in his typically engaging and open way, immediately struck up a conversation with Don Angel and Tomás, whom we had never met before, and I, in my typically more reserved fashion, tagged along. At some point, the landlord, who lived with his family in the front of the house, joined us. This was typical of the landlord who seemed to enjoy gabbing and relaxing with us on weekend afternoons as we gathered around a picnic table and earth pit, in which, on very rare occasions, he would roast a *cabrito*, "kid goat." At some other point, we were joined by the landlord's youngest child, a preschooler, nicknamed "Baby." Curiously, the name "Baby" was not an uncommon nickname for young children of Mexican immigrants in Angelstown. At any rate, on the tape recording made on that afternoon, Baby's mostly indecipherable commentary as well as birds can be heard in the background along with an occasional passing car or jet descending toward or departing from O'Hare Airport about an hour's drive away.

We joked and laughed together considerably that afternoon. At one point, the landlord told a joke about an apple vendor hawking his goods while disparaging the goods of another apple vendor from California. Because the Mexican vendor clearly got the better of the California vendor, the joke seemed to be tinged with Mexican animosity toward the United States. Don Angel took the story of this vendor as a cue to interject another vendor's joke that was filled with *albures*. As the other men listened, they tossed in another *albur* or two. I should note here that Edmundo played a pivotal role in the evolution of the game, as he always did, for both Edmundo and Don Angel enjoyed baiting each other with *albures*. Indeed, they used these games to create a very deep kind of *confianza*, "confidence." (A note on transcription and translation: I have tried to represent somewhat literally the verbal play of a few minutes by including most of the false starts, ungrammatical language, and incomplete thoughts. In addition to Edmundo and me, two others—both of Mexican origin and graduate students at the University of Iowa, Jorge Calles and Raymundo Rosales—have tried hard to create an English translation that might be adequate to the original Spanish. The task, to say the least, has been most difficult.)

Don Angel:

El lechero era de Zacatecas, "Leche, leche," y otro que de–

The milkman was from Zacatecas, "Milk, milk!" *(his voice changes as if to imitate a vendor calling out, "Milk! Milk!)* and another one *(heckler)* that–

Edmundo:

Es de Jalapa.

He *(heckler)* is from Jalapa.

Don Angel:

Decía "A arrear las sacas, a arrear las sacas," es que dijo, "Oigame–"

He *(heckler)* said, "Get it up, get it up" *(again, as if calling out)*; he *(milkman)* said, "Listen"–
(Everyone has been laughing and now there is even more laughter.)

Tomás:

Es de Jalapa, Veracruz.

He *(heckler)* is from Jalapa, Veracruz.

Don Angel:

Que se enoja, que se enojan también. Dice, "Oigame por qué jijos de," lamiendo

He *(milkman)* gets mad, they *(both milkman and heckler)* get mad too. He *(milk-*

se saca. "Leche, leche," "a arrear las sacas." Que se encuentran, "Oigame hijo de la . . . ¿por qué?"

man) says, "Hey, what the hell?" (laughter all around) lapping it up like a calf. "Milk, milk." "Get it up." (Don Angel shifts voices so as to indicate, first, the milkman and then the heckler.) (laughter) They run into each other, "Hey, you so and so, what the hell?"

Edmundo:
Es que anda de sacatón, eh?

He's a wus, eh?

Don Angel:
Era Zacatenco.

He was Zacatecan.

Edmundo:
Zacatenco.

Zacatecan.

Tomás:
Zacatecas.

Zacatecas.

How to explain the intricacies of this seemingly insignificant moment when a joke was told? On the surface, it appears that a milkman and a heckler are exchanging quips. Beneath the surface, however, there are a number of formulaic words and phrases through which an *albur* gets signaled. For instance, in the sequence transcribed the formulaic terms are: *lechero,* "milkman"; *Zacatecas,* "a state and city in Mexico"; *leche,* "milk"; *Jalapa,* "a city in Mexico"; *sacas,* "take out"; *sacatón,* (difficult word to translate but "wus" is one possibility); and *Zacatenco,* "one from Zacatecas." The literal meanings of these terms, even in Spanish, express nothing special. In this sense, these words at one level, then, are merely normative, for, like other verbal signifiers, they rely on standard meanings in order to permit conventional communication. In short, two actual Mexican locations are described, *Zacatecas* and *Jalapa,* as well as a milk vendor attempting to sell his milk. However, these words are also coded terms: for instance, *leche* also means "sperm" or "come"; hence, a *lechero* might be understood as "one who is full of sperm/come" or "one who is selling sperm/come." In addition, buried inside the terms *Zacatecas, sacatón,* and *Zacatenco* is the root word *saca* or *sacas,* whose *albur* meaning might be understood as "taking out one's dick" as during the act of fucking or during a blow job or masturbating. And the root term inside *Jalapa* is *jala*, "pull," with an *albur* meaning very similar to that of *Zacatecas* or the verb *sacar*, "to take out," but referring, perhaps, a bit more specifically to "jerking off." In other words, if the first level of meaning can be called normative, the second or *albur* level might be called transgressive.

With this preliminary understanding, let us return to the transcribed sequence in order to explicate some of the transgressive details that the translation has failed to capture. Don Angel's audience knew immediately that the *lechero* from Zacatecas referred to someone selling his own sperm. The heckler exposed this insulting "truth" to the *lechero* when he yelled back *arrear las sacas*. The phrase is a hard one to translate, for it contains some intricate punning. For instance, *arrear* sometimes refers to the herding of cattle, *vacas*, and, more generally, to urging or hurrying something along. The heckler's insolence occurred, then, in dropping the word *vacas* and replacing it with an *albur* whose sound is quite similar, *sacas*. In short, the heckler was urging the *lechero's* dick to come as quickly as possible. Even though the word *vacas* never appeared in the joke, it seemed to be suspended throughout because of its association with the word *arrear* and, most importantly, because of its association with cow's milk or the udder of a cow. Don Angel's phrase *lamiendo se saca*, in so far as it suggests the sort of lapping that a cow does, was one example of how those connotations seemed to persist. I need to point out, however, that it was hard to determine exactly the boundaries of the joke. At one level, the *albures* that were tossed back and forth occurred between the *lechero* and the heckler, but at other times they also occurred between Don Angel and his listeners. In short, the *albures* were performed both inside the joke and outside the joke, making the boundaries between the two levels fairly permeable.

At the normative level, then, the joke was not particularly funny, indeed, maybe not even a joke. The humor occurred at the transgressive level—or, more accurately, in the way the transgressive took advantage of the normative. A vendor attempting to hawk his product was made into a fool by a heckler whose one-upmanship functioned scatologically. But, more importantly, it was the joke teller, Don Angel, speaking through the voice of the heckler who performed the leveling. Given the context of the afternoon, humor was created as soon as Don Angel tossed out such code words as *Zacatecas, lechero*, and so on because the normative meanings of these words got leveled by their formulaic, transgressive meanings. Somewhat like the wise-guy heckler who pokes fun at the vendor, skewering him, until the vendor cannot reply except with anger, Don Angel became a momentary wise guy making dirty talk out of conventional meanings and sometimes aiming these at his listeners. But let us also consider Edmundo's role in the making of the humor. He arbitrarily tossed in *Jalapa*, for it was not necessary for the joke's structure, nor was it Don Angel's intention, that the heckler be from any specific locale. The heckler as *jalapeño* was tossed into the evolving humor, therefore, in the hope of goading Don Angel's imagination further so that the inventiveness of the game might increase. It was a moment of repartee, of subtle but affectionate challenge, that could have evolved into a full exhibition of the dueling art of the *albur* but never quite made it. This particular sequence seemed to remain mostly constrained to the joke itself, whose structure, as joke, seemed to limit possibile improvisations. Edmundo's offering of *sacatón* continues the playful punning embedded in *Zacatecas* and emphasizes nicely that the *lechero* has been leveled, made a fool of, skewered, by the power of the *albur*. In this sense, the *lechero* as *sacatón* becomes emblematic of any loser in a game of *albures*, and, as can be projected from Tomás's rather limp performance in this sequence, we will next examine the real squirming—fucking over—of someone (Tomás in this case) caught in the jaws of an *albur*.

Don Angel:

Mira a ese carro cómo le rueda la rueda de enfrente . . .

Look at that car, how the front wheel is rolling. *(A car passes and the group of men look at it. Seven-second pause.)*

Don Angel:

Oh my goodness.

Oh my goodness *(sighing)*.

Edmundo:

¿La rueda se le va a venir quedando atrás?

That wheel is going to fall off (roll to the rear)?

Don Angel:

¿Tú crees?

Do you think so? *(Laughter, ten-second pause, and a jet plane flies by.)*

Tomás:

Mañana tengo que ir a trabajar.

Tomorrow I have to go to work *(sighing)*. *(Seven-second pause.)*

Don Angel:

El trabaja en el rancho de Rozamelos, eh?

He works at Rozamelos farm, eh?

Tomás:

¿Qué rozamelos?

What Rozamelos?

Don Angel:

¿Cómo se llama?

What is it called?

Tomás:

Se llama jes . . .

It's called jes . . . *(Tomás does not complete the thought.)*

Don Angel:

¿Cómo?

How do you say it?

Tomás:

Rousonelos.

Rousonelos.

Don Angel:

¿Cómo?

How do you say it?

Tomás:

Rousonelos, y tú dices Roza Rozamelos, qué Rozamelos.

Rousonelos, and you say roza rozamelos, it's not rozamelos.

Don Angel:

Rozármelos, él también habla muy bien el inglés.

Rubmyballs *(someone claps his hands)*, he also speaks English very well. *(Don Angel changes slightly the speed of his pronunciation in order to make the pun clear: rozamelos = rub my balls.)*

Edmundo:

Si habla muy bien.

Yes, he speaks very well.

Don Angel:

El sí.

He does.

Edmundo:

Y el español lo habla muy bien ya me doy cuenta.

And he speaks Spanish very well, I'm noticing.

Don Angel:

El inglés, también.

English too.

Tomás:

Mira así dice Rousonelos, como dice.

Look, this is what it says, Rousonelos, look here. *(He pulls out a piece of paper, scribbles something on it, and shows it to Edmundo.)*

Edmundo:

Rousonelos.

Rousonelos *(as if reading it with a more American-English pronunciation).*

Tomás:

Rousonelos.

Rousonelos.

Edmundo:

No dice Rozamelos.

It doesn't say rozamelos.

Tomás:

No dice Rozamelos.

It doesn't say rozamelos.

Edmundo:

Uh, uh.

Uh, uh.

Ralph:

Rousonelos.

Rousonelos.

Tomás:

Yeah, Rousonelos.

Yeah, Rousonelos.

Ralph:

Rousonelos Farms.

Rousonelos Farms.

Tomás:

Uhm uhm.

Uhm uhm.

The first transcribed sequence from a Sunday afternoon spent in verbal play concerned the telling of a joke. However, the entertainment and art of a game of *albures* occurs most especially in moments of improvisation. This second transcribed sequence, then, particularly in the wordplay between the actual name of a local farm, Rousonelos Farms, and Don Angel's very clever Spanish pronunciation, *rozamelos*, offers an excellent example of improvisation. *Roza* is a verb form of *rozar*, "to rub," and *me los*, means "those that are mine," with *los* having a more specific *albur* meaning of testicles or balls. *Roza me los*, or more in the spirit of Don Angel's pronunciation, *rozamelos*, then, might be translated as "rubmyballs" with its understood subject, "you," specifically addressed to Tomás.

But the sequence contains more *albures* than this very clever one. Immediately prior to this sequence, the landlord and Tomás discussed the geographic location of the Mexican states in the vicinity of Don Angel's home state of Aguascalientes. The conversation was factual and started by Tomás's seemingly sincere wish to locate the state of Zacatecas, which is, indeed, next to Aguascalientes. Interestingly, this large area in central Mexico was also the region in which the landlord and his wife were born. At any rate, listening to it on the tape recorder the conversation seems a bit idle until, after an eleven-second pause, Don Angel offers his comment on a passing car whose front wheel had an odd roll to it. At the time, I couldn't see any problem with the car, and even today it remains unclear to Edmundo and me whether or not Don Angel was fishing for an *albur*. Within a brief time, however, Edmundo seized the opportunity and instigated an *albur* whose approximate meaning might go like this: *rueda = wheel = testicles* or *balls; venir = to come = orgasm; atrás = behind = butt* or *ass: My balls are going to end up in your ass.* In short, *rueda*, *venir*, and *atrás* as formulaic terms signaled the presence of an *albur*, while "my" and "your" were understood because, as we have seen, a game of *albures* is a game of one-upmanship in which each contestant tries to verbally "fuck" the other. Don Angel's reply, *¿Tú crees?*, was not particularly effective because it is not a formulaic *albur*. In effect, Edmundo had the last word, and Don Angel lost.

Within a few seconds, however, another round of *albures* began. Tomás, somewhat plaintively and without any *albur* in mind, informed us of the fact that he had to work the next day. Within a few seconds, Don Angel, knowing where Tomás worked, improvised a very clever *albur* that depended, as I explained earlier, on the fact that an English name could be pronounced so as to sound like a Mexican *albur*. I do not know if this translation of Rousenelos Farms by Mexicans living in the Angelstown area was a standard joke. Given, however, Tomás's final reaction to Don Angel's wit, there is considerable evidence to suggest that Don Angel invented the *albur* at, perhaps, its moment of telling. (In Angelstown, there were examples of standard jokes that played with the sounds of English/Spanish. For instance, an Anglo lawyer, Brad White, who often serviced Anglestown's Latino community, was known as *pan blanco*, "white bread." Indeed, White even played along with the joke by advertising himself on his lawyer's "shingle" as *pan blanco*.)

At any rate, Tomás seemed to be caught by surprise and spent much of the time afterwards squirming, albeit playfully. I say squirming because his need to reassert the English pronunciation at the expense of the *albur* pronunciation seemed to be a vain struggle to regain some control. But Don Angel had clearly scored a coup, and his insistent request to hear the pronunciation again (*¿Cómo?*, 'How do you say it?') allowed Tomás himself to tighten the jaws of the *albur*. Don Angel's ironic quip, then, about Tomás's skills in English capped the play, exposing Tomás's self-skewering and his emergence in this sequence as the *sacatón*. Incidentally, the word *cómo*, "how" or "what," often functions as an *albur* in Mexican Spanish, for it puns with another *como*, a verb form of *comer*, "to eat," and can be used at a transgressive level to suggest the eating of ass or dick. In this particular sequence, however, Don Angel did not seem to be suggesting that line of punning, but rather relentlessly pursuing Tomás's self-skewering. As a final clarification of this transcribed sequence, I ought to add that a subtle ganging-up on Don Angel began to form after Tomás showed the piece of writing to Edmundo and both agreed that Rousenelos, not *rozamelos*, was the correct name. But the consequences of what that ganging-up might have led to did not occur because I intervened in complete ignorance that a subtle game of *albures* had just taken place. My own commentary, then, caused a detour in the evolving game. It took less than half a minute, however, for Tomás to recover:

Tomás:

Ah! . . . qué Angel ya lo, yal siempre va con la larga allá adelante. Que Rozamelos.	Oh . . . that Angel, he always likes to have the last word. Man, rozamelos.

Edmundo:

Agárrele la palabra a aquel señor, Don Angel. ¿No oyó lo que dijo?	Listen to the gentleman, Don Angel. *(Tomás and Edmundo start to laugh.)* Didn't you hear what he said?

Don Angel:

No oyó este sordo.	This deaf person didn't hear. *(Laughter)*

Tomás's phrase *va con la larga allá adelante* might be translated as meaning "having the last word" or "to have the advantage" or "being in control." Tomás was simultaneously acknowledging Don Angel's wit as well as pitching him another *albur*, for *larga*, "long," has an *albur* meaning of "dick." In short, Tomás was goading Don Angel by describing him "as always going about with his dick in front of him." Edmundo's contribution *agárrele la palabra*, "grab the word" or "seize the opportunity" or "listen," contained a well-concealed *albur* beneath an otherwise very sensible conversation. At the normative level, Edmundo was challenging Don Angel to not let Tomás's last words go by without comment. At the transgressive level, however, *agárrele* is a formulaic *albur* meaning here something like "grab the man's dick." Moreover, the subtle conspiracy to gang up on Don Angel, which had emerged earlier between Edmundo and Tomás, implied that if Don Angel could not reply, the two of them would verbally fuck him.

Don Angel was no one's *sacatón*, however; nor was he to be denied. He played gracefully and quickly with Edmundo's "Didn't you hear what he said?" At the normative level, as if offering a natural reply to a prosaic question, Don Angel deftly responded, "This deaf person didn't hear." But, of course, Don Angel was not deaf, nor was he speaking hyperbolically about not having heard Tomás. Indeed, he was pitching back his own *albur*, for *este sordo* has a transgressive meaning, namely, "this dick." In effect, Don Angel implied that "his dick didn't hear a thing" or "I didn't get fucked, but I just fucked both of you." Edmundo and Tomás had no reply, and this left Don Angel, who *siempre va con la larga allá adelante*, untouched.

The last transcribed sequence starts up after a brief and somewhat curious detour in which Tomás and Edmundo talked about the last names of different nationalities. The instigation here probably had something to do with the name Rousenelos and my own inquiry into whether the name was Italian. According to Tomás, the name was not Italian but Greek; however, for whatever reason, Tomás seemed interested in all the "elli," "eni," and "ini" sounds that one might hear in the final syllables of Italian names. As stated earlier, Edmundo and I had never met Tomás nor were we ever to see him again, and so our understanding of his person and interests (or even his reason for having dropped by to visit Don Angel) were never clear to us. On the surface, however, he seemed a nervous man of big build, and the verbal detour that he pursued seemed to reflect a kind of nervous discomfort with silence—or so goes my interpretation. At any rate, I have chosen to not transcribe the detour that occurred but, rather, to pick up the conversation at that moment when Edmundo attempted to give Don Angel an opening:

Edmundo:

Entonces qué Don Angel?   *(Twelve-second pause.)* What do you
                                           think Don Angel?

Don Angel:

¿Cómo ese apellido de Minalga?

What about that Minalga name?

Tomás:

Hay la mmm ¿Cómo dijo?

Oh the mmm *(almost a sputter as if caught by surprise)*—What did he say? *(Laughter and someone claps his hands.)*

Don Angel:

Ahí apenas.

Right there.

Tomás:

Que te digo cómo se sale.

I tell you he comes out.

Don Angel:

Aquí está el taquito de Sa a Santa, San Nicolás.

Here everyone eats *(laughter)*.

Tomás:

Oh god.

Oh god *(barely audible)*.

Edmundo:

Mire cómo se sale con la suya usted, eh?

Look how you get the last word, eh? *(laughter) (Don Angel is returning to his apartment.)*

Tomás:

¿Qué cómo dijo Nalga, qué, qué dijo?

Look how he said ass/pussy, what, what did he say?

Don Angel:

Mi nalga.

My ass. *(As he opens the door, he repeats it for Tomás's sake and comic effect.)*

Edmundo:

Yyy, ya se enojó.

He got angry. *(The landlord laughs.)*

Tomás:

Es muy rabioso, no?

He's an angry person, right?

Edmundo:

No, ahorita sale.   No, he'll come out in a minute.

Tomás:

¿Sí?   Yes?

Edmundo:

E, es muy bueno para los—   He is very good for the—

Tomás:

Albures.   Albures.

Edmundo:

Los albures, no? Es fino. A veces . . . está   The albures, no? He's good. Sometimes
platicando conmigo muy en serio, hijos.   . . . he is talking to me seriously, man.

Tomás:

Y sale con sus, y y los dice que ni se rie,   And he comes out with his, and he says
parece que es la mera, la mera verdad,   them without even cracking a smile, it
pero no.   seems like it's the real truth, but it's not
                                           (laughter).

Edmundo:

Tiene buen estilo este, el señor.   The man, he's got style.

Tomás:

Y buen humor.   And funny *(laughter)*.

Edmundo:

Se le está derramando la bilis, pero no de   He's busting inside, but not from anger
coraje si no de aguantarse la risa, bub   but from holding back from laughing, bub,
bub.   bub. *(He imitates someone about to burst
                                           because of holding back laughter.)*

Tomás:

Sí, ¿verdad? Está que se quiere reir y se   Yes, right? He's ready to bust and he's
la está aguantando.   holding it in.

Remember that the prior talk between Edmundo and Tomás was about last names, *apellidos*, and did not contain *albures*. After being invited into the talk, Don Angel immediately launched an *albur* while managing to stay on the same subject. Don Angel asks, "What about that *apellido* called *mi nalga?*" *Mi nalga* most often means "my ass," but Mexican men may also use it as a slang term for "girlfriend." In this latter context, "my squeeze" might be an approximate translation, although it does not capture the affectionate vulgarity contained in the Mexican term, and "pussy" might be another, although it seems almost too vulgar. In the same statement, Don Angel also played with the formulaic *albur* described earlier (*como*, "I eat"; *cómo*, "how" or "what"), which on the normative level functions with its non*albur* meanings, but on the transgressive level means always "I eat —." So what was Don Angel saying in this statement that clearly caught Tomás and Edmundo by surprise? A translation is difficult, but it might run something like this: "What about that last name, eat my ass/pussy?" And because it occurred in a contest of *albures*, one might understand him to be saying, "I just ate your ass/pussy." But Don Angel did not stop here, for after the initial expression of his rivals' surprise, he tossed out another formulaic *albur, ahí*, "there," whose transgressive meaning is, once again, "dick." And, then, he tosses out still another, *aquí está el taquito de San Nicholas*, even while Tomás, in particular, remains surprised by the earlier *mi nalga*. This last quip by Don Angel was fairly outrageous and seemed to operate at several levels. Both *ahí*, "there," and *aquí*, "here," have transgressive, formulaic meanings: "dick." Don Angel was referring to his own dick to be eaten like a *taco*, but there was also the suggestion of eating St. Nicholas's dick. *San Nicholas*, of course, was the name of the Catholic church only a block away and whose rather elaborate garden Don Angel had created. The area in which we lived could rightfully have been understood as belonging to the parish of *San Nicholas*. Hence, still another meaning might have been "here's the wise-ass of this place," for *taquito* may sometimes mean "swear word" or, more specifically, "one who says outrageous (smart-ass) things." The best translation, however, may have been "Here everyone eats" or "everyone eats my dick," meaning, of course, "no one beats me at a game of *albures*, I fuck everyone."

Edmundo simply could not top this flurry of *albures*. His *mire cómo se sale con la suya . . .* , "look how you get the last word," has a transgressive meaning that might be translated as "look how you pull out your dick" (*la suya*, "yours," once again means "dick"). But Edmundo's final *albur* was a feeble return, more an affectionate admission of defeat. He knew he got roundly "fucked" by Don Angel's wit. Meanwhile, Don Angel had become preoccupied by Baby, the landlord's youngest child, whose scurrying about had taken him into Don Angel's apartment. (Don Angel had always been annoyed by Baby because of his tendency in the summers to open the screen door of Don Angel's apartment and wander in. Such acts truly violated Don Angel's sense of privacy, fastidiousness, and control.) Don Angel, then, was returning to the apartment to shoo Baby outside and check on any damage. Don Angel's last *mi nalga*, which might be translated as a kind of final "kiss my ass," was made at the door itself, and it was playfully tossed back to the rest of us as a well-timed exclamation mark punctuating the conclusion of the game. The very revealing commentary that followed between Edmundo and Tomás in which Don Angel's skill was discussed tells us much of what we need to know about a game of *albures:* he's laughing inside but holding it back or, as Tomás specifically said, "he says them without even cracking a smile, it seems like the real truth, but it's not."

Tomás's description opens up my own analytic approach: *parece que es la mera, la mera verdad, pero no,* "it seems like it's the real, the real truth [the truth itself], but it's not." Tomás here made a clear distinction between the appearance of truth (or true meanings) and some subterranean dimension, or, in my language, between the normative and the transgressive. The normative, then, is the place where standard meanings occur. It gets codified in dictionaries and schools, has a grammar, and is orthodox. The *albur*, as emblem of transgression, however, is more private in the sense that it occurs mostly during moments of confidence and among males. It is the site of the carnivalesque and the centrifugal, whereas the normative represents the centripetal, in short, the social and linguistic structures associated with proper behavior.[17] I mentioned earlier, however, that the *albur* too has been highly codified (in books) and made public (movies, comic routines). Nevertheless, it is marked as the source of dirty humor whereas the normative is unmarked. In this sense, the *albur* is dependent on the normative. Its very performance cannot occur without, as Tomás suggested, the semblance of truth. In order to deviate from the truths of the normative, then, degrees of attentive listening and verbal labor become necessary, and when these fail, as is bound to happen and as we saw in the transcribed selections, periodic breakdowns occur. An important aspect of the art of the improvised *albur*, then, might be understood as a masking of the labor necessary to create it, in short, a masking of itself so that the normative and the transgressive maintain parallel worlds without revealing the separation that constitutes them. The best *albur*, then, disappears into normative conversation and does not reveal its other world unless one has been initiated. The normative provides the stable center on which the transgressive can perform. The *albur*, then, is performative on normative life and, thereby, creates its humor. Hence, the *albur* is a special moment clearly marked, but it too disappears and the normative returns because conventional life is an enormous presence that provides the stuff on which counterdiscourses perform transgression or resistance.

A closer examination of the *albur* may more clearly reveal the parallel worlds that coexist, one of which is cloaked. These parallel worlds (the normative and the transgressive) seem to maintain separate but dependent grammars and semantics. Although the following analysis strains a bit to show literally what seem to be parallel grammars and semantics, my point in the end is to show how normative and transgressive meanings generally, not literally, function inside the same *albur*. Take, for instance, the exchange among Tomás, Edmundo, and Don Angel:

Tomás:
Siempre va con la larga allá adelante. (He always likes to have the last word.)
Edmundo:
Agárrele la palabra a aquel señor, Don Angel. ¿No oyó lo que dijo?
(Listen to the gentleman, Don Angel. Didn't you hear what he said?)
Don Angel:
No oyó este sordo. (This deaf person didn't hear.)

Edmundo's normative statement at the syntactic level contained a subject, verb, direct object, and modifying prepositional phrase. Nothing unusual here; likewise, at the semantic level, the exchange proceeded without surprise. Don Angel's reply was conventional, for he answered Edmundo's subsequent interrogative with his own statement. In short, the thread of conversation revealed no ruptures. At most, the naive listener might have noticed a certain hyperbole, hence, irony, in Don Angel's reply. But the dominant impression, as Tomás said, was *la mera verdad,* "the real truth" or "truth itself."

But cloaked beneath the normative syntax and semantics was a transgressive syntax and semantics. For instance, at the semantic level the *albur* always cloaks something else: *Zacatecas* cloaks *saca,* which, in turn, cloaks another set of terms; *Jalapa* cloaks *jala;* and *este sordo* cloaks "my dick." This transgressive semantic is coupled to its own transgressive syntax that might be displayed, artificially perhaps, this way: *este sordo* = this deaf one = my dick = my dick just fucked you. Precision in what is at work here is hard to establish because it most often depends on the context, but the *albur,* because it functions as a verbal joust, seems often to implant pronouns—for instance, I, me, and you—and possessive adjectives and pronouns: for instance, my, mine, and yours. Moreover, these implicit pronouns and possessives function, typically, with an implicit verb, say, fuck. This deep cloaking at two levels never gets specified but remains, to the initiated at least, understood. All that is needed to set off the particular transgressive grammar and semantic is the formulaic word or phrase, in short, the *albur.*

Let us examine a less formulaic *albur:*

Tomás:
Mañana tengo que ir a trabajar. (Tomorrow I have to go to work.)
(Seven-second pause.)
Don Angel:
El trabaja en el rancho de Rozamelos, eh? (He works at Rubmyballs farm, eh?)

The seven-second gap between Tomás's factual statement and Don Angel's *albur* may have been significant. Such a fissure may have indicated the mental labor that Don Angel needed to think up the *albur.* Don Angel apparently already knew where Tomás worked (Rousonelos Farms), but whether he had ever converted its English sounds to a Mexican *albur* is unknown. At any rate, an ideal game of *albures* would flow from speaker to speaker, each speaker topping the other while maintaining normative and transgressive meanings without missing a beat. The transcript that I have been examining, however, contained numerous breakdowns that may have signaled the amount of labor needed to create a game of *albures,* and this seven-second gap may have been due to a breakdown.

Despite not being ideal, however, the name Rousonelos and its *albur, rozamelos,* provided another example of a normative semantic cloaking a transgressive grammar and semantic. Tomás said something factual about his life via adverb, subject, verb, and infinitives. After a pause, Don Angel pretended to elaborate further information concerning Tomás's work. Within the elaboration, however, he played with English sounds to make a Spanish meaning, *roza me los,* "rub mine" or "you rub my balls" or "touch my balls." With just the slightest shift in pronunciation, a grammar appeared that contained an understood subject, verb, direct object, and possessive adjective. In short, a new skeletal or syntactic structure appeared that supported a new and transgressive semantic. This other grammar and semantic, then, was buried inside a normative grammar and semantic, but, unlike the more formulaic terms that we have seen, *roza me los* depended more on the proximity of sound between an English word and a Spanish phrase. The more important point to make, however, is how completely the normative structure cloaked the transgressive so that an outsider, such as me, could remain completely fooled. Only after Edmundo showed me the transcript and poked fun at me for not getting it at its moment of happening did I realize what I had missed. For me, it had been a serious conversation. I never heard the transgressive grammar, much less its semantic. What my fundamental mistake suggests is how thoroughly the conversational level, when done well, can mask the *albur*. Like Tomás suggested, it is the cloaking of the *albur* that comprises its art, an art that requires participants to listen carefully for and play subtly with phrases, single words, and even clusters of syllables, and not necessarily the entire sentence.

Games of *albures* could be examined in far more depth, but my intent here is to suggest the gist of two *albures* rather than a thorough understanding of the genre. A more in-depth analysis of the Mexican *albur*—its written versions, its use in comic routines and movies, its occurrence among other groups of males in Angelstown—would, indeed, change the brief analysis provided here. To enter that deeply into the *albur*, however, would shift the focus of this study away from Don Angel as an embodiment of socioeconomic and historical forces. A game of *albures* in this text is not so much a language genre to be analyzed as another example of language use embedded in material and temporal conditions. As Halliday has suggested, language study for the sake of understanding the linguistic system is necessary, but language study for the sake of understanding something else, say, the social system and its distribution of power, is also necessary.[18]

From the perspective, then, of using the study of language to examine the social system, what sorts of things might be said about an insignificant and somewhat private game of *albures* performed one Sunday afternoon in Angelstown? I wish to consider this game as structured along normative and transgressive lines not only linguistically but socioeconomically as well. I have shown something of the highly specialized structure of such a game and argued that the amount of fluency and labor needed to improvise required a kind of initiation. Here, it seems, was a cultural practice that preserved itself more distinctly than many other *mexicano* cultural practices simply because not everyone could perform or even understand a game of *albures*. Variations of the game surely have existed in many Mexican-origin communities in the United States, as Limón has shown,[19] but the ability of the game to move out of *mexicano* culture and to adapt to the cultural material of others would seem to be limited.

If my point has some validity, what might its implications be in the context of an urban space such as Angelstown where the cultural materials of various ethnic and socioeconomic groups were in close proximity and, thus, fluid relationship to each other? In terms of language use, Bakhtin used the term "inter-animation" to characterize these sorts of linguistically fluid conditions, these borrowings and exchanges of language.[20] One language or dialect could "inter-animate" another. On the one hand, the transcribed moment that I have been analyzing seemed to be a bit of cultural material that resisted the currents and eddies of interanimation. For instance, the wordplays of *Jalapa/jala* or *Zacatecas/saca* would seem to be firmly rooted in *mexicano* practice and not easily transplantable. On the other hand, the *albur* of Rousonelos/*roza me los* emerged precisely because of the close contact of languages and cultures, indeed, was an example of outside cultural material brought inside *mexicano* culture. Appropriated in this way, the *albur*, however, could not be easily translated because it was too specialized as a cultural and linguistic practice. Here, then, was a small pocket of linguistic resistance. Here was the joke of a *mexicano* insider, Don Angel, manipulating a verbal art form that was cocooned in the context of Angelstown, and, thus, a pocket of *mexicano* male culture was preserved.

But the particular socioeconomic context of Don Angel must also be taken into consideration. Through games of *albures*, Don Angel momentarily found respect as a man of intelligence and words. His socioeconomic position (as janitor, dishwasher, and most recently nurseryman) made little use of his intelligence and words, but in a game of *albures*, more often than not, he won. The new socioeconomic order that paid his wages was a giant leap beyond the traces of *viejito* life that he could only sentimentalize because they had been left so far behind. In trying to participate in this new order in whatever ways he could, he joined the migrant stream to the United States and, thus, entered other sorts of discourses, including the genre of the *albur*. But the *albur* and *mexicano* life have functioned, generally speaking, as part of the physical labor of that socioeconomic order and not its mental labor. In so far as physical labor has had little prestige in this order, Don Angel has appropriated prestige during those moments of *mexicano* life that have gone unheard by those who manage the order. And, I believe, it was significant that the name Rousonelos of Rousonelos Farms, Inc., a large migrant labor camp in the area, provided the pivotal *albur* around which much of the entertainment occurred. These farms had the authority to both provide and determine the wages of others, including Tomás's. Although the *albur* was not primarily aimed as a playful leveling of the farms, there were hints of the *albur* having pushed authority down into the scatological and the enjoyment of that kind of action.

But there were other aspects of *mexicano* discourse that I wish to point to. For instance, three seemingly insignificant slang terms were often spoken by *mexicanos*, including Don Angel. I consider these slang terms, whose frequency of use made them almost invisible, another sort of opening into *mexicano* life: *agárrame la onda*, "get my meaning," *se me borró el cassette*, "I forgot," and *muchacho nilo/muchacha nila*, "nylon boy/girl." The literal translation of *onda* is "wave," and it can be applied to waves of water as well as radio waves. The image that Don Angel and others provided for explaining *agárrame la onda* was that of tuning into the frequency of a radio station until one eliminated the static. A metaphor of tuning in, then, was applied to the experience of two speakers trying to understand each other (somewhat, perhaps, like the phrases "Catch my drift?" or "Are you tuned in?"), and so the phrase was often a substitute for *¿Me entiendes?* "Do you understand me?" *Se me borró el cassette*, "I forgot," means literally "My cassette tape recording was erased." *Muchacho nilo/muchacha nila*, "nylon boy/girl," begins with the notion that nylon fabric is attractive, hence, stylish. To be *nilo/nila*, then, was to be smart, modern, or "with it." The first two slang phrases borrowed from the imagery of technology to characterize mental behavior: in the first phrase, the negotiation of meaning or the interpretation of another's words; in the second phrase, the cognitive act of forgetting. The third phrase also used a recent technological invention to characterize behavior, namely, exterior behavior, including one's personality, sense of style, and looks.

There was nothing especially remarkable about these phrases, despite their humor in English translation, but when they are considered in the context of what I have been calling the broader cultural and historical conditions of Don Angel's layered discourses, new insights emerge. Much of the imagery in Don Angel's traces of *viejito* discourse, as I have suggested, consisted of working the land and some sort of invisible relationship between humans, objects, and animals. If *viejito* discourse had something to do with the retrieval of the past, the struggle toward the modern was more evident in *mexicano* discourse, in its *albures* and its slang thick with modern imagery. Although my interpretation runs the danger of making too much of seemingly innocent slang terms, these terms used the imagery of technology to characterize interior and exterior conditions of the individual. In Mexico, the *viejito* lifeways have both resisted and adapted to the forces of modernization. Technological innovation in Mexico and elsewhere has become a powerful trope penetrating everyday language with images of modern life. But a man like Don Angel, who was inhabited by both *viejito* and *mexicano* discourses and performed them skillfully, was marginalized in both Mexico and the United States because in the eyes of others his own traces of *viejito* discourse acted as a kind of friction slowing the push toward modernization. Interestingly, however, the modern needs the unmodern

(Don Angel and others like him) as its labor class. This entire ideology, if it can be called that, has acted upon him until he too has accepted its claims about who he is and is not. In this sense, then, this push toward the modern might be described as hegemonic, for it not only defines the sorts of "truth" schemes that help to structure the semiotics of power but, in so far as these same schemes are accepted by the less powerful, they help to structure that semiotic as well. For instance, like a *muchacho nilo* Don Angel's prized shirts and pants were made of nylon, perhaps because they were cheaper to purchase but also because of their association with stylishness. In short, Don Angel in these very small actions and uses of language interiorized the hegemonic beliefs around him in order to acquire a degree of status, but he could never quite remove his *viejito* traces. In accepting those hegemonic beliefs as truths, he helped to create his own marginalization, but, and this is important in my analysis, this very interiorization of the modern was what allowed him to make his way—to earn wages, retire, engage in a game of *albures*, and meet those who had more socioeconomic power than he, especially in his work as a gardener. These actions were significant, even if also marginalized, for they contained what he defined as some of his talents. In finding talented parts of himself in these actions, then, he found moments that allowed him to individualize himself within conditions of apparent hegemonic oppression, or to create respect under conditions of little or no respect.

Thus far, I have explored two discourse styles that were conducted in Spanish. As I have tried to make clear, I have separated these two styles artificially by noting that, for Don Angel, the specialized genre of *albures* was learned not among the *viejitos* but among other Mexican males sometimes in the context of work. Clearly, however, the fact that both discourses were conducted in Spanish means that the cleavage I have made is useful for analytic purposes but artificial for understanding the reality of his discourse performances. I am ready to turn to the last discourse "layer" that completes my analytic scheme.

The third discourse style was clearly demarcated as different. It occurred in English and might even be characterized as nonexistent as discourse since it consisted of isolated words and phrases, many of which were formulaic. Here is a short list of Don Angel's English repertoire: "How are you?" "Nice to meet you," "Good-bye," "Welcome," "Go ahead," "Ten minutes," "You talk to Norma," "Okay, show me," "Oh my goodness," "mall," and "vacuum." These words and phrases were associated specifically with janitorial work, and I presume there were other words associated with gardening, dishwashing, and his earlier work as a field laborer. My point, however, is not to list every term and phrase that he knew but to suggest the fragmentary quality of his discourse in English.

I wish to consider the relationship between Don Angel's fragmented English discourse and the stream of English words, oral and written, that surrounded him. Don Angel's limited ability in English suggests, metaphorically at least, that the language of coworkers, managers, and the media existed as an almost unmanageable, victimizing flood. Indeed, it was not hard to find evidence to support this image. For instance, there was the day that he requested help from Edmundo and me in interpreting his car insurance bill. And there was another day when he asked me to help him fill out a form to send with a cash payment to the local diocese. In fact, interpreting phrases heard at work, filling out forms, writing official letters, interpreting at lawyers' and doctors' offices or at car repair shops were frequent activities that Edmundo and I engaged in not only for Don Angel but many others in the neighborhood.

If the potential for linguistic and socioeconomic victimization, as a consequence of knowing limited English, was always present, one should expect to find Latinos/as suspicious and resistant of the Anglo world and that some of this should be formulaically structured in their talk. Indeed, I wish to interpret a selection of formulaic jokes and puns used by Don Angel and many other Latinos/as in Angelstown as containing elements of suspicion and resistance. One of the most common of these jokes/puns, and one that I have heard most of my life, was *no me chinglés*. The pun combined *No me chingues*, "Don't screw me," "Don't cheat me," or "Don't fuck me over" with *inglés*, "English." The meaning of the pun, then, was "Don't cheat me or fuck me over by using English." Another joke/pun was *anglosangrón*, which combined *anglosajón*, "Anglo-Saxon," and *sangrón*, which is related to *sangre* "blood" and describes a person who is ruthless, impolite, or of "bad blood." Still another common pun was the subtle pronunciation of Chicago as *sí cago*, or "Yes I shit." All of these wordplays contained, of course, a kind of biting resistance to Anglo ways and authority. Lastly, the following joke should sound familiar to English speakers because it contains ethnic stereotyping and a four-part structure set against a backdrop of crisis. (Rather than translating from the Spanish, I have summarized the joke in English.)

> A Spaniard, Frenchman, Mexican, and American are in need of help. The Spaniard prays to the Virgen de la Macarena, and she comes and helps; the Frenchman prays to Santa Teresa [I believe this refers to a French nun canonized in 1925 and known in Spanish as Santa Teresa del niño Jesús], and she comes and helps; the Mexican prays

to the Virgen de Guadalupe, and she comes and helps; the American,
realizing that he has no one to plead to and that this is his last chance
asks the Virgen de Guadalupe, "Hey, what about me?" The Virgen
replies, "Sorry, I no speeke English."

I take these jokes and puns and others still to have been ventings of resistance, small moments when frustration can be released via words. *No me chinglés* and *anglosangron* pointed to a general distrust of the English speaker, a fear that the American will take advantage of the Spanish speaking. However, "I no speeke English," spoken by the Virgen de Guadalupe, a religious and national symbol of Mexico, took the underlying fear and suspicion and transformed conditions of helplessness into conditions of dominance. The phrase "I no speeke English" is common among both English and Spanish speakers. Typically it pokes fun at the more helpless Spanish speakers when facing more dominant English speakers. "I no speeke English," then, summarizes Latino/a powerlessness, but what is not often noticed is that it may also be a strategy of self-defense, a moment of acquiring a modicum of power within a more generalized condition of powerlessness. In this latter sense, the phrase means, in effect, "I will not cooperate, you will have to go elsewhere." In the mouth of the Virgin, however, the phrase "I no speeke English" suggests even further dimensions. Her associations with Truth itself, particularly at the moment of death, suggest that the English speaker has been the helpless one all along (partly because of Protestantism, atheism, or secularism). The Virgin's words, then, are ironic, for they transform the formerly helpless into a position of dominance and the formerly dominant into a position of helplessness. In short, she wreaks a kind of righteous vengeance, and in so doing she summarizes Mexican desire. Indeed, all these puns and jokes were a kind of vengeance, a venting of resistance via language, a put-down of North American ways and English speakers, indeed, a symbolic reconquering. *A caveat: Moments of derisive laughter via formulaic jokes may tell us something important about communal beliefs but they do not finally tell us much about* individual *beliefs and frustrations among those who tell and laugh at the jokes. Such jokes may tell us something about the communal, but not necessarily how deeply the communal is shared by the individual.*

I need to return here, however, to my central point about Don Angel's fragmented English. Thus far, I have argued that the image of a resentful victim almost helpless in a surrounding flood of English was, at least, an adequate characterization that has been captured in a selection of formulaic jokes and puns. In many ways, however, this analysis and imagery are misleading. To a considerable degree, Don Angel—and others even more so—navigated the flood through a series of improvisations and appropriations, which were rather similar to my description at the beginning of this chapter of his manipulation of identification cards. The improvisations used were not surprising but commonsensical, the sorts of things that most language users would try in order to navigate the straits of another language. Here is a summary of how Don Angel accomplished his job as a janitor despite his fragmented English discourse:

1

Most of the janitors (about thirty) that he worked with were Latino/a or of Latino descent. Almost all, including one supervisor who was Mexican, knew at least some Spanish. In being linked by Spanish, the workers created a highly informal network of information that enabled the hiring of new employees; the filling out of applications and other bureaucratic forms; the dissemination of company rules, work orders, and changes in work procedures; and the reading of product directions as well as instructions on how to use dangerous chemicals properly.

2

If someone from this network was not available to explain how to use, for instance, a new product and Don Angel could not understand the English explanation, he resorted to his formulaic "Show me." A demonstration of the job to be done by someone who knew how was a good substitute for a verbal explanation of the job.

3

Because many of the cleaning products in the United States were also marketed in Puerto Rico and Mexico, Don Angel and the other janitors already knew how to use some of them. Three products that Don Angel mentioned were Bleach, Clorox, and Windex. These products and others, then, belonged to an international economy. Their names, purposes, and dangers might be described as small examples of a kind of shared knowledge that bridges the linguistic, cultural, and socioeconomic differences that separate the United States and Latin American countries.

4

Over time, new products and terms became memorized. For instance, since Don Angel read little English, he had never encountered what he called "soap hand." Quickly, however, he memorized the words and what they signified. He may not have known how to pronounce these words, but sight recognition was enough. One result was that when the cleaning company changed its suppliers, Don Angel often continued to identify the product, its uses and dangers, without anyone's help.

5

Related to his memorization of basic terms was a subtler method of comparing ingredients, descriptions, and directions for using two products, one that he was already familiar with and another that he had never used before. He may not have understood the terms nor known how to pronounce them, but their visual similarities helped him to decipher what a new product was and how to use it.

6

Don Angel also used color and smell to help him determine if a new product was meant to replace another one.

These commonsensical responses to knowing little English might also be described as creative adaptations or even "poachings."[21] In Don Angel's experience and that of many others, English and Spanish were hierarchized. They demarcated social stratification as surely as the other elements that constituted what I have been describing as the semiotics of the more powerful and that of the less powerful. In such conditions, English potentially was a tool of exclusion and manipulation, and these were the festering sources from which the Spanish jokes and puns described earlier emerged. The motive behind the jokes and puns was the leveling of social stratification, but it was the sort of leveling that remained bound to words and bound to one's circle of intimates who understood Spanish.

If, in contrast, one were to search for actions and words that actually realized a degree of leveling, one might start, perhaps, with the practices that made English intelligible to a nonspeaker such as Don Angel. These practices were private and extremely localized in so far as Don Angel's absorption of "janitorial English" occurred spontaneously when a particular situation demanded it. Such practices were difficult to document, for their inventiveness, privateness, and unpredictability constituted a kind of "poetics," which de Certeau called "the practioner's constructions of a text."[22] These practices appropriated that which had been distanced because of social stratification. A man like Don Angel selected from the distant and drew it near. This space called the "near" might also be called the "site of awkward translation"; hence, Don Angel remembered "hand soap" as "soap hand" and, as he himself said, often knew the visual representations of words but not their pronunciations. These were personal inventions, then, approximate routes full of detours that also found their way to the making of meaning. Because they were private, local, and unpredictable, they would have eluded the kind of documentation that has been often cited by government and business leaders as proving that Americans in general—and particularly those who belong to minority and immigrant populations—suffer from a literacy crisis.[23] Don Angel's fragmented discourse, his approximations and appropriations, would go unmeasured because standardized tests cannot measure the overwhelming number of nonstandard routes that also lead to the making of meaning. But these routes, elusive and almost untheorizable, are also a set of actions by which power and the ciphers that preserve it are momentarily deciphered.

Here at the completion of this long analysis of Don Angel's "layered discourses," I encounter the theme that started my investigation. Hernadi created an image of ominous state control rooted in the inability of immigrants to decipher bureaucratic documents.[24] The observation was shrewd because the recording of individuals through print and numbers and their representations through ID cards and so on does facilitate social management, a management that is all the more insidious because it can link itself readily to the well-being of individuals and society through such examples as police protection or voter registration. But social control and who benefits the most from it is a debate that I am not equipped to treat. My more central point concerns those moments when state control and social stratification that favors the powerful experiences a kind of leveling at the hands of those deemed less powerful. Don Angel's manipulation of ID cards or his fragmented English discourse were signs of a vast "poetics" that I understood as a hermetic terrain in which everyday life improvised a series of escapes that were difficult for immigration officials to observe or would have been difficult for experts documenting literacy figures to observe. In some ways, Don Angel's life, like an *albur*, maintained a mostly normative surface through which a certain amount of transgressive play occurred. In claiming this condition for Don Angel, I have begun to lay down a major theme that will be developed in a variety of ways throughout the rest of this book.

4

A BOY AND HIS WALL

Ralph:

Why did you put everything up on the wall?

Valerio:

I put it because it looks better.

R:

You like it that way?

V:

Yeah, cause if I don't, it looks, it looks plain. Just like the water, it looks plain.

R:

Just like plain water?

V:

Yeah.

R:

What's the first thing that you put up? Do you remember?

V:

First thing that I put up is, is these two posters right here, this one and that Ferrari . . .

R:

The Ferrari?

V:

Yeah, the one ripped.

R:

And that one up there?

V:

That's a Porsche.

R:

OK, then, the Ferrari went up first and then the Porsche?

V:

Yeah, well I put them at the same time.

There were two walls in Angelstown that framed a life. In fact, all over Angelstown there were literal and metaphorical walls framing the lives of individuals I cared about. These walls were symbols of confinement, of the deep fissuring that separated those who have more power and socioeconomic standing from those who have less. Their power to confine heightened a certain fantasy-making. But desire and fantasy-making are a kind of scaling of walls. Walls as confinement, then, walls of a pressure cooker that caused the imagination to bubble.

I turn, therefore, to two walls in a bedroom. They belonged to Valerio Martínez, who was fourteen when I first saw the walls. He was born in Mexico and arrived as a five-year-old with his parents in 1980.[1] Valerio and his two brothers shared the same small bedroom, while the two sisters slept elsewhere. In this sense, confinement was literal, and everyone in Valerio's family talked about it. A two-bedroom apartment is too small for seven people, they said. When I was with Valerio or members of his family, my feelings became shaped by theirs, curved like the curved doggedness of their stocky bodies. I never felt this anywhere else in Angelstown: something Saturnian, relentless as the overpowering heat that emerged from the bakery ovens and vats of *carnitas*[2] and pushed me drenched out the door of the cooking shed behind the grocery store where Valerio's father worked when I first met him—or like his mother's common observation that the family was *muy tapada*, "closed," "stupid," "thickheaded."

But people find ways to subvert what pains them. One day when I walked into the apartment, Valerio's father asked me how I liked the walls. I looked. He had found cans of leftover paint and painted a few walls in pastels or bright colors. He grinned. It reminded him of the colors used in Mexico he said. Valerio's family had also trained vines (varieties of pothos, which are a kind of philo-dendron) to frame entire entrances to some of the rooms in the apartment. Don Angel similarly trained vines to a cord that ran up to the ceiling of his room, across to the central light fixture, and over to a second wall. And there was the dance teacher of the local Ballet Folklórico who had no place to put all the props of his troupe, and so he arranged his brilliantly colored props along the walls of his apartment. Walls, then, may confine, but they are also "blank spaces" on which imagination can write out a desire and protect the self. If these individuals protected themselves with the traditional and nostalgic, Valerio, as we will shortly see, protected himself with images of the modern.

Within their home nostalgia provided Valerio's family with beauty and comfort in the form of colorful paints and winding green vines, but how vulnerable is nostalgia as it moves outside the privacy of one's home and becomes public, hence, susceptible to the derision of others. For instance, Valerio's father was labeled *chero*, and Valerio probably was too by his peers who wore hipness on their bodies. (Valerio hated the word, and his animosity suggested, to me at least, personal encounters that had stung him.) For youth, in particular, the label *chero* was threatening because it was an ever present reminder of what it means to be unmodern. I recall an afternoon when, during an open-air performance of the local Ballet Folklórico, gang members sitting in the front row poked fun at the dancers in their colorful, quaint costumes, and the dance teacher lost his cool. I had never seen him rant and rave. That day he was trying hard to shame his critics, pointing to what he imagined to be their dissolute lives. He didn't understand their own need to separate themselves from all the quaint imagery of Mexico that locked them into backwardness and a kind of systemic humiliation structured by the power differential that separates the United States from Mexico more exactly, if invisibly, than any border.

Valerio's narrow bedroom walls seemed to mirror the psychological and socioeconomic confinements that boxed his life, while the montage of posters, newspaper clippings, and mementoes that he scotch-taped to the walls revealed his imagination's work in subverting that confinement. Valerio constructed a narrative about himself in these posters and clippings. In a sense, he wrote himself out on these walls. In school, he did not write himself. There, he was labeled learning disabled (LD), as was his older brother, and they both said being LD meant being a "dummy." They talked about getting out of LD classes, but I knew that doing so would entail passing a battery of special tests, tests that had already designated them over the years as LD. The histories of these tests had become parts of their perceived personas, and such histories are hard to overthrow because they are official histories, products of the most up-to-date testing instruments that educational experts have devised.

Approximately two years before Valerio began covering his walls with posters, I talked to the language therapist/pathologist in charge of LD at Valerio's school. An attentive and playful person—Valerio's favorite teacher he had said—she spoke in her smokey voice of her affection for Valerio, but she also told me, so to speak, about the wiring of his psyche. According to the test scores, Valerio had a learning disability in the language area but not in other areas. We started to look at some of his recent test results. On the digit-span test, for instance, he exhibited poor memory skills. On the similarity test, he had trouble finding the overarching category that would link, say, a ball and a wheel (roundness). In addition to a poor memory, then, he had trouble labeling and finding exactly the right word. We started to examine some of the details from one of the labeling tests. He typically got things, as she said, only "sort of right." A "cash register" became a "casher"; "tweezers" became "eyelashes"; a "stadium" a "field"; an "anchor" a "hook"; a "stump" became "bark"; a "well" a "fountain." We turned to another test to examine his problems with categorizing. He couldn't say, for instance, what "hot," "cold," and "warm" have in common. The answer is "temperature," but he said "opposites" and "liquids." For "mother," "aunt," and "cousin" he provided no answer, and the speech pathologist explained, "Sometimes he just quits. . . . It's just like an overload. Too much goes in and he doesn't absorb anymore, so he just quits."

Valerio also had trouble, she said, with explanations, definitions of terms, and reading comprehension. Reading for him, she surmised, was not reading for meaning or enjoyment but reading in order to fill in blanks and hoping that he got it right so that he wouldn't have to do it over again. While I listened to the language therapist describe Valerio's "disabilities," I thought about the magnificent circularity of schooling, that schooling historically has trained students into a fill-in-the-blanks conception of reading and then complained when students have thoroughly absorbed that training. But even as she specified Valerio's learning disabilities, she noted some of his strengths. His nonverbal skills were at least average, she said, and he scored well on yes/no answer tests and, interestingly enough, on activities that required connected discourse. It was as if in the everyday world where discourse is largely performative and social, constructed in groups or dialogically, he did well, but in the school world of metadiscourse—where discourse and its parts become the objects of study or, in short, testing grounds for evaluating individual competence—he started to short-circuit. Notice, for instance, that in her own summary of Valerio's strengths and weaknesses she made a distinction between comfort and worry

for many second language learner [handwritten marginal note]

almost as if his learning disabilities might vanish within a context that was not a testing ground: "I think there's more ability than the testing indicates. There is more in there than we're getting out. . . . But his ability to communicate to you and to define and explain his thoughts is very difficult because he lacks the vocabulary, he lacks the memory and he lacks the specific labels to tell you what he would like to. And when he feels comfortable with you, he doesn't worry about it. And that's when you get all the questions . . ."

Ah, the questions! Such a peculiar charm they had over me. Valerio's incessant questions were central to his person and one of the things that made him so attractive. Even his teachers and administrators in his school were especially fond of him, and everyone, including his parents, pointed to his incessant questions. "Where do you work, Ralph? What are the people like over there? How many people are above you, how many below you? How much money do you make? What do you do at your job? What makes your computer work? How does a plane fly? Who owns airplanes? How big is your house? What's inside a baseball?" Without my asking, the language therapist offered an interpretation of his incessant questioning: He seems to be trying to establish and reestablish bits of content in his memory bank because he has a short-term memory problem, she suggested. At the time, I was puzzled by her interpretation. Now I offer another one: Questions are probings of the unknown. What was unknown to Valerio? I return to the image of the wall, in this case, the invisible wall that separated Valerio, his family, and many others in the neighborhood from the sources of power. For me, his questions did not emerge from some sort of miswiring but from socioeconomic and ethnic differences. Each question was a potential bridge thrusting over the wall and tapping sources of power that weren't his. The world as circumscribed by expert knowledge was his unconscious target, and from his distance he fantasized its importance, became polite and docile—just like other family members—in its presence, and humiliated and *unnerved* by its existence. I never made a careful study of his questions, but I remember, in particular, questions about my income and employment. Were my answers to these questions simply inadequate, and so he asked them again and again? Maybe. Did he ask the same questions of his parents, uncles, and aunts that he asked of me? I do not know. Were these questions explicit socioeconomic probings leaping the wall manufactured by power differences and bubbling up from an invisible but ongoing humiliation, which, in short, was his side of the wall? I think so.

I spent two vigorous hours with the language therapist sorting through a messiness that was less Valerio's and more mine. Was LD actually there as something inside Valerio's psyche and the psyches of other Latino children?

I've spent twenty years here. . . . I have seen the number of children with this kind of a problem increase. . . . The Hispanic population has increased here so . . . if you put the two together, mostly what I have are Hispanic children. . . . If you would do a strict test for retrieval or word finding, what you would do would be to take words that you know that the child already knows . . . "cat" and "book" . . . these types of words, and what happens is that you show these to the child and you take the latency time, how long it takes them to come up with them. . . . This kind of a child . . . they just have trouble thinking of the right word at the right time. It's gone. . . . Valerio will just tell you, "I don't know, I forgot." . . . It's really more than just learning the labels, it's a skill of being able to come up with one word or two short words opposed to telling me that this is something flat with four legs that you eat at. It just doesn't work for storing information. So it's more than just knowing the labels. You can already know the labels, but the latency time is so great they're useless.

The language therapist had some doubts about LD "reality." For her, LD test results were unimportant and unconvincing if a student's classroom performance or the practical judgments of teachers said otherwise. Moreover, some teachers, notably from the bilingual staff, rarely recommended LD testing for their students. They sensed, apparently, that LD "reality" was more messy than officialdom acknowledged. Nevertheless, terms like "word retrieval" and "latency time" cycled through the official discourse, amplifying its authority. Such terms seemed to reduce the appearance of messiness, but there may be an irony here: in the process of elevating the exactness of one's terms, a new kind of messiness sweeps in. For instance, for the Latinos described by the speech pathologist, might "word retrieval" and "latency time" problems have been official but obfuscating descriptions of being half-out and half-in a language? Oral history interviews, for example, revealed that since the 1920s the problem of not fully knowing English had been a characteristic of Mexican students in Angelstown's schools.[3] As one elderly gentleman, who knew only Spanish prior to entering school, put it, "I'd come home with my hands all blistered up, you know, and Ma says, 'What happened?'—and I says, 'Well they slapped my wrists 'cause I couldn't remember, or I couldn't pronounce, or I couldn't say it like the (other) kids." In the context of Valerio and others, then, were "word retrieval" and "latency time" mystifying terms belonging to a discourse of measurement that reconfigured a simple problem of not knowing a second language ("I couldn't remember," "I couldn't pronounce") as a kind of miswiring?

More significantly, might LD "reality" get constructed, in part, in the moment of discourse between examiner and examinee, between the test and the test-taker, in that moment of worry that the language therapist talked about? On the one hand, much of the authority of LD "reality" rested, in part, on objectively assessing something actually there inside Valerio and others. In contrast, to suggest that LD may also be created in the moment of dialogue between participants who are unequally powerful means that LD may be less "there" in the tested subject and more in the social/political contexts in which the testing occurs. This suggestion also begins to undermine LD as implacable authority, which was the image under which Valerio labored.

Of course, my naiveté about LD undermines this text, but as the language therapist and I worked through the messiness of Valerio's and others' LD "reality," it occurred to me, finally, that those labeled LD did not see its representation as messy or ambiguous. Here, then, was the most significant issue: if the language therapist, bilingual teachers, and I had access to several representations, Valerio and his family did not. LD as a "reality" was the only representation he and his family knew, and although in official discourse it had replaced, with good intentions, the stigmata of "dumbness," the distinction between LD and "dumbness" had become in everyday discourse too subtle to distinguish. For Valerio and his family, LD was equivalent to the old stigma. Moreover, there was the mother's own term *tapada* that was intractable because it could absorb more modern and subtle terms, such as LD, and continue to replicate the belief that one was stupid.

Participants on both sides of the wall, then, contributed in their different ways to the making of LD "reality," fixing it ever deeper as an authoritative label whose messiness was hard to uncover. On one side of the wall, there was the family's conviction of failure, ever flexible in its ability to discourage, distanced from any other representation except the one given to them by the authorities. On the other side of the wall, there was the authoritative system itself that, like most such systems, creates its specialist vocabularies and other means for erasing its own messiness. Hence, in the minds of Valerio and his brother (and others I presume), the LD designation became a subtle oppressor whose weight might have been lessened if they could have only peered into the possible messiness that was hidden by the wall. In effect, the single representation that authority offered was a magnifying lens through which outsiders beheld insiders. In the end, the good intentions of the experts who had first articulated the conditions of LD and devised the diagnostic tests were unable to deflect real-world appropriations—or so goes my interpretation.

The language therapist and I also looked at some of Valerio's writing. My fieldnotes for that afternoon (29 January, 1988) describe formulaic, cramped, unmotivated "essays" of single paragraphs as if the object were to get them done and leave. Unfortunately, I was unable to make copies of those early writings because of school policies put into place to protect the students. In order to provide some grounding for my observations, however, I offer other examples of Valerio's writing. In September and October of that same year, I received two handwritten letters from Valerio. I had just moved from Angelstown to Iowa, and these letters were the beginnings of a very modest amount of correspondence between us. I doubt that anyone can convincingly argue why in these letters certain discourse characteristics occur and others do not, nor do I believe that we can reliably perceive his school essays through a very different genre, namely, the personal letter. Nevertheless, I offer these letters because I recognize the Valerio I knew in them. That is to say, I recognize—between the lines, so to speak—the same self-conscious hesitation (cramping worry) through which he felt this world of unequal power. And this condition of power difference, as I argued earlier, periodically motivated fusillades of questions. (I have copied his writing exactly, his spelling, punctuation, paragraphing, and so on. He was approximately twelve years old at the time of these letters.)

Sept. 12, 1988

Dear Cintron Family,

It was nice to hear from you Ralph. I liked hearing about Iowa.

Im in sixth grade this year. My teachers names are Mrs. Hume and Mrs. Home. I'm a Lieutenant for school patrol this year.

My dad likes his job. My mom is going to go to school to learn English. My dad might buy a new car.

I would like to now more about Iowa and your house.

Sincerly,

Valerio and family

October 10–88

Dear Ralph Cintron

It give me good pleasure. That you wrote to me. It give me good pleasure That your family gets alone well. In the picture your house looks big and nice. Angel wen't to Chicago with my mom and dad.

> Polonia is very well said the doctor. Next month they are going to
> open a new clinic in Hubertville for cistis fabroses. Ralph one day we
> are going to your house.
>
> Ralph you said that you want to know about the baby. The next
> visit is at Jan. at the new clinic Angel is going to transalte.
>
> Ralph thats it for now.
>
> Ralph when are you coming to visit us.
>
> > Sincerly
> >
> > Martinez family
> >
> > Thank you

According to the language therapist, Valerio's school essays were compara-
ble to those of other students his age although teachers might have expected
more than single paragraphs. As I sat reading the single-paragraph essays that
Valerio had written over the years, I began to wonder more deeply about LD.
For instance, the language therapist had two functions: she administered the
LD tests to Valerio and others, but she also tutored their writing and reading.
This latter service was particularly practical and very valuable to the school district. In short, it could be argued that designating students as LD helped to
maintain a bureaucratic niche, that LD was less a clearly defined disorder and
more a generic term or rationale, a bureaucratic ploy by which Valerio could re-
ceive the help of a language tutor, help that he, indeed, needed.

However, recalling at this later date that meeting in January 1988 with the
language therapist, I believe that doubts should be raised about the tutoring
help that he received. Valerio, it now seems to me, had come to understand
rather precisely what his school meant by language training: Before one could
learn connected discourse, one had to lay a foundation in unconnected discourse (labeling, defining, categorizing, and so on). Indeed, the language therapist stated several times how important it was for students to practice these language skills, which I earlier called metadiscursive skills. Such a conception of
language instruction might be called structuralist, and the next structural unit
up, so to speak, is the paragraph. (Interestingly, when the language therapist
showed me the paragraphs of other LD students, her main concern was with sequencing—beginnings, middles, and ends, as she put it—and a concern with
sequencing seems to affirm, again, a structuralist orientation.) Valerio's one-
paragraph essays were formulaic and unmotivated, then, for the reason that the
school's structuralist orientation had been drilled into him so extensively that
he felt no additional and personal motivation connected to writing. In fact, one
day, according to the language therapist, he pulled out an early "essay" and said,

"Remember when I could not write?" What he meant by writing was the quality of his handwriting. A preoccupation with structure had prevented the emergence of what might have been a more motivating concept, namely, writing as meaning-making.[4] It occurs to me now that perhaps Valerio was cycling nicely through the circularity of schooling: (1) He had clearly experienced trouble in the classroom, but the trouble had been defined according to a structuralist conception of language instruction. (2) The LD tests located the trouble because they were constructed to measure student ability in handling the structuralist aspects of language. Further, the scientistic aura of the tests elevated the importance of the structuralist conception for language instruction and made it a verity. (3) The therapy or tutoring that was offered was similarly conceived within the same womb—as well it should have been because tutoring is meant not to interrupt the cycle but to return the student to the fold. The three components of the cycle, then, were mutually reinforcing, circular.

Moreover, Valerio's parents tacitly reinforced the same assumptions. Before meeting Valerio's language therapist, I had discovered that his parents' language instruction in Mexico had also followed a largely structuralist conception in which language drill, correct spelling, handwriting, and so on played prominent roles and meaning-making did not.[5] Valerio's cramped, dutiful, self-conscious, and uninspired paragraphs—as if nervousness and fear had written them—seemed to me consistent with his parents' experiences with schooling that somehow had induced, at least in his mother, the conviction that she was *tapada*. Valerio's school may have wanted to see confident students in command of their pages, but in Valerio's case the methods for producing that student coalesced with a family history in which regimented rights and wrongs were seen as natural. The result was paralysis, not confidence-building. A certain heaviness of life, the Saturnian quality I named earlier, had been etched onto the Martínez family because this is how life had managed them. The heaviness seemed dense, buried, and not graspable because reflective and self-reflective languages had not yet emerged.[6] Despite its intentions, schooling for Valerio continued to etch the same theme of heaviness even deeper with a new tool called LD. Here, then, was another real-world appropriation in which the good intentions of schooling—whether enlightened or not—were bent until they conformed to massive social and historical forces. If one accepts my perhaps overpsychologized interpretation, all this (and much more that was hidden from me) was present, I believe, in the life of Valerio.

But people find ways to subvert. The very walls that confine can also become blank spaces whose prodigious size can be used to magnify interior life and make a spectacle that can be read by its author and others as well. Valerio did not so much read the spectacle that he made on the walls of his bedroom that he shared with his brothers, for his own self-reflective language had yet to jell, but the spectacle itself might be understood as a first salvo of an inarticulate interior starting to articulate itself. Interestingly, the spectacle was a montage of posters, articles, artifacts, and mementoes, a kind of fragmented discourse whose coherence was not so much built into and across the fragments but resulted more from an act of my own interpretation. In short, if Valerio had difficulty shaping a version of himself according to the conventions of oral or written narratives, he managed to create a more perplexing text, an implicit narrative whose themes were not original but rather floated around him in the culture of his peers. The fact that the themes were not original but part of a collectivity that I knew well allowed me to make the implicit narrative explicit, in short, to interpret not only the particularity of Valerio but also the generality of others his age in Angelstown. It is this two-pronged interpretation, therefore, that I will pursue throughout the rest of the chapter.

Ralph:

So tell me Valerio, how come you're the only one to put things on the wall?

Valerio:

I like it, it's a reflection of me.

R:

How is it a reflection of you?

V:

Makes me feel strong.

R:

Makes you feel strong?

V:

Yeah.

R:

What makes you feel the strongest?

V:

The ground Marines.

R:

The Marines? How come?

V:

The helicopters . . .

R:

Why do you want to feel strong?

V:

To do work.

How does one create respect within conditions of little or no respect? This question and its many versions constantly appear in my fieldnotes.[7] One answer is to appropriate images that are larger than life, such as those on Valerio's walls. These larger-than-life or hyperbolic images circulated throughout the Angelstown neighborhood where the Martinez family lived. In my interpretation, such imagery enabled one to dream oneself beyond one's conditions. Either such dreaming was mostly a male preoccupation or I had greater access to males. Either way, males, old and young, seemed to invent giant scenarios for themselves, even as they mocked, with different mixes of gentle humor and anxiety, the likelihood of achieving these scenarios. Sometimes the scenarios became real success stories. For instance, I recorded the graceful and cultured story of a print shop owner, the hardscrabble story of a man who had a small company that laid down *chapapote*, "asphalt," and the mysterious story of a man who, although arriving from Mexico with little, came to own a number of Mexican-oriented businesses. His particular success story was cut short when he was professionally murdered.

If these particular scenarios were realized in the sense of providing an income and a degree of independence, most scenarios were not realized. Among the *mexicano* adult males I knew, there was often a piling up of scenarios, dreams about starting small restaurants or grocery stores, about becoming computer programmers, notary publics, doctors, or exporters/importers, dreams about fixing one's house (with fancy tiles in one instance and, in another, fixing the attic and basement so that a two story house could be stuffed with renters on four floors.) However, even among these adults, one common scenario typically came true: money earned in the United States was put to use in Mexico. This money allowed families to purchase land, to build homes for themselves and relatives, to purchase gifts and critical needs for relatives in Mexico, and to acquire retirement incomes for use in Mexico. Sometimes the money was used to start small businesses there.[8]

The common factor, of course, in all these scenarios, realized or not, was the making of money that was often transformed self-mockingly into becoming a *millonario*. But this transformation of the reasonable into the far-fetched was only one example of Angelstown scenarios flowing toward the hyperbolic. In short, in Valerio's immediate surroundings, imaginings such as the ones mentioned and many others—rather than their realizations—were prolific.

I raise these points, then, about the circulation of hyperbolic imagery throughout the neighborhood to problematize Valerio's own comment, that the objects on the walls were a reflection of him. What kind of a reflection? The one that Valerio might see in a mirror, or a reflection of the fantasy life invisible to the mirror? Obviously, I think the objects on the walls mostly reflected his fantasy life, for the life that the mirror would have reflected was one that included three painful labels: that of *chero* applied to him or his family by peers, that of learning disabled applied by his school, and that of being *tapado* given to him and other children in the family by his mother. These views in a real mirror, then, were a few of the images from which his imaginary life tried to free itself to make him "feel strong." In my interpretive scheme, then, "feeling strong" pointed decidedly toward the hyperbolic, and in the hyperbolic Valerio found three main constellations of images: Marines in tough poses who could "hit the ground running" from high-tech machinery, baseball stars whose heroic skills earned them vast sums of money, and expensive, exotic cars whose smooth shapes could slice through limiting nature, wind and all, having retrieved from a fantasized future a technological design that could master and overcome natural limitation.[9]

> **Ralph:**
> Why do you like them [cars]?
> **Valerio:**
> Cause . . . they look, they look smooth.
> **R:**
> What is it that looks smooth about them?
> **V:**
> The shape.
> **R:**
> Can you point out the kinds of things that you particularly like?
> **V:**
> The whole car, convertible . . .
> **R:**
> Oh, the convertible top, OK.
> **V:**
> I like the shape, I like the rims, and I like the lines that goes like this.
> **R:**
> Kind of like a circular–

V:

Yeah, that line . . .

R:

You like those.

V:

Yeah, I–

R:

Almost like fins?

V:

I like the shapes.

Of course, the attraction of the hyperbolic is not limited to this fieldsite, as Susan Stewart's analysis of the gigantic suggests.[10] One can read signs of the hyperbolic in the culture at large, for instance, in such exhibitions as monster trucks and tractor pulls, such sports as professional wrestling, body building, and karate, and such toys as Ninja Turtles, Transformers, and the Garbage Pail Kids. All these images and artifacts were parts of the hyperbolic spectacle inside and outside the fieldsite as I conducted research. In my view, the aggrandizement of mechanical mass and power, and the aggrandizement of human body mass and power seem to share the same hyperbolic structure; similarly, the lure of the horrific, which is what sold the brief fad of the Garbage Pail Kids (cartoonlike figures whose popularity lasted from the late 1980s into the early 1990s and who depicted "disgusting" bodily excesses: drooling, throwing up, and so on), was another kind of aggrandizement. Many of the children I knew in the neighborhood purchased toys or eagerly watched television shows that relied on this kind of hyperbolic imagery. In my view, the hyperbolic was a generalized system of seduction temporarily releasing young males, in particular, whether they were *mexicano* or not, from the everyday and mundane. In short, Valerio and his brothers consumed this generalized imagery as readily as others every time, for instance, that they hooted their enjoyment while watching televised professional wrestling or wore a T-shirt depicting a lunging Frankenstein with a nail driven into his head or another T-shirt saying "genuine bad cat." (*A question: When the generalized hyperbolic becomes globally marketed, as these images became, does it lose its mark of hyperbole—its difference—and become itself the mundane?*)

I believe, then, that the images of tough Marines jumping from helicopters on Valerio's walls synthesized the aggrandizements of both mechanical mass and body mass. Moreover, I would argue that this imagery was common and longstanding among many of the males in the neighborhood. For instance, most of the young males I knew saw the military and police work as highly attractive careers. Even those in the midst of illegal activities, or on its edges, envied the Marines and the police, imagining their work as tough and dynamic. A few older men of Mexican origin who had grown up in Angelstown also talked of their youthful idealizations of the Marines and more generally of the military as well as of the police. Their accounts of growing up differed from what contemporary young males told me and what I observed only in the recently increased violence from street-gang warfare. One of these older men became a Marine and another chose a career as a policeman. The persistence of these idealizations across generations says something about a persistent innerscape paired to—but not determined by—an equally persistent outerscape of social conditions that were loosely structured around ethnic, socioeconomic, and power differences. In short, I would argue that the need to "feel strong," as Valerio described his own "innerscape," was paired as a rather precise response to the conditions of his outerscape. "Feeling strong," then, was one way to *create respect under conditions of little or no respect*.

But I wish to concentrate particularly on one constellation of images, that of cars and more generally high-tech machinery. In addition to the pictures of a Porsche and Ferrari on his walls, Valerio also displayed pictures of a Cadillac, Beretta, Honda Accord, and Desoto Club Coupe. The Desoto was of much older vintage and, hence, an apparent anomaly in this constellation of contemporary cars. When I asked Valerio why he displayed an old-fashioned car alongside contemporary ones, he said that he would like to have been in the old times because they made "neat stuff" back then, like the Wright brothers. (Valerio had always been interested in airplanes and the history of aviation; hence, alongside the cars, he had the pictures of a jet and O'Hare Airport.) Sometimes he imagined himself an inventor living in the "old times" but, interestingly enough, never in the present. For Valerio, it was as if reference books (*The Guinness Book of World Records* was one of his favorites) could reduce the amorphousness of history into a set of verities so that certain characters, moments, and actions from the "old times" were now labeled as important on a historical trajectory. From such assuring texts, Valerio could imagine a place in history for himself, but the present held no assuring text, no place to clearly locate his future worth in the eyes of others. Hence, the "old times" were another place of the imagination where one could "feel strong," as strong perhaps as when one is surrounded by images of hyperbolic, high-tech machinery.

Valerio's fascination with cars, however, deserves even more extended analysis. Such an analysis, I believe, will not only uncover more of Valerio's particular innerscape but also a kind of collective innerscape of many of the young males in the neighborhood. The car, it seems to me, acquires importance in the imagination precisely because it can move through public space generating images that might camouflage private space. The car, obviously, is a practical tool as well, but its practicality can never fully explain, as we will see, the use of a car as a site for self-display. The car, if the owner wishes, can be a mobile display of an artfully constructed self. This self can safely cruise public space because it knows that there is not enough knowledge out there to unveil the camouflage. The car, then, is a particularly useful site for the creation of hyperbole. For instance, Valerio's older brother, Angel, at the time of the wall interview was shopping for a used red sports car. I was told that he had saved enough money from a variety of jobs to purchase such a car. I never did find out if Angel's search was successful, but I had also come to know him well over the years, and I knew the power of a red sports car to hide what he, like Valerio, was eager to hide. He and Valerio were unusually close, and both had absorbed the same sorts of indignities, but Angel always struck me as being the more vulnerable of the two, as if he had recorded a bit more deeply the hurts tossed out by his mother and the schooling system. (But I hesitate here even as I offer my analysis about a sharp difference between public and private spaces—for instance, that the first is a camouflage of the second. Such an analysis may distort how one space vibrates sympathetically with the other. For example, the ability to muster enough cash to construct whatever self Angel hoped to display was itself a partial realization of his fantasized private space. The public realization of one of his private dreams would certainly contribute to a partial healing of his vulnerability. Can one confidently say, therefore, that the private spaces hidden behind the public displays are, in some sense, always an emptiness kept at bay because once unveiled they would reveal the pretense of one's displays?)

I will take my argument about the significance of the car one step further: One unforgettable day I rode with some thumpers. In Angelstown, the term "thumper" was used for a certain kind of car and was also sometimes extended to describe the driver. On weekend afternoons in the summer, the thumpers of our neighborhood cruised the corner where Don Angel had his small apartment, which was about half of a mile from where Valerio and his family lived. Oftentimes they would park outside a small Mexican grocery store across the street. According to my friend Martín, who knew all of them but was not himself a thumper, they had been hanging out in front of this store since they were little kids on bikes. (Later, after I had taken a small peek into their lives, it occurred to me that the expensive, flashy thumpers that they now drove extended old rivalries from their bike days. For instance, against the backdrop of a never-ending crapshoot just to the side of the store, I witnessed at different times an exquisite display of a difficult give and take between genuine camaraderie and one-upmanship.) On the unforgettable afternoon I'm recalling, Martín signaled one of the thumpers to pull over as he drove by. Martín introduced me, and I started taking pictures. Suddenly, thumpers were all around me, more than I had ever collectively seen, and I was peeking into the mysteries of Alpine sound systems whose speakers quivered from the backs of the cars. Here was the source of that "thumping" bass that could vibrate an entire block or two with concussions more to the body than to the ear. The preferred music, as I already knew from Martín but which was verified by the drivers themselves, was "hip hop," "heart throb," "techno," and "rap." In Angelstown, thumpers also often had specialized hydraulic systems powered by an array of hidden batteries. These systems could tilt the car left or right, front or back, or jack the entire car up and drop it herky-jerky fashion. When raised high, the car became harder to drive, fragile, overly sensitive to the conditions of the road surface.

I turn here to fieldnotes written the day after I first talked to Manuel, the owner of one of the thumpers I rode in. The fieldnotes are lightly edited:

> Of all the thumpers, clearly the best guy to talk to is Manuel. He has an 82 green Jaguar. I ask him to take me for a ride. I conduct an interview as we ride around. No tape recording on this one. At one point, I ask him to crank up the sound. It's loud, but it is also behind us. We can't really talk while hearing it, but it doesn't totally blast us away either. In the interview, he tells me that he listens to it when he feels stressed out. It makes him feel better. He knows no one in the neighborhood has a car like his. His is the only Jaguar. The car cost him $3,500. ALL OF A SUDDEN IT OCCURS TO ME THAT THAT IS A PRETTY CHEAP PRICE FOR A JAGUAR, NO MATTER THE YEAR. He has put more money into the car than that though. The figure I have in my notes is $4,000, but I do not recall if that was 4,000 more or 4,000 total. He did not do the work himself, and that seems pretty typical of all the thumpers. Professionals tend to detail the cars, to put in the sound systems, and the hydraulics. What's interesting about his car is that it is pretty modest in comparison to some of the others. For instance, his sound system is not one of the louder ones. He doesn't even want to be heard two blocks away before he arrives. The paint job is not one of the fancier ones. All in all, his car is pretty functional, no hydraulics, for instance. As he drives around, he listens to hip-hop, heart throb, and techno. This is pretty much the list that Martin provides for his group, which is counter to the alternative music group. For Manuel, the Jaguar has

both status in the neighborhood as well as practical comfort. In fact, his buying decisions revolved around three types of cars: Jaguar, Mercedes, and Cadillac. He was not going to look at any other car except these three, because other cars simply don't drive as well. Besides, girls like them. He sometimes goes into competitions at McCormick.[11] Another car, which he later sold, also went into competition. Perhaps one of the most interesting things that he says about car status is that it's all in the surroundings. For instance, around here—and as he says it, he points to the neighborhood—a Jaguar or Mercedes, or Cadillac is a big deal, but in a neighborhood where Jags, Mercedes, or Caddies are common, they aren't such a big deal. I really like this sensitivity to context. As I talk to him seated on a little concrete embankment, I point to the houses and talk about their run down nature, the run downness of the neighborhood. I ask him if having a sharp car was a way to counteract the decay around oneself. He said yes.

With a thin waist and bulging biceps, Manuel was an experienced weight lifter. His tight T-shirts seemed to be consciously chosen to show off his bulk. Almost as if he had been scripted by the poster image of the tough Marine on Valerio's wall, he seemed to have realized Valerio's dream of "feeling strong." For Manuel and his friends, the body was a visual space to be meticulously controlled. Manuel was less "displayed" than his friends, who in their clothes and hairstyles presented themselves as far more self-consciously constructed. However, his car, just like theirs, served as an articulated visual space and extended the possibilities of the body simply because a car can cover more public space in less time than the body. Hence, the detailing of the cars, the flashing lights around license plates, the hydraulics, the sometimes tinted windows, and so on expanded the thumpers' ability to *create respect under conditions of little or no respect.* In this sense, the sound system was a brilliant extension of the self's ability to occupy space because the special signifier of the thumper was its domination of a plane beyond the visual, that of sound space. What was at work here might be explained this way: The ego (I use the term metaphorically not psychologically) as a kind of aura frames the body, and certain artifacts expand the ego's presence in public space; in short, the body, car, and thumper sound system were transitions from the biological to the technological, from the visual to the aural, allowing the ego to occupy ever-increasing amounts of public space.

Under such conditions, public space sometimes became noisy. The noise was both literal (as I said earlier, a cranked up sound system could be heard two blocks away) and metaphorical (egos barking at each other, insisting that their presence be felt and known). No wonder, then, that the thumpers who gathered around the grocery store in front of Don Angel's apartment were oftentimes described as drug dealers or gang members by those whose own egos inhabited smaller, more routine spaces. On the one hand, some of these descriptions were factual. Indeed, according to my friend Martín, who had grown up with the thumpers and whose own bragging ways could not deceive but only be a source of affection between us, some of the thumpers had flirted with gangs, and others had been caught selling drugs (Manuel had supposedly sold steroids, for instance). On the other hand, Martín, himself a former small-time drug dealer who had recently been arrested, claimed that his thumper friends and he too had been mostly clean and were now all clean. I believed him. The rumors that the thumpers were gang members or drug dealers seemed to me to be woven with bits of envy. Circulating these rumors seemed to be one way to undermine the excesses of ego that overflowed onto public spaces and crowded out more restrained egos whose bodies and styles of dress seemed to argue humility as a virtue. The rumors, then, were leveling devices that undermined the pretentions of Caddies, Jaguars, and other kinds of new cars in the neighborhood while simultaneously revealing deep-seated envy. In short, rumors functioned rhetorically, revealing the inner and outer worlds of those who gossiped as surely as the bodies, cars, and sound systems revealed the inner and outer worlds of those gossiped-about. Ironically, it seemed to me, the dialectic of gossipers and gossiped-about could only emerge from profoundly shared worlds (shared innerscapes and outerscapes) that were differently inflected and, therefore, strained.

Thumper cars, of course, are related, particularly in their hydraulics, to the low-riders driven by the Pachucos of the forties and fifties and the Chicanos of the sixties.[12] The differences and similarities between the two styles are more than I can delineate here, but when I saw one of the local low-rider clubs parade their vintage Chevies and Fords, their style seemed frozen and nostalgic, a tame hobby of males in their fifties. The thumpers, in contrast, were flashy and modern, in part, because their thumping sound systems dominated sound space more thoroughly than any low-rider. Nevertheless, it is this idea of domination, which the more powerful sound systems of thumpers have heightened, that links the two generations of cars. This domination suggests that what I defined earlier as a pairing of a persistent innerscape to an equally persistent outerscape loosely structured around certain social conditions was as alive in the Angelstown I studied in recent years as it had been forty years earlier. What the Pachucos and low-riders had initiated, the thumpers seemed to extend. Did they not share the same sad and exuberant need to splash themselves visually and aurally across one's "hood" and to occupy it with a thick panoply of symbols that signaled some in-between space that had broken away from the ethnically traditional while simultaneously refusing to assimilate into the dominant culture? And in spending all that effort to invent and dominate an in-between space, was it not inevitable that sometimes explicitly illegal acts should occasionally combust on the social scene? The Angelstown thumpers, then, it seemed to me, whether really dangerous or not, wore danger as part of a historical costume that they had updated in order to signify an in-between space that had refused to pass away.

Before returning to Valerio's wall, I want to discuss one other car group in order to amplify my thesis about the circulation of hyperbolic imagery. In addition to thumpers, there were cars in Angelstown that belonged to a specialized club called Too Low Flow. To this day, my knowledge about these cars and their owners remains sketchy. What I wish to discuss here, therefore, concerns less the reality of Too Low Flow and more of how these cars were imagined among those I talked to. Among those who admired them, Too Low Flow cars exaggerated the styling characteristics of thumpers. This evaluation seemed to me accurate because the various times when I saw these cars, I too noticed that the hyperbole of Too Low Flow seemed to be written with an extra difference. For instance, in addition to the sound system and the careful detailing of the cars, Too Low Flow club members used brightly colored (oftentimes pink) windshield wipers and chrome rims on low profile tires that lowered the car. At times, the cars were exuberantly comical because some owners, in addition to installing whistles and chirps, had individual control of eyelids covering the headlights. The total effect included, then, high-pitched sounds, winking eyelids, manic windshield wipers, and, sometimes, almost at the very limits of comedy, hydraulics shaking the entire car to the right and left or up and down. This translation of visual and sound space into comedy was, in its own bizarre way, a part of the same in-between scene that I described earlier, for these cars too were crafted by young Latino males of the neighborhood. As far as I could tell, Too Low Flow was strictly Latino and never a part of the African-American or Anglo styles. A Too Low Flow car, then, seemed to be a kind of Latino carnival whose excesses, although inflected differently, were the shared theme that linked low-riders to thumpers to Too Low Flow.

Most importantly, however, owners of Too Low Flow took extra precautions, I was told, to keep their cars fanatically clean. Engines were spotless, and the bodies of the cars, ideally, were not allowed to show water spots, much less rust—or so I was told. I was particularly fascinated by these descriptions of fanatical cleanliness. I was even more fascinated by the kind of respect that these descriptions generated among the youth who looked up to the Too Low Flow. Why would fanatical cleanliness be so openly admired?

My answer is a complex one that will slowly evolve over the course of this text because it embraces more than the Too Low Flow. I have already introduced hints of my explanation, but I will now more directly address a major point. Cleanliness, quite simply, was an important ingredient in almost all the hyperbolic imagery that I have been discussing. It represented one more type of control over one's outerscape. Through such control, the innerscape could gain authority, in short, acquire *respect under conditions of little or no respect*. Of the many ways by which one might express control, dominance over nature and its plenitude of decay (in this case, rust spots) was an attractive route. Recall here the scene with Manuel who owned a thumper and not a Too Low Flow. As we sat on the little embankment about ten yards east of the grocery store where he and his friends even as children had gathered on bikes, the store that had been the backdrop of their never-ending crap shoot, Manuel was quite explicit about his "raggedy" (his word) neighborhood. The thumper he owned, a Jaguar, and the thumper his brother owned, a two-door Cadillac, were explicitly contrasted to a specific context. On one side, were the cars; on the other, was the neighborhood. In short, the cars were elements in a larger system of display that also included clothes, hairstyles, and conspicuous displays of jewelry. All these displays signified control, the dominance of the "neat and clean" over the raggedness of the neighborhood. For me, however, the descriptions of Too Low Flow seemed to take the rhetoric or semiotic of the "neat and clean" one step further to reveal with unusual clarity the urgent need to camouflage with large public displays all those traces of raggedness and decay that lurked in one's private spaces. In short, these private spaces, too often crafted by systemic humiliation, created an urgency to exert control over public spaces and to craft in a hyperbolic style the emblems of such control.

How did the pictures of cars on Valerio's wall fit into this larger portrait of cars in the neighborhood? These posters were not of thumpers and Too Low Flow;[13] instead, these posters of Porsches and Ferraris imaged an exotica that was even more out of Valerio's reach. Europeaness, exorbitant cost, and streamlining were a few of the characteristics that these posters could excite in the imagination. Valerio pointed to these characteristics, and I interpreted him to mean something of the following. As exotica, these characteristics helped define Valerio's present as mundane and in so doing offered a rupturing of that present: Europeaness as emblem of sophistication and difference; exorbitant cost as emblem of the amassing of capital; streamlining as emblem of futuristic design and perhaps technological mastery of nature. In short, Porsches and Ferraris were outside the limits of the real, whereas thumpers and Too Low Flow, even as they exoticized the reality of the neighborhood, had become common features of that reality. At most, Porsches and Ferraris inhabited only magazines and posters, not the streets—Valerio was quite explicit about this. It was the exotic distance of Porsches and Ferraris, then, that made their images valuable and provided the reason for bringing them into one's living space.

We might understand all the images on his bedroom wall in somewhat the same fashion. If the bedroom walls were, figuratively, the confinements of his present, they were also blank spaces upon which to write out an implicit text of his desire, a desire that was not just his own but shared the clichés and conventional tropes and topoi of his neighborhood. Indeed, his was part of a collective desire ready to be filled, a vacuum, so to speak, for drawing in the phantasmagorias produced by inventive marketplaces whose reach was global. One could just as easily find, for instance, similar posters and images—and probably walls—in Mexico as in Angelstown or, for that matter, in many other locations. Despite global production and circulation of the phantasmagorias, however, their consumption is probably best understood according to local conditions and meanings. For instance, Valerio's notions of "feeling strong" and of his bedroom walls being a "reflection" of him, and his incessant questions—which I interpreted as probes thrown over his wall of difference in order to understand what constituted that difference—were aspects of his particular style for consuming the phantasmagorias. But his own style was part of a larger system of desire and consumption that operated on the streets of his neighborhood, and it is the simultaneous analysis of these two sites that has been my goal thus far in this chapter.

The next large constellation of images on Valerio's walls consisted of baseball heroes. He had taped to his walls newspaper clippings and pictures of Jerome Walton, Will Clark, Mike Bielecki, Jose Canseco, and Kevin Mitchell. Valerio also owned baseball cards that he kept in a safety deposit box in a bank. Two of these cards were of Mark McGuire and Ryne Sandburg. Walton had either won the rookie of the year award the year before or was the leading candidate that year, and Bielecki, another Chicago Cub, was having a career season of pitching. The other players were established stars in baseball. Canseco, for instance, had accomplished the phenomenal statistic of forty home runs and forty stolen bases in one season and was earning $23 million, and Sandburg some day will enter the Hall of Fame. The point is that the images of these baseball players were another phantasmagoria cycling through Valerio's imagination along with those of exotic cars and tough Marines and their high-tech machinery. Remarkable physical prowess, staggering incomes, fan adulation, and so on were some of the major ingredients through which baseball stardom manufactured its exotic distance; hence, like other conventional phantasmagorias, the images of baseball stars could be globally marketed.

Because Valerio and I were both Cubs fans, I sometimes watched parts of baseball games on television with him. As I reconsider those moments through the lens of this analytic moment, at least one insight into the workings of exotic distance and the special magnetism that constitutes phantasmagorias is worth exploring. Baseball broadcasting on television depends largely on the juxtaposition of the long shot, medium shot, and close-up. The long shot helps to fabricate exotic distance and, perhaps, is its metaphor. The long and medium shots, which more or less replicate the overview of the fan sitting in the stadium, keep the viewer separate from the intimate details of the game in order to provide a more general understanding: for instance, the strategic positioning of infield and outfield players. The close-up, however, provides a different kind of understanding: for instance, the emotions of a hitter or pitcher or the specific detail of a runner sliding into second base. But the "close-up" can be defined in broader and more interesting ways than just the close-ups of televised baseball. I would like to include here the "close-ups" of baseball cards and the "close-ups" of newspaper articles and photographs. All three of these "close-ups" were actual aspects of Valerio's life that fed his imagination. In interesting ways, these "close-ups" help to fabricate the exotic distance of baseball stars and their global marketing. For the consumer, the close-up reaches across exotic distance by providing a fleeting intimacy and a sliver of knowledge concerning the object hidden by exotic distance, and, thus, the close-up removes the slightest of veils. The sliver of knowledge might be as minuscule as batting-average statistics, and the intimacy as insignificant as the feelings of the baseball star on having been traded the year before or the grimace of a frustrated batter. Nevertheless, these little stories and facts are the close-ups that begin to fill the emptiness of the consumer with an identification, a relationship with the exotically distant. If the desire of the consumer and the goal of marketing is to fill such emptiness, the close-up makes the exotically distant more familiar and simultaneously generates the desire for even more familiarity. Out of this want, an entire economy is manufactured in which the exotically distant is peeled of its abstraction so that it can begin to inhabit intimately the very life of the consumer. These forces were at work in Valerio's own life, for over the years he had consistently expressed the very conventional desire of wanting to be a professional baseball player and, indeed, played first base that summer for a local church team.[14] Moreover, cycling through the culture at this time was the very revealing refrain "I want to be like Mike" from a popular television commercial that relied on close-ups of Michael Jordan, the Chicago Bulls basketball star. The refrain summarized brilliantly the marketing of mass images that evoke and depend on an "empty" consumer "wanting" identification with something almost totally out of reach, the exotically distant Michael Jordan. Of course, sometimes the selling of a star does not work, and an intimacy between star and consumers never materializes. This fact points to the agency of the unpredictable consumer, for the emptiness that is inside all of us always chooses how it desires to be filled and with whom and what.

I have pointed to three constellations of images that dominated Valerio's wall. In addition to these constellations, however, there were other images, artifacts, and one prominent constellation of images that I have yet to discuss and that deserves analysis. Some of these more miscellaneous items were congruent with the constellations that I have been analyzing, but others were less congruent. For instance, there were a series of Christmas cards, several from me and other cards from clients on his newspaper route. These cards did not project fantasy images of tough Marines, baseball stars, high-tech machinery, and cars; rather, they were sentimental acknowledgments of appreciation for the real being that was Valerio. But an even more prominent acknowledgment of self-worth was a set of eleven awards. Two awards recognized his school-patrol work, another was for physical fitness, and still another was given to him by the local newspaper for being one of their newspaper boys. The newspaper awards and even the newspaper route were regarded almost indifferently, except for the fact that the route had provided him cash with which to buy his own television and other items. (He was far more proud, for instance, of having been a member of the school patrol for several years.) However, there were also seven LD awards that must be discussed, given what I said previously about Valerio's lack of school success and seeing such lack as one more humiliation in the mirror of his real life.

Just how successful or unsuccessful in school was Valerio? Valerio described only one of the LD awards as being significant to him: The Highest Achievement Award in LD math. The reason for its importance, he said, was that he did not expect to win anything, that he thought he was having trouble in math. The other LD awards were mostly in reading and language arts, and these subjects, to him, were not as important. Valerio and his family, particularly his mother, saw with a suspicious eye the school system's tradition of award-giving as well as the passing marks that her children received in LD classes. For instance, his mother pointed out to me that Valerio's passing marks on report cards were in LD classes, not regular classes. I did not realize this until after several report cards, and when I looked more closely, indeed, I saw the stigmata of LD stamped on the cards. That stamp in her mind explained everything, an everything that others in the family had been made keenly aware of. (For instance, Angel, Valerio's older brother, too was LD, but, after learning certain "tricks" about representational painting, he painted some highly creditable landscapes, and later his mother expressed withering skepticism that he had, indeed, painted them.) For the family, then, the awards and passing marks were more fictitious than real, the ploys of a school system whose good intentions to encourage and nurture were undermined by social and attitudinal realities that could not be easily displaced. Nevertheless, Valerio displayed these awards prominently, and that act contained, perhaps, a significant desire: that of projecting back to him some sort of worth that others had actually seen in him. In my interpretive scheme, then, these cards and awards, projecting memories and images of self-worth acknowledged by others, were juxtaposed and scattered among fantasy images that implied, as I argued earlier, an emptiness that wanted to be filled. It was as if Valerio could fill his emptiness with two sets of images: one an acknowledgement of real worth, the other more of a search for worth not in mundane reality but in the planes of the hyperbolic and the astonishing.

Almost as interesting as the Christmas cards and awards was a pseudo Oriental print of birds sitting on branches amidst sparse but new foliage. This framed print had originated the entire project of wall decoration, preceding even the car posters. The framed print had been given to Valerio by his mother and still occupied a central place on one of the walls. Valerio during the interview implied that he identified less with the print and more with his mother's desire to have it hung. As I looked at the print, I was struck once again by the global marketing of imagery, in this case, the hint of Orientalism, and the fact that it hung alongside other conventionalized global images: for instance, Batman images culled from cereal boxes; a two-dollar Canadian bill given to him by an uncle who had had to reenter the United States via Canada because of immigration problems; pictures of the Fatboys, an African-American rap group; calendars that displayed traditional Mexican images (*charros*, "Mexican cowboys," on one calendar and, on the other, *señoritas* with big flowers in their hair, dancing in brightly colored dresses); and a three-dimensional devotional icon of the Virgen de Guadalupe.

The three traditional Mexican images deserve some commentary. Whereas the colorful pictures on the calendars were disparaged by Valerio as being too *chero*, the Virgen, another traditional image, was not. Why was this? For Valerio and others, the Virgen was the locus of the sacred, the magical grantor of petitions and favors. Valerio, for instance, kneeled every night for approximately five minutes before her image to say his prayers, prayers that were meant to protect him and members of his family. In short, the Virgen was, arguably, the most powerful image on his decorated walls. The Virgen, then, may have been just as traditional as the Mexican cowboys and the dancing *señoritas*, but these latter images were also secular whereas the Virgen was sacred; hence, her sacredness protected her and made her icon difficult to disparage as *chero*.

My deeper argument, however, pertains to the international circulation of local iconographies, for instance, the hint of Orientalism that becomes mass produced or the stereotypes of Mexican traditionalism that, likewise, become mass produced and, finally, disseminated beyond their cultural and geographical boundaries. One could just as easily point to the mass production of European icons (Porsches, Ferraris) as to American icons (baseball stars, rap music, Batman, and so on and so on). From this perspective, Valerio's walls displayed not only an array of conventional hyperbolic desires but also an array of local iconographies that had become internationalized. Local iconographies, of course, have been circulating through global arenas for hundreds of years. But the proliferation of such iconographies has become so extensive during the twentieth century that the sites for producing them are not necessarily located within the cultures and geographies from which the iconographies emerged. One result is that we are mostly immune to the difference that the iconography may have once represented because the iconography has become our own.[15] Valerio's walls, for instance, were not unusual but commonplace as were the cheap plaster knickknacks of small puppies and other figurines sometimes decorated with a red heart and the words "I love you," all located in the Martinez family's living room. In mentioning knickknacks, I ought to emphasize that I am not writing about "good taste" or "bad taste." My interest is in the production and circulation of iconography, the complexity of forces by which the manufacturing of goods encourages spectators to become consumers and finally citizens.

Perhaps I can clarify my point by turning to a specific encounter with a figure whom Edmundo and I called El Arabe. He was, indeed, of Arab descent but born in Mexico, and, according to him, someone who had traveled the world as part of the Mexican diplomatic corps. As strange as it may sound, we never inquired his actual name. El Arabe was an itinerant street vendor who had been appearing every now and then for twenty years on the same busy street corner in Angelstown selling a variety of goods to his Mexican clients. His home base was Chicago where he owned a liquor store managed by others. Because of the store, his street vending was not necessary, he said, but was more of a pleasure.

During the year he made a long circuit that might include stops in Mexico to visit relatives and to purchase goods to be sold later in Tennessee, Ohio, Chicago, Angelstown, and other places where he knew of a Mexican community. He traveled in an old Cadillac, which he stuffed to the brim when closing shop. His most conspicous products were birdcages and cheap tapestries of the Virgen de Guadalupe. Rather surprisingly, he also sold cheap tapestries depicting an overview of Mecca and its holy shrine. His vending site was located next to a Mexican restaurant, a favorite of mine and Edmundo's. Because he sold cheap goods at a conspicuous site, I was particularly interested in his relationship with the city because of the passage of recent ordinances requiring the licensing of street vendors and because city hall at the time was decrying the deterioration of the neighborhoods on both sides of this major artery leading to the downtown. Indeed, some city officials were advocating the creation of an entirely new gateway, one that would bypass the minority communities and the empty buildings sometimes dressed in graffiti. El Arabe's replies to these questions did not confirm any suspicions but, instead, suggested benign treatment on the part of the city. His selling of tapestries and other cheap goods may have been an eyesore in some eyes, but the city was not actively running him off. After several visits and long talks and after the prices of his goods had dropped considerably and Edmundo and I had purchased too much, a more interesting story began to take shape for me.

El Arabe was a transporter of cultural stuff. I knew of no one like him in Angelstown, a man who derived much of his labor from a peripatetic style. The labor of everyone else I knew tended more or less to make people stationary. He shuttled back and forth between the United States and Mexico and maintained in some fashion connections to the Middle East. He boasted often, for instance, that only he knew how to get the tapestries of Mecca. For him, they were special and he was proud of them. When Edmundo and I examined them closely, we could only find Arabic script, which suggested to us that, indeed, they were manufactured in the Middle East rather than Mexico or the United States.[16] His biggest selling item, however, were the tapestries of the Virgen de Guadalupe. I was astonished when I compared the tapestries of the Virgen and those of Mecca. Other than the iconography, I could not see a significant difference between the two. Both were very inexpensive, both relied on the same materials (some kind of cheap cloth and bright colors), both were infinitely replicable, and both depicted immediately recognizable icons. It was as if a style that could circulate internationally had been in place for a considerable time to create the genre of tapestry painting whose subject matter was local iconography. As far as I could tell, it made no difference whether the local iconography was Elvis, the Virgen de Guadalupe, Mecca, Daniel in the Lion's Den (a tapestry that hung above a sofa in the home of another family in the neighborhood), Harley Davidson motorcycle riders, or some other immediately recognizable cultural or geographical icon. Tapestry paintings, as I later found out, have indeed become an international genre largely manufactured in Turkey and sold by large retailers in the United States who display iconographies from around the world in their catalogues. Tapestry painting, then, with a manufacturing center(s?) in Turkey, represents a distinctive homogeneous style, that has absorbed and reproduced local iconographies. As a universal class marker, the tapestry allows those of more modest means to decorate their living spaces and in so doing imitate the practices of the more wealthy. Of course, this need to decorate living space is itself a somewhat recent phenomenon dating, more or less, to the emergence of the bourgeoisie. If bourgeois taste has become increasingly an international style through which wealth, success, and cultivation display themselves through the purchase of art objects, then circulating among the working classes, is one of its international counterparts: tapestry paintings. The important point is that the desire for consumption and display are vast ensorcellments affecting divergent levels of society.

El Arabe may have been a minor but unique actor in this global drama, but my interpretation of him allowed me to understand better Valerio's bedroom walls, the living room decorated by his parents, and the living rooms of other families I knew in the neighborhood. Tapestry paintings were only one component in a larger system of envy and imitation of the bourgeoisie. Also within this same system were the knickknacks, mentioned earlier, that were sometimes displayed in glass cabinets; fat, velvety living room furniture that could be bought at a downtown store whose enormous, blinking neon sign had been targeted—according to a Latino city official, a friend of mine—by a city ordinance as too large and gaudy; landscape paintings bought in resale shops and drugstores; large, plastic gold and black clocks flanked on both sides by Pegasus; and, in particular, a set of brightly flowered, inexpensive pitchers and a bowl that imitated seventeenth-century European designs and was described by one family as examples of *lujo*, "good taste," a "luxury item." All these items and many more with their hints of the Orient or Europe or Mexico or whatever and whenever (local iconographies now internationalized) were parts of the unnoticed conventions of everyday life. These objects of so-called bad taste created their special seductive power by imitating the art objects of an internationalized bourgeoisie. In a larger sense, however, such objects performed a political role in so far as they ushered in and maintained an identification with a political and economic structure that could deliver, if not the real objects of an internationalized bourgeoisie, then at least its imitations. In this sense, imitations are quite political in ways not normally imagined.

Let me explain my point further by returning to my earlier statement about the production and circulation of iconography and the complexity of forces by which the manufacturing of goods encourages spectators to become consumers and finally citizens. In my analysis, those without sufficient cash to purchase the goods—either bonafide goods emblematic of the internationalized bourgeoisie or their imitations—remain spectators of the circulating iconographies. In contrast, the consumer has sufficient cash to purchase at least some of the goods. If the amount of cash is not satisfactory, such a consumer (and spectators as well) may also have all sorts of explanations and rationalizations by which to recoup self-worth and dispel frustration in the face of economic inequities. My central point, however, is that the circulation of a common iconography, like a common language, encourages consumers to identify with a people and a nation, and this sense of identification is what I loosely define as a kind of warped "citizenship," warped because it does not proceed along lines of any sort of participatory democracy but along lines of consuming a particular iconography. Even if some "citizens" resent the social and political inequalities that both separate and tie the larger group together, a desire for the common iconography is still pervasive. Here, then, is a subtle form of identification: the complex but shared iconographies that swirl about us encourage a kind of attunement to the forces of production and consumption that mark modern economies. It becomes difficult to imagine life lived in any other way. We recognize its markers in those just like us and even those very different from us, and from this sharing of an iconography—whose separation into "good taste" and "bad taste" merely postpones the recognition of what is shared—emerges our passivity and warped "citizenship."

Let me return to the case of Valerio and his older brother. Both were born in Mexico, but they had no desire to return there to live. Both described Mexico as too traditional, too boring, and lacking in good jobs, their favorite phrase being "there's nothing to do there." They identified more with the United States than with Mexico, more with the ways of life here and their friends with whom they had fabricated a common ground. These identifications ran deeper than the fact that both were more fluent in English than in Spanish. And these identifications were also resilient, for they persisted despite small and large humiliations: for instance, the knowledge that they were labeled learning disabled or that their parents did not have much economic status in the context of the United States. Such humiliations had not unraveled the knotted forces of identification with such iconographies as the United States Marines "hitting the

[handwritten in left margin: Cultural citizenship]

ground running" and American baseball stars. In my view, then, these specific iconographies were but small examples of a more general hyperbolic spectacle resembling dramatic sparks flying from an accelerating machine that manufactures and consumes goods. If this machine can be called "modernity," it, of course, is no longer owned by just the United States and Europe. Wherever the machine finds itself, its magnetic field draws many into its orbit even as it polarizes and displaces others. Valerio and his brother knew all about displacement, for the word *chero* and other humiliations reminded them of their uncomfortable position somewhere in the periphery of that magnetic field. They also knew, however, that their parents inhabited a space even more peripheral. They knew, for instance, that they were not the spectators that their parents had been when growing up on the same *ranchito* in an obscure area of Mexico. For instance, when Valerio bought his own television with his own money and installed it in his bedroom alongside his highly decorated walls, he acted out the role of consumer in a way that his parents as children had never done, and it was through such actions and abilities that an identification had emerged, a kind of warped "citizenship" aligned as much with the forces of modernity as with a geographical and cultural entity called the United States. Of course, such "citizenship" remained fragile because it depended on the machine of modernity cranking out not only its iconographies but also the ability to realize some of its icons. To produce the first without the second would have encouraged cynicism. In the case of Valerio, however, it seemed to me that the machine could keep cynicism at bay, could hide its duplicitous side from Valerio not only because it limped along but, more importantly, because it was being perceived by a dutiful and even buoyant personality.

may 1995

Shortly after the summer of 1990, I lost track of Valerio and his family. At some point, I heard that they had moved, but no one could tell me where. In one sense, I was not eager to find them. Valerio's mother occasionally had expressed annoyance with my fieldwork, the repetitious questions, the ever-present tape recorder. I found her suspiciousness and occasional negativity that ran below the general politeness of the household subtly disconcerting. Moreover, my own awkwardness while doing fieldwork—the difficulty, for instance, of explaining my highly hermeneutic conclusions in any other language except writing—made it difficult for me to explain to her the what, why, and how of my research. Better to move on, I thought.

By late May 1995, however, I felt less sensitive about old awkwardnesses, and I looked for Valerio diligently. The family was easy to find. They had bought a two-story house across the street from their formerly cramped apartment and were renting out their top floor to young *cheros* recently arrived from Mexico. The scene was immediately recognizable: the purchasing of a house, the renting of the top floor (the hottest one in summer) to others like oneself in order to pay for the mortgage. The sorts of conditions that had first marked Valerio and his family and so many others I knew in Angelstown were being inherited by the next wave of legal and illegal Mexican workers. Valerio's family had cranked up the political and economic machine of modernity and were now shyly and quietly acquiring even more of that iconography by which spectatorship gets left behind.

Edmundo, Valerio, a high school friend of Valerio's, Valerio's brother Angel, and I moved out of the house to sit on the front stoop. Valerio had changed dramatically, had become muscular by lifting weights, but, more than that, had lost his boyishness and found a presence, one of "feeling strong" as he had described it years ago. He was on the verge of graduating from high school and had managed as a junior to escape LD "reality." He described all those LD years as feeling like "one of the dumbest students in school. . . . that I was not going to go on to college and that I was not going to be very successful in life." The escape was initiated by Valerio himself who, after receiving decent grades in a few regular classes, asked school officials to be removed from the LD rolls. He had to fight for the change, but now, on the verge of finishing high school, his intentions were to study biology at the local community college and hopefully move on to a regular university to study nursing. I found my mind drifting at times as I became more interested in watching my feelings becoming unusually rich as the different people around the stoop spoke. Edmundo and I had been doing this work together for five years now, and I had started three years prior to that. There across the street was the cramped apartment where I had first met Valerio and his family and later saw the walls that became this chapter. But the scene was moving on, and whatever I had hoped to record and interpret seemed less significant now than the affection between Edmundo and me for all the crazy years spent together, and the affection we both felt for all the people we had come to know, and even the affection we felt for the literally killing streets of Angelstown.

Were there still walls of confinement framing the family? Of course. The power differential by which mainstream America drives the political and economic machine of modernity (some might say postmodernity[17]) was still humming. The well-being of the machine depends too much on the selection, for instance, of low-wage earners who can be managed by others. Since schooling helps in the selection process, it too helps to maintain the power differential.

Had LD been part of the selection process for Valerio, his brother, and others like them? That is my interpretation, although an ambiguous one because it simultaneously offered one-on-one attention even as it stigmatized. But it was his response to LD reality and a host of other small and large humiliations that spurred a sort of imaginative dreaming that is no longer distinctly American but now internationalized. In a sense, he dreamed himself beyond his immediate conditions, beyond even the American node as producer of modernity. And yet even this dreaming helped the machine to motor forward, for it belonged to a certain complicitous acceptance, a charming yet painful optimism and naivete that I could still hear in Valerio's voice. There was still doubt in his eyes despite the recent accomplishments (which is, of course, true for all of us), and I felt a whole battery of questions residing there still, some of which he actually voiced: How am I doing, Ralph? What do you think of nursing? Will it work? He was still pitching questions over the wall, I thought. My reply, although not then but now: *échale Valerio, no te agüites.*

so cool!

What I have tried to depict in my story of Valerio and his family and others in the neighborhood is the imaginary life, a kind of elusive ether, that Appadurai labeled a "key component of the new global order."[18] Any account of the reality we inhabit must include an account of that imaginary life that flows at the greatest depths of reality. Accounts that do not contain something of the imaginary life may appear less speculative, but they are not necessarily more precise or believable and certainly they are not more complete. At any rate, it seemed to me, that that which most fired the imagination of those I lived with in Angelstown was a power differential—or at least its perception—that magnified the social standing of those who seemed to have power and demeaned those who seemed to have less power. Without such a differential, the hyperbolic fantasies, the in-between spaces so distinctive in their appearance, and the circulating iconographies, which help to bind us into a kind of warped "citizenship" even as its icons remain unequally distributed and, therefore, divisive, would not have been so sharply drawn. It was the heated imagination of others, therefore, that heated my own.

learned from them

5

THE LOGIC OF VIOLENCE/
THE LOGIC OF TRUST

"A lot of times I've asked myself," he says with the expression of a
man with regrets, "who it is that has done such damage to my sons?
Is it me for being weak of character? Is it my wife for having spoiled
them all of their lives? Or is it this country? I don't know what it is, but
something has certainly harmed them."
—Ramón Pérez, *Diary of an Undocumented Immigrant*

There were times in Angelstown when I did fieldwork with
people who seemed difficult and not very likeable. What was I to make of values and beliefs that seemed to run contrary to my own? It seemed to me that as
long as I could summon a certain generosity, fieldwork could continue, but
there were times when I came very close to stopping the pretense of generosity
and walking away. I never took that walk, however, and now, at this writing moment, those same social scenes seem more illuminating than what I imagined
back then. But I am left with this predicament: How does one textualize such
encounters, such people? How do I render the density and subtlety of life lived
if, as the observer, I felt that mostly nastiness and short-sightedness were to be
found there? Call this my prejudice, but it seems to me that some of the most
important human encounters are those that cause anxiety even anger. At these

moments, we encounter all those limitations that define us. Anxiety and anger may protect our most vulnerable places, but they also encourage us to root ourselves ever deeper inside limiting definitions that rationalize against that wilder stuff that calls to us from just beyond our narrow selves.

Let me translate this human problem into the context of ethnographic research. An ethnography of the emotions would begin with the assumption that emotions have a public dimension, that anger and nastiness, say, do not just well up from the interior of a person but are distinctly shaped along systemic lines. One of the special interests of this chapter is to locate the complexity of inner life as largely driven by ideological forces. I hope to deflect any interpretation that might otherwise pathologize a set of individuals and instead to emphasize the workings of ideology. In the various scenes to be presented, then, a kind of nastiness among and between certain individuals will be evident, but my analysis will point less to "nasty" individuals and more to the "ideologics" that shaped their conditions, beliefs, and actions. In short, ideological analysis becomes one way, my way for now, for setting aside my rationalized behaviors and my judgments of others so as to listen more keenly to that wilder call that I might otherwise not hear.

a long evening

Valerio's story in chapter four ended in May 1995. The next story that I wish to tell starts, more or less, at that same time. Edmundo and I had been spending some rather feverish days catching up with different individuals. No research I had told him, no tape recorders, just gossip, some joking, and, if lucky, some really good food. There was one visit, however, that worried both of us: a seemingly obligatory visit to the Juárez, old friends of mine since 1987. But before I open the door, imaginatively at least, to the Juárez home, let me set the stage for understanding their special troubles that became clearer to me the more familiar I became with my own fighting spirit and that of the streets.

María and her husband, Alberto, for as long as I have known them, have been a stylish, young-looking couple. Their ways were considerably different from the traditionalism of Don Angel or of Valerio's parents. María's more modern hairstyle, Alberto's leisure suits, his associate's degree in computer programming, and the fact that most of their children had Anglo names seemed to signify, particulary in Alberto, a fierce and very conflicted desire. As a teenager, Alberto had arrived to a farming community in central Illinois from Mexico and, by his own account, was immediately scarred by schooling troubles. Instead of being sent on to high school, as he should have been, he was sent back to elementary school. He felt picked on because of his Mexicanness and his lack of English, and in that ironic way by which some individuals convert the insults thrown at them into a badge of defiance, he converted his Mexicanness into a kind of rallying point for the making of defiant dignity. His defiance, however, was fragile, for it was mixed with shame and anger concerning his poor English skills. In his eyes, his Mexicanness had, indeed, kept him from getting ahead. Later, in Angelstown, he had been poorly paid at a factory, had gone on disability for a number of years due to an injured back, had completed technical courses that had been taught in Spanish but could not help him enter the Anglo labor force, and was most recently working as a chef's helper in the kitchen of a nearby gambling boat. Against all this, he defiantly asserted his equality with all Americans despite huge power differentials that made him just another laborer. But his situation was more complicated than this, for fueling his imaginative horizon was the success of a brother in Mexico who was a medical doctor. For Alberto, then, inhabiting the middle class was not an unreasonable expectation, but the obstacles remaining were formidable. The result was that he despised his place within the working class, vehemently asserted his Mexicanness even as he distanced himself from other aspects of Mexican traditionalism, and envied the American middle class. But he also despised the latter for creating, as he saw it, the obstacles that kept him, and others like him, out. Moreover, he was smart enough to construct a kind of protocritique with a certain bitter logic capable of exposing inequality. As he asserted one time in Spanish, "So you tell me, what is white? These Americans think it is so important. Here's a sheet of paper, this is white. No American is this white. So they can't tell me they're white. They're not white." Certainly, Alberto was speaking some sort of skewed truth, but as he drank his beers in the evening, exposing each injustice at work and celebrating his verbal defiances, I would grow tired of this vision in which everything deserved a tongue-lashing.

Edmundo and I visited them last in 1995 on a summer evening that soon became particularly difficult. María led us up the back way, as she always did, to the second-story porch. They had owned their home since 1989 but had always lived on the second floor. They rented the first floor to another Latino family and never claimed the income on their taxes, but few landlords in the neighborhood did. There at the landing, just outside the door to the apartment, was a cage enclosing seven or eight frantic finches. They seemed a disturbing but appropriate symbol, as if the sheer noise of the household and the layers of bickering had spilled outward to infect the finches themselves. The birds were killing themselves in their confinement, it seemed to me, and worse yet the Juárez had so numbed themselves to their own situation that they no longer could see

mad a our people

the mirroring finches. Yeah, I was being judgmental, but the Juárez family had always summarized for me a certain innocence and trouble whose points of origin were deeply embedded in the larger social system. The forces that were twisting them and others were obscure, difficult to see, but Edmundo and I often discussed the cipher of the Juárez as if a sympathetic decoding might lead, eventually, to a decoding of the macro-system itself. At any rate, as I passed the finches I knew that I was about to enter a kind of crazy hospitality. I knew that within an hour or so after gathering at the kitchen table I would feel, as I usually did, a mounting headache and that I would then retreat to some corner of the apartment. María had asked Edmundo, knowing that he was a professional counselor, to help her understand her husband and perhaps to talk to Alberto about his treatment of her and the children. Edmundo knew it was a doomed effort, something that María rather than Alberto had initiated, but Edmundo could not comfortably refuse. After several hours, Edmundo, exhausted, gave up. The next day Edmundo dubbed Alberto's discourse style as *sí pero*, "yes but." No matter what anyone said, Alberto always found a rejoinder, a *sí pero*. Not many other thoughts could coexist with his, and in so doing he denied his own potential for suppleness.

But Alberto was not the only one responsible for the noise and for turning the apartment into a symbolic cage. I was closest to the family from March 1987 to August 1988 when I visited twice weekly. During that time there were four boys under ten years of age, and they functioned as a kind of force field lurching from living room to bedroom to kitchen with nonstop television in the background. Within a year or so, María gave birth to her fifth boy. They had their basketball team, joked María and Alberto. When the little girl that had been her goal finally arrived a few years later, the joke became a basketball team with cheerleader. Time to close the factory, joked María. But long before the last two children arrived, she and I had had long conversations about her life history and her frustrations about living in the United States and managing the force field. She had come from a large, more or less middle-class family in Mexico and was not familiar with the United States before marrying Alberto and traveling north to be with him. Rather quickly her idealism was shattered when she discovered, via rumors that were soon confirmed, that Alberto had been married and divorced. At first, she felt abandoned, and she longed to return home to her large family and the conditions that she was used to. She never made that decision, however, and what she got instead were years of having to depend on Alberto. He knew English, more or less, could reasonably navigate American ways, and knew how to drive (she didn't learn until years after). Her own spunkiness, independence, and her favorite outlet—talking to friends, family, and neighbors—became curbed in the new country. In contrast, Alberto's authoritativeness became more prominent, partly out of necessity. Quite often, he would teasingly document her misinterpretations and blunders with American idioms and ways, and although María, Edmundo, and I laughed at the kitchen table, Alberto through such discourse and our cooperation reinforced his authority and competence and her dependence. By her account, having children gave her new meaning and purpose, but the energy of the boys soon became a relentless burden. Working at a nearby factory allowed her to escape the burden. With her female coworkers, she could reexperience her sociable side. Responsibility for the children, however, was mostly hers, and this coupled with her fears of street life and what the boys might get into meant that she had to constantly scold, monitor, and herd. She was the mother finch trapped in a cage designed, although not consciously, by everyone in the family, including herself, as well as the world outside. Everyone was driving each other nuts, and Alberto's ritualistic, evening *tragitos*, "drinks," did not help. They scared her, reminding her too much of her own father's alcoholic binges when he would disappear for days at a time.

Finally, a few months prior to our most recent visit in the summer of 1995, a near catastrophe occurred. The oldest son, Andy, to whom I had been very close years back, was shot in the head during a dispute involving street gangs. Andy survived, and although his actual involvement in street gangs was never clarified, Alberto and María did what was common in Angelstown. They shipped him to Mexico to live with Alberto's brother. The whole episode confirmed María's fears about the neighborhood and left her deeply perplexed. Why were all these shootings occurring, she asked. What was happening in Angelstown and the rest of the United States? Why all these gangs? Why was Andy shot? Edmundo and I also had been searching for clarity but of the more abstract variety. In contrast, her search was driven by urgency, fear, and love.

I cannot possibly answer why Andy was shot, but I can render a set of suggestive scenes recorded by my tape recorder or written in my fieldbook. I will start, then, with scenes from that summer evening that began to unfold shortly after we passed the caged finches. There at the kitchen table with a hearty meal in front of us, Edmundo and I listened to Alberto as he opened the conversation by locating *la culpa*, "blame." First, there was the three-hundred-dollar telephone bill. Andy, now living in Mexico with his doctor uncle, Alberto's brother, was homesick and feeling very confined by the strictness of the new household. María had felt the need to soothe her son and accepted his collect calls—all with Alberto's permission, or so she thought. *"Mentiras.* [Lies.] *Nooo María*, you are

Elements of machismo

always inventing things, changing what we agreed on, or changing what occurred. I never said such a thing," said Alberto. And so the conversation went back and forth, a kind of power struggle over the "reality" of who had agreed to what. Because the struggle, I presume, could not be factually resolved, it was, as usual, Alberto's tenacity that crowded out competing interpretations.

Second was the disagreement concerning what the boys should wear. Again Alberto found fault with María's handling of the situation. "The boys need to wear what's in style, *de moda*," Alberto said, "If the pants are a little baggy, that's OK." María countered: "But how can you say that? Those clothes are a sign of gang involvement." María laughed, "Alberto buys whatever the boys want, but then he has to take it back because some of the teachers have said that the clothes contain gang colors." "*Nooo María*," he replied, "you are trying to control everything they wear, you are overprotecting them."

Third, we listened to their disagreement over the division of labor in their marriage. "*Oiga María*," Alberto said, "you are always talking about 50/50 between men and women. OK, well you fix the washing machine, the transmission in the car, the electrical work that needs to get done." He laughed: "And what about the day I grabbed two wires and shook myself up? Well, women can do this work just as easily as men." María countered: "Don't be silly Alberto, I do not even understand how to do those things." "*Sí pero*," he replied, "that's no excuse. Women are just as intelligent as men. You have to stick with it until you finally get it." We listened as Alberto twisted María's plea for sharing household duties that both were capable of doing into a put-down of what she did not know how to do. He was urging her, unfairly, to extend quickly her knowledge base so that it might resemble his own. In so doing, he disrespected what she did know and, moreover, made her 50/50 plea appear to be somehow inherently contradictory and something to be ridiculed. His manipulative logic mangled and silenced what had been a straightforward request.

Fourth was Alberto's criticism of the boys. "*Nooo*," he said, "not understanding is no excuse. The boys aren't willing to work hard enough at their lessons. I won't sit down with them to go over their lessons until they have gone over it two or three times, and if they don't understand after all that, then I am happy to show them how, but reading it once and saying you don't understand, *nooo*, that won't work. You have to learn how to do things on your own because we won't be around all the time to help. *Nooo*, the boys aren't willing to work hard enough." Again Alberto saw only what his boys could not do and expressed no more respect for their strengths and differences than for his wife's.

Fifth, we listened to Alberto concerning the children's need for attention.

Edmundo said: "The children want some attention, some sense of belonging to a family. When you have to punish, agree beforehand, the whole family together, what the rules are and the punishments." " *Y por qué* [and what for]," Alberto replied, "My father never paid attention like that to us when I was growing up. You do not need that to grow up responsibly. He never sat down to play with us or anything like that. And he did not discipline us either. My mother did that. She was always at home." As I listened to Alberto insisting on the absurdity of expecting a father to provide loving attention for his children, I knew that I was not listening to an overly negligent father. Indeed, as he spoke these words, he held the youngest, his little girl, Vivian, for a very long time with *cariño*, "affection."

Sixth, there was the disagreement between Edmundo and Alberto concerning the need to have children so as to carry on one's name. Edmundo had just gotten married and had inherited the children from his wife's previous marriage. Neither he nor his wife were interested in having additional children. This sentiment surprised Alberto and María. Alberto replied: "It is important to me that the family name continue, that it not die out, that the bloodline goes forward. Yes, we already have six children, but if the factory weren't closed, I would like to have more." María, who did not want to have more children, replied: "And if I hadn't been able to have babies, would you have had children with someone else?" Alberto replied, "*Sí.*" María reacted with shock and enormous hurt. Alberto seemed dimly aware that he had truly said something off limits, and his responses at this point became embarrassed. Edmundo replied: "Bloodline does not mean much to me, what gives me pleasure are my actions, the chance to train children to be honest, responsible people." But Alberto remained unconvinced.

Last we heard Alberto's complaints about his job as a chef's helper on a gambling boat. Alberto argued: "If you make sandwiches, you get paid as much as me. But I do more and I know more. I spend all my time cutting vegetables, but I get paid less. That's not right. They have French cuisine with French names on the menu, and I've memorized those dishes so that the chef sometimes asks me for the recipe. Yes, I know a lot, and sometimes I cook them here in the house too. And one day the manager asked, 'Who made the such and such? Was it you Alberto? Did you make sure that you did it exactly the way you were told to?' And he was hovering over me, the way he always does, always looking over your shoulder. And so I said sarcastically, 'Yes it was me, and, you know, I understand English, and I fixed it exactly the way I was told to. The only stuff I didn't understand was the stuff you never told me.' From that point on, he has not dared to talk to me again. No one can talk to me like that."

These small verbal victories seemed to fill Alberto with glee. They amplified his self-esteem, his desire to be somebody in the world, his sense of being right rather than wrong. He spoke as if his words consistently pointed to the reality of things independent of any bias and as if he had the right, indeed, the exigence, to speak the truth. From this conviction, he could justify his *sí pero* and, thereby, reestablish order, which meant that he rarely listened. He seemed to think that truth, spoken this way, had the power to settle chaos without considering that it might also, under the right circumstances, stir it up.

In order to amplify my observations, let me turn to a translation of a short conversation that occurred in late April 1987. I have made only slight changes in order to make it more readable. The discussion concerned schooling in Mexico and gradually became a disagreement about the teaching of algebra. María, who completed junior high but went no further, maintained that, as she was graduating, algebra was being introduced in the elementary grades. Alberto vehemently maintained that she was wrong, and they both interrupted each other considerably as they tried to make their points:

> **María:**
> Yes, but in what year would they start teaching algebra? When they started with mathematics, they began with algebra.
> **Alberto:**
> Nooo—
> **María:**
> In what year?
> **Alberto:**
> One thing is algebra and another is mathematics (*becoming heated*). Algebra is what I have learned, it's pure letters, numbers—
> **María:**
> Well, what is it that they are learning now (*becoming heated in return*)? Wasn't your father telling you how different it is, that the classes now are very different?
> **Alberto:**
> Algebra, nooo—
> **María:**
> Yes. It's not the way it used to be—
> **Alberto:**
> Nooo—
> **María:**
> Yes, it's not the way it used to be, now it's very different. (*A five-*

second, confusing exchange because the children are also very noisy.)

Alberto:

Yes, but algebra is not very simple, woman . . . it takes a lot to get it into one's head.

María:

Exactly, and so why do they begin with little children? I don't know why. Why does one need algebra?

Alberto:

What do you mean why?

María:

Well, why? So that they can learn it as children?

Alberto:

They are equations that are used, like the scientists use pure letters and numbers. That is what algebra is used for, to make formulas and all that . . . (*Alberto continues, but his statements are unclear, in part, because María interrupts.*)

María:

The last year I went to, the last year I went to junior high . . . HOLD IT (*addressed to Alberto who won't stop talking*) HOLD IT; the last, WILL YOU HOLD IT? The last year I went to junior high, they told me—I was now among the older ones and I could no longer stay in that school, it was a special school for workers, this was the last year to take any special courses because already those in the elementary grades were advanced in those classes—the schools had changed a lot—

Alberto:

In what year was your brother Tito?

María:

He was in high school. You didn't know that?

Alberto:

Well, I had seen things of his that were in algebra.

María:

He was in high school.

Alberto:

Then, why do you say that they teach those things first in primary school?

María:

I didn't say it was the first thing taught, I said that when they start teaching mathematics. For instance, they start teaching adding and subtracting. (*She starts to become more heated.*) They start with the small things, but I am not sure if they do this in first or second grade. Whenever they start, they start. Ask one of my nephews or your nephew, you can ask one of them.

Alberto:

Ma . . . the . . . ma . . . tics (*He pronounces it syllable by syllable in order to emphasize the word.*)

María:

Well, it may be mathematics, but it's like algebra.

Alberto:

No, it's not like mathematics, there are a lot of differences.

María:

No, this is what I've been trying to tell you.

Alberto:

And this is what I've been telling you.

María:

And this is what I've been saying because I don't know what algebra is. All that I am saying is that it is like the numbers that you have shown me. It's that I don't understand it. And when they were teaching me in school, yes, I understood it well, but when I got here, well, it's that they teach very differently here . . .

Alberto:

Well, there's pre-algebra.

María:

Well, I don't know. I'm not going to read something that I don't understand. (*She starts to become heated again.*)

Alberto:

There's pre-algebra.

María:

I'm only saying that the numbers that you were showing me that you were saying were algebra—

Alberto:

That gives a value to a letter—

María:

No, leave that orange there. (*She turns to one of the boys to stop him with the same tone of voice that she has been using to argue with Alberto.*)

Alberto:

There's pre-algebra, what they call here introduction to algebra. It's very different.

(*In frustration, María leaves to tend to the children. She shortly returns, but the discussion of algebra is over and the conversation turns to the differences between Mexican and American schooling.*)

What might be glimpsed inside these verbal exchanges between Alberto and María? More than likely, Alberto, indeed, was correct, and María wrong, about the starting point for the teaching of algebra. But their disagreements, in my interpretive scheme, were less about algebra and more about the damaged chemistry that fused them together and even more about the damaging social system in which they lived. At the core of their troubles was a set of power imbalances distinctly evident in the above conversation. The first power imbalance functioned privately because it repeatedly wounded the intimacy that they both desired. At this level, Alberto, under the cover of being "correct," could disguise his tenacious need for authority, which was realized too often at the expense of María. María, always spunky, used snappishness to counter his one-upmanship, but these back and forth jabs resolved little except to prepare the arena for the next round. The second power imbalance functioned at the socio-economic level as an omnipresent reminder that equality with majoritarian or mainstream society was not easy to come by.

But let me address more specifically how the above exchanges enacted these two power imbalances. Alberto's exposure to technical expertise (the study of algebra and computer programming) made him knowledgeable in ways that undermined María. He used his knowledge to enhance his authority ("one thing is algebra, another is mathematics" and scientists use algebra for equations and formulae). However, it is important here to distinguish how Alberto wielded technical expertise to maintain authority from how he maintained authority over daily affairs. For instance, the seven disagreements that I earlier stitched together from an evening's interactions were, I would argue, examples of trying to control daily life. In contrast, his authority derived from technical knowledge was rooted in larger systemic forces operating in modern culture. What drew him to the study of algebra and technology after passing the High School Equivalency Exam was not just talent and interest in these subjects or the lure of a good paying job. There was also the prestige of these subjects, the fact that they represent one of the foundations of the modern. The topos of technical expertise, particularly the semblance of power and economic betterment that seems to be attached to this sort of knowledge, was very attractive to someone like Alberto who aspired to the middle class. He clung to this topos tenaciously, if tenuously, for it represented one of the few props by which he could *create respect under conditions of little or no respect.* His need for authority over home life and his authority in technical matters melded, then, to create the stomping, if fragile, personality that I have been attempting to describe here. I say "fragile" because Alberto was distinctly splintered from the Mexican culture that he understood best, and so he inhabited, instead, and very tenuously at that, the American version of the modern. In short, the tenuousness of his position was a major source of anxiety, and so his style of logic was mostly angry and obdurate as it tried to cover up the insecurity. For instance, his answer to María's "Why algebra?" could only dimly explain how and why scientists and others use algebra. Like the rest of us, perhaps, when we lack expertise in a given subject, he mostly bluffed an answer that hid its shaky foundations even as it trumped the challenges of others. If he appeared to be mean, then, and I certainly think he was and do not wish to excuse it, we need simultaneously to point to the structural meanness of what may be a chaotic modernity that is always divisive, in that it is always awakening and then frustrating desire in order to maintain its consumerist ethic, and is always in need of workers, sometimes immigrants, who lack cultural and economic capital and, therefore, desire to acquire more. Alberto's meanness aimed at María, then, was also a structural meanness caging many, including the Juárez, who themselves had caged, in my symbolic reading, at least, a family of finches.

As for María, her knowledge base was different, and she seemed to have trouble competing on the terrain of technical expertise ("Why does one need algebra?" "I don't know what algebra is." "I don't understand it." "I'm not going to read something that I don't understand"). She had less education, no technical training, and no interest in acquiring it. Her work experience was on factory lines, and when she aspired to a career, she typically and idealistically mentioned the owning of her own shop and the art of buying and selling. If her husband was competitive and authoritarian, her self-described gift was her sociability. For instance, she enjoyed factory work because of the friendships that she had made with other women, and she idealized the owning of a business as an extension of sociability. Her knowledge base, then, did not consist of specialized training. It remained practical, consisting of those abilities acquired at a variety of factory jobs as well as those numerous, if unnamed, skills she had acquired while growing up in a large family and taking care of younger siblings. Most importantly, it included a talent for laughing, joking, and making others feel comfortable, in short, sociability. In the eyes of Alberto—and, perhaps, even within the larger cultural imaginary—María's knowledge base as opposed to his own was differentially loaded, meaning that greater power is awarded to technical knowledge because it is so much at the foundation of the modern. These conditions can be critiqued as unjust, and yet such a critique does not easily dislodge what I described earlier as a kind of structural meanness located inside a chaotic modernity that is particularly dependent on technical expertise. Alberto and María, then, seemed to be caught in a private drama, a rather conventional one at that, in which a traditional husband asserts his own supposed competency but not his wife's and thereby establishes his respect by disrespecting her; simultaneously, they seemed to be caught in a larger, social drama, a structural meanness, that could only exacerbate the private one.

At this point in my analysis, I wish to examine how language operated in many of these scenes. For instance, Alberto verbally muscled his way through confrontation after confrontation—whether the exchanges were with María, the boys, or his manager—by mobilizing, what I call, certain "realist effects" through which he located the real, true, and correct. Realist effects are abundant when language is used for naming and arguing. Perhaps the single most important realist effect occurs via the verb "is," whose simple power is the location of facts, conditions, states of existence, and so on in some space apparently independent of the speaker (one thing *is* algebra, another *is* mathematics). Realist effects create an apparent identity between signifier and signified, an identity that occults the third and most important part of any naming, namely, the namer. In that occulting, the real, true, and correct emerge as seemingly independent of being named. They emerge as names not chosen from a range of potential names, as names not chosen by a specific speaker speaking from specific motives, predispositions, and speaking conditions. They emerge as if they had named themselves without human mediation—a most impossible condition to say the least. In short, in most propositions, but surely not all, it is the appearance of the real, the true, and the correct and not the really "real" that gets named, and probably most speakers and listeners, in the heat of arguing, cannot distinguish between the semblance of the real and the real itself. Here, then, is one of the results of the discourse of power: As it names the world, a semblance of reality appears to be more than a semblance. The extent to which this transformation occurs, then, is one measure of the amount of power to be awarded to a particular speaker and his or her claim. Alberto's discourse sought power wherever it could be found, and so he was mostly incapable of letting go of his need to name the real. Hence, Alberto ran roughshod over the mistakes of others: María probably had made a mistake about algebra in elementary school. But even when the others had not made mistakes but were, indeed, presenting reasonable perspectives (for instance, even if María was overprotecting the boys, she had good reason to do so given the dangers of the neighborhood), he continued to locate truth and reality in his own point of view and to ignore María's perspectives. The result was a kind of powerful but crude dictatorship of the real, true, and correct that took precedence over any acknowledgement of María's fears and needs and too easily dismissed her own semblances of reality that deserved to be heard.

But how did Alberto's discourse of power, which fought off all challengers in order to maintain authority, and María's discourse of power, which jabbed back in order to acquire a modicum of authority, insinuate themselves into the lives of the children? At the time of the algebra conversation in 1987, Andy was in second grade, Emmit in kindergarten, Jason was four years old, and Alberto, Jr., was still too young to play. Since I was interested at the time in the acquisition of written and oral language, the three older boys and I spent many evenings at the kitchen table drawing, writing, and reading stories, building masks, talking about the neighborhood, and so on. If we happened to be outside, we spent time playing games, repairing bikes, or visiting a local ice-cream dairy. Virtually every picture drawn or every story written by the boys concerned some sort of monster destroying something or some superhero saving something else or some transformation of self into a monster or animal. (Ralph: "Why do you like to draw whales Andy?" Andy: "Because they're so big and can kill people with their butts.") Around Thanksgiving in 1987, Andy wrote the following story at home. I am unable to replicate the visualness of the text, the fact, for instance, that in two places Andy wrote "sp" and boldly capitalized the W at the beginning of one of the sentences much like a teacher when correcting a student paper. Of greater interest is the fact that the arms of the T on THE END were drawn as a swastika and the N was crowned with a three-pointed crown. The reversed swastika was also the symbol of the Maniac Latin Disciples, and the crown a symbol of the Almighty Latin King Nation. I am not certain what Andy meant by these symbols, if anything. At the least, he may have placed them into his text because they were part of his neighborhood's environment:

> I will sneak on all the turkeys. I will turn into a bat. I will hide in then.
> When they come I will suck the beaueitiful, nice, yummy blod.
>
> THE
> END
>
> I like you? do you like me?
> Yes or no

At the time, I paid little attention to these frequent stories of monsters, superheroes, and large animals. I was skeptical of interpretive frameworks that might either overinterpret or resemble the psycho-talk of popular culture. Hence, I left the stories alone, and they became part of the detritus of fieldwork. In comparison, the boys' school writings and drawings were the sorts of polite work that one might expect. They were passionless, as if the vitality of emotional life had been dampened by schooling itself. If the schools needed to preserve order in the classroom, I had, in ways that I did not fully comprehend, given permission to the performance of urges and needs that were "disorderly," less socially acceptable. Almost from the beginning in 1987, in a matter of three or four visits, the boys' relationship with me became, to a significant degree, built around the impermissible. I became their outlet for dirty songs, burps, farts, and sarcastic remarks about parents. The boys had learned quite well the generic rules for displaying the impermissible; they knew equally well, of course, the socially acceptable scripts and the rules for censoring the impermissible. Or as Emmit might say after something naughty, "uh oh, spaghetti-o," an interesting script that critiqued naughtiness by grafting it to a slice of American advertising. Emmit was labeled the *payaso*, "clown" or "cutup," by his parents. Quite often, as Andy diligently wrote and drew monster stories or read children's books, activities that he seemed truly to enjoy, Emmit would burp, say naughty words into the tape recorder, or draw depictions of what he called "caca," penises, and 'pee." When caught by parents, Emmit might say in a very slow, rhythmic, insistent, and annoying way, "SORRY . . . SORRY . . . SORRY . . . SORRY . . ." Andy often chastised Emmit as crazy, but he also laughed with him. In short, I was the boys' permissive audience, and any explanation of their performances, like any other explanation of rhetorical encounters in the midst of fieldwork, needs to be understood as partly fabricated by all participants in the scene.

By the summer of 1995, as I said earlier, Andy had been shot and sent to Mexico to protect him from possible gang trouble, and the family had increased by two. On the typically contentious evening I previously described, I left Edmundo in the kitchen wrangling with Alberto's need to pass on the family name by having as many children as possible, and slipped away with a headache that was growing more insistent. Alberto's overbearingness had worn me down until I felt muted, dull, and almost helpless. I had lost my footing for making counterarguments or even reasoned replies, and I would wager that these same feelings were periodically felt by María and were perhaps at the root of her dissatisfaction with her marriage. At any rate, I went looking for the older boys. They were in their bedroom, a kind of sanctum, it seemed, where fantasy life could escape the noise of mother and father and the younger children. Emmit, who had just entered his teen years, was shy and very reticent, while Jason, not quite a teenager, was eager and more open. I had not seen them in a while, and yet they seemed eager to pick up where we had left off. Without any encouragement from me, Emmit busily copied a remarkable likeness of Spiderman, and Jason, eager to play with my laptop computer, wrote a story in which a hero called Jason invented a special stove for the making of "creepy crawlers" who saved the world by defeating the monsters created by "Mozinroth." At one point, the boys pulled out a remarkable binder filled with plastic sheets that held cards representing a large number of cartoon action-heroes, including Spiderman. The documentation and ordering of all these heroes had been carefully attended to. I took a picture of the two of them holding their binder open to the camera because they were so proud of their work and energy. In my interpretive scheme, it was in this sort of careful, deliberate work—Emmit patiently copying Spiderman, both boys carefully mounting and preserving action-hero cards—that the boys created a sense of control, pleasure, and privacy in an otherwise very unprivate household. The marketplace had provided them with a certain style of escape, one that was sharply demarcated from adult interests and that relied on fantasy heroes whose hyperbolic exploits both defeated, even as they mimicked, the darker forces that roamed the universe. I interpreted the need for this special style of privacy and fantasy as embedded inside the discourse and dynamics of the entire family. All the boys, Andy, Emmit, Jason, and even Alberto, Jr., who occasionally joined us as we talked about Spiderman and other superheroes, seemed to have handed a certain genre down from the oldest boy to the next and so on until all had been sutured into its hyperbolics, a genre that included monster stories, superpowers, and fantastic battles between good and evil. I am not saying that each boy played with the genre in the same way, but I found it remarkable that so much was so broadly shared. Hence, it seemed reasonable to me to regard the power struggle between Alberto and María as having morphed into a complicated dynamic in which the boys used naughtiness and sarcasm as forms of resentment aimed against their constantly chastising parents, and used monster stories, superheroes, and fantasy battles as ways of escaping into a private world of power safe from Alberto's seemingly infallible power that always eroded whatever challenges María and the children could muster. Symbolically and literally the apartment was claustrophobic, for the needs of others had little space in which to live. Under these conditions, any sort of escape that the boys might effect made good sense to me. According to my interpretive scheme, then, if Alberto's uncompromising search for the real, true, and correct exerted hyperbolic violence upon the world, the boys had found, in response, a genre, also hyperbolic and symbolically violent, through which they might experience power and meticulous control and, thereby, resuscitate their otherwise pinched lives.

another long evening: martin's vengeance

Another evening, one spent with my young friend Martín who introduced me to the thumper drivers, was as difficult as the evening with the Juárez, but perhaps also more illuminating. It occurred on 9 April 1993, almost two years prior to the 1995 visit with the Juárez, and marked the first crystallization of what I am calling here "the logic of violence and the logic of trust." Indeed, it was during this evening in 1993 that I first used the terms. That evening Martín spun a story of vengeance, and as I listened, it occurred to me that vengeance itself, despite being typically characterized as a powerful emotion, was the result of a decision-making process that might be described as a kind of logic, and if imagined as a logic, might there not be some counter logic to dampen its violence? I responded to Martín by using the terms "logic of violence" and "logic of trust," but even as I did so I wasn't sure if I meant the word "logic" in its denotative sense, or as a fertile, organizing metaphor. I suspect the latter, for what interests me here is how cognitive life and emotional life function together and, more importantly, how both of these are not just private experiences but thoroughly social, indeed, parts of a larger "ideologic." At times, our conversation was heated, and sometimes it took me back—and all too uncomfortably—to my own struggles with violence and trust during earlier moments of my life.

After that evening and for the next few days, I used fieldnote writing to clarify these opposing systems of violence and trust. I remember those struggles clearly, for it seemed at the time that if I could not articulate the difference between these systems and establish a firm ground for the logic of trust, then, somehow, I could not recover a moral order that might save my friends and myself from endless cycles of unhappy violence. I was in a kind of mini-crisis. On the one hand, listening to stories of vengeance with a supposedly neutral ear seemed morally bankrupt; on the other hand, since I had never articulated a system that both understood vengeance and opposed it, I didn't know how to reply to such stories. Moreover, as I struggled to articulate a territory that was unknown to me, I also struggled to balance the merits of relativism (and its virtue of tolerance) against moralism (and its virtue of clear standards). At any rate, during three or four days of fieldnote writing, the terms "logic of violence" and "logic of trust" emerged and were elaborated upon, and since then they have become a useful heuristic by which to understand not only my experiences with Martín and the Juárez but other occurrences in Angelstown as well.

The conversation with Martín occurred inside Don Angel's apartment below the bare bulb that illuminated his bedroom/living room. Earlier that week Don Angel had left for Mexico to help bury his mother, and so Edmundo and I had the apartment to ourselves. Martín had dropped by to shoot the breeze, for awhile, but as the evening wore on, our talking began to "click"—at least in my head. I began to understand how pain rumbles through a body and psyche, how it might transform itself into fear or violence, and continue outward to sweep up the rest of the social body in its own thickening wake. Our talk was not particularly revelatory to any participant except me. To most observers, the talk would have seemed cluttered, like most late-night gabbing, with boredom, sleepiness, exasperation, small amounts of anger, joking, and large blurry hubris, particularly on Martín's part. Nevertheless, Martín without knowing it seemed to be laying out the structured emotional logic by which violence gets justified, and as he spoke I began to understand what had coursed through the lives of others off and on for years. My goal in the rest of this chapter, then, is to link my earlier analyses of the Juárez to a more specific analysis of Martín and others and a small number of their exploits in order to present a larger portrait of the logics and ideologics of violence and trust.

Our visit with Martín began, as I said on 9 April, and lasted well into the morning of the tenth. I want to begin my account at two or three o'clock on the morning of the tenth in that apartment that did not separate bedrooms from living rooms. Martín, in the self-important mode that he sometimes laced with self-parody, had already awakened inside of me my impatient and dismissive side. I could tell that Edmundo had also become, on occasion, irritated. Both Martín and Edmundo are physically large, and I sensed that Edmundo would have enjoyed pinning some of Martín's self-inflated imaginings and rationalizations to the floor like a heavyweight wrestler. So Edmundo and I were both somewhat worn out with Martín when he began to unfold the story that I have edited here in order to convey it more easily. The story concerned Martín, Fidel, and Gonzalo, formerly close friends, who had been arrested months earlier for peddling narcotics. Martín, for whatever reasons, was being charged far more severely than Fidel and Gonzalo. Martín was bitter about this apparent unfairness. Moreover, the other two had never come around to console him for taking the bigger rap and, worse yet, Fidel had spread "lies" that Martín was behind the bust and had collected Crimestoppers' money for the betrayal. In short, he had received "no respect, no consideration" from Fidel and Gonzalo.

At one time, all three had had big dreams of making big money, and this particular sell was to be a small step toward ever bigger sales, toward becoming, as
Martín put it, "Godfather the Sequel." A fourth character, Andrés, appears
here as a messenger who, for a short while after the arrest, passed along the esca-
lating suspicions and threats that began to emerge between Martín and Fidel.

> Fidel never confronted me saying, "Hey Martín, I think you got money
> out of this shit, out of setting us up." That's all he kept saying to
> Andrés. Andrés would come and tell me. . . . Fuck this shit, I got fed up
> with it. So I told Andrés, "Hey, can you get me Fidel's plate number?
> You know what car he drives, I know what car it is, but there can
> always be more than one. . . . I need you to get the license plate of that
> car for me, act stupid, drive around the parking lot." . . . So I got it set
> up, fine, and he [Fidel] was driving around in his girlfriend's Mustang,
> and I asked him, "What the hell happened to your car?"
>
> "Oh it's in the shop," he says, "getting work done. I'm dropping
> the car lower."
>
> "Where the hell do you have your car?"
>
> "Well, I got it at this and this place." . . .
>
> "When's your car going to be out?"
>
> "Well, my car will be out about this time because they got to go
> through the suspension. They got to make sure that the weight of the
> car can handle the spindles."
>
> "Well cool, are they going to do a good job?"
>
> "Oh well, they are only charging me so much and so much."
>
> Fine. . . . This was Fidel's Too Low Flow car, a Caddie, a red Cad-
> die. So in the car, he had a Alpine pull out, two Alpine amplifiers, one
> for each speaker with two twelve-inch pyramid faze 3 pro series
> speakers and a kicker box and I had some guys take care of that, steal
> his shit out of the car, steal his alarm, and fuck up his car, in other
> words, key it up. They scratched his rims, they slashed his tires, they
> broke his windows, they fucked up the interior. . . . Because he kept
> insisting that hey, number 1, that I had set them up because I wanted
> money [$1,000 from Crimestoppers for turning others in] and 2, in
> other words, he was calling me a pussy, hey, you know, "Why you turn-
> ing us in?" this and that, "Why be a stool pigeon?" you know, 'cause
> that is the kind of interpretation I took, and I was thinking the only
> pussy here is Fidel because he does not want to come forward and
> tell me, you know, face to face: "Martín, I think you got money out of

this shit." . . . I can call him a pussy because he doesn't come up to me forward and say, blah, blah, blah. . . .

I did do something wrong (sell dope) and I got busted for it. And at this present in time, not proudly to say, I am facing up to a . . . maximum of five years in the state with thirty months of probation and $2,000 fine to follow, and he thinks that I set him up and that's why I'm going to jail, that's why I'm facing a jail sentence while those motherfuckers are out like a free bird. Shit, we'll see who's a pussy, you know, we'll see who's a man when he come out of jail or whatever. . . . But for one thing I know for a fact, if Fidel and Gonzalo were to go to jail, they'd be fucking jailbait, they'd be what you call the inmates' bitches, they'd be the ones getting [laughs] popped, because they're all pretty boys. . . . That seriously wouldn't scare me. . . . Hey, I'd fucking just kick ass any dumb fucker who'd try to do that shit with me. That's the kind of attitude you'd have to take in jail. For the fact of gaining respect. . . .

I still got a score to settle with them when once I come out of jail. Right now I'm just hanging low profile, but his car got fucked up real good. It got fucked up nice, I mean, just to replace all the things he lost, the paint on the car, the tires, the rims. It was enough money to spend getting a new car. . . . And he asked me later, "Have you seen any of my shit?"

"Naw, what happened?"

He go, "Man, right where I had my car stored in the garage. . . . It got fucked up, got keyed and everything."

"No, bullshit, are you talking about your Too Low Flow?"

"Yeah, man, the paint job, the interior, the speakers, the fucking tires and shit." . . . I said, "Damn, who the fuck would do that shit?"

"I don't know dudes . . . I'm not really going to worry about it 'cause I'm going to report it to my insurance." . . .

And that was it. I mean I didn't literally, literally, literally take any action, any physical action on the car, but you could say I was the one calling the shots about the car getting fucked up like that.

What was hiding behind Martín's discourse that seemed at times almost comic, as if he had been acting out the banal passions on the latest soap opera? As he spoke to Edmundo and me, he postured considerably like a quintessential tough guy "taking care of business," even packing a pistol in case Fidel found out who had called the shots. In my interpretive scheme, however, the posturing and the clichés of male ego are important aspects of ritualized vengeance. Indeed, tales of vengeance were common in Angelstown. One could hear it, for instance, in female fight stories,[1] such as the one told to me by Celestina of how she and her enemy almost came to blows, and there were stories far more gory and vindictive from friends of mine like Humberto who talked of his own angers and those of the Insane Deuces or those of Ricardo, a Latin King, who was later put in jail on murder charges. In short, as I heard Martín's story, these stories and others started to coalesce almost as if they were parts of a recurring cycle, a highly structured and common ritual that had been there all along without my seeing it. In responding to Martín, then, I had to struggle (and I sometimes lost) not to shame or dismiss his words and actions because, simultaneous to the posturing, there was also an unfolding, albeit unconsciously, of a specific ritual—vengeance—whose natural language is mythopoetic: A wounded someone wants to open a wound in someone else, and in opening that wound, there is a kind of ravishment, even a freedom. To release the blood of another is to release oneself—all this is primal, and strangely communal, for those who speak the discourse of pain desire pained others to accompany them. Call it, then, a need to make others hurt as much as one hurts, a need to make pain communal.

In my interpretive scheme, then, Martín spoke of "gaining respect" in order to face down being a "pussy," and, in so doing, he mobilized the ritualized language of the neighborhood that often went like this: "So and so ain't showing me respect, no consideration"; "So and so's telling lies, talking trash. They ought to come talk to my face and I'll set them straight"; "You gotta show 'em they can't fuck with you"; "I got my rights"; "No way so and so's going to take advantage of me." The language was typically brittle and never pliant. It seemed to me that behind its brittle assertiveness, however, one might find the skeletal structure of the logic of violence, in short, the network of assumptions that might lead to an act of vengeance. I offer the following as a tentative list of these core assumptions:

how to survive...

Life is tough.

Most people are not to be trusted.

Always be wary.

Defend yourself or get beaten up.

When someone (Andrés in Martín's story) reports the offensive remarks or actions of someone else, that someone reports faithfully without distortion.

Your enemies have simple motives: to hurt you.

Your enemies are basically "low lifes" and not much else.

When done wrong by your enemies, you occupy the moral high
ground, a place of righteousness.

The wrongness of your enemies deserves punishment.

You always have the right to inflict such punishment.

You show more "heart" (honor, courage) when you take care of your
own "business."

If the above is, indeed, a rendering of the skeletal structure of the logic of violence, what is missing is the real-life intensity in which all parts of the structure fire almost instantaneously. When such moments occurred in Angelstown,
particular retributions appeared to be quick, just, natural, and obvious responses to offensive actions. The moves through the structure were so quick
that often when I heard these stories, particularly from Humberto, I felt empty
and helpless. I simply nodded. Counterarguments eluded me. Conventional
moralistic replies simply seemed anemic. Speed, decisiveness, and a lack of self-
doubt seemed to characterize the offended party, and, frankly, I felt over-
whelmed. Sometimes I rationalized my empty nod and lack of a response by
thinking that in not arguing back I was being more objective, like a good social
scientist. Below these rationalizations, however, was a simple helplessness and
an annoyance at myself for not being able to reply. If, as a guiding ethos, the
logic of violence seemed to lead to endless cycles of vengeance stopped only by
exhaustion, I needed to say so firmly and quickly, but for whatever reasons I had
been unable to do so prior to this special evening with Martín. In simplest
terms, if Martín felt sure of his "righteousness," I felt less sure. Here, then, was
a key tension between us, a dialectic, if you will, that demanded elaboration.
But I was also compelled to show Martín "respect" because I was genuinely
fond of him and because if I could not show respect, I would run the danger of
initiating a different sort of violence. Hence, these cautions monitored my
analysis as I spoke to Martín, and they monitored me even more as I wrote in
my fieldbook during those days after 10 April when I confronted my own mini-
crisis whose intensity was exhilarating.

The logic of violence represented a kind of brute cause and effect relationship in which the humiliation of someone called for an equivalent humiliation
of the offender. Its ethos was "an eye for an eye, a tooth for a tooth," and I
grudgingly admired its mythic, destructive clarity, its ability to sweep away ambiguity so that what is left is clear, stark, and empty. In contrast, the logic of
trust deflected the momentum and inevitability of the logic of violence by calling some of its premises into question. In a sense, the logic of trust interrupted

the relationship between a cause and its effect; it destabilized judgment and punishment and made both less sure. In short, by acknowledging doubt it muddied the entire logical and automatic structure of ritualized vengeance. Let me display here a series of doubts that could have been mobilized by Martín in order to slow the speed and inevitability of his decision to seek vengeance: (1) Did Martín have clear access to Fidel's mind so that he could be certain that Fidel's motives were as singular and intentional as suspected? For instance, might Fidel have been idly grousing about his arrest rather than intentionally "dissing" Martín? (2) What of Andrés's reports—no distortion there? (3) If Gonzalo and Fidel were patented "low-lifes," what had they been before the arrest when Martín had been good friends with both as they dreamt their big dreams? (4) Why should an offended person be on a higher moral ground? An offending person may, indeed, be pretty low, but the elevation of the other person, as if on the other end of a seesaw, is not automatic. Perhaps in occupying a higher moral ground, offended parties can whitewash their own roles in the making of the dispute. (5) Which "right" is it that grants us the right to inflict punishment or to take care of one's own "business"? "Rights talk," of course, has become part of the discourse of our times perhaps because it can quickly ennoble any gripe. Rights talk seems to evoke the eternal and transcendent and, thereby, smacks of truth; but rights themselves are not grounded in some transcendental place, indeed, are more like matters of agreement that have evolved contentiously from within a specific cultural setting and have a longevity that cannot be assured.

I could continue with my list of doubts, but perhaps it's best here to summarize: It is the very clarity and certitude of the logic of violence, its admirable swiftness and decisiveness, that makes it problematic. It depends, for instance, on go-betweens transparently reporting the words and actions of others; on the clarity and factualness of a particular offense; on a coherent and purposeful offender; on the erection of a great divide separating the low-life offender from the moral high ground of the offended; on the distance and difference of "righteousness" from which the offended party can judge the offender with moral force and certitude and determine the appropriate punishment. In contrast, the logic of trust weakens the scaffolding by finding doubt and heretofore unimagined complexity. It is not as swift, decisive, obvious, nor, of course, as divisive.

But more to the point, the logic of violence might also be understood as an ideology that explains real events, feelings, and social conditions. In this sense, the logic of violence represents a very tight knot of emotion, reality, and ideological interpretation. It makes sense of "the way things are" and are expected to be. In short, it functions as a kind of commonsense interpretation of street life. Creating another interpretation, cutting that knot, is no easy matter. Indeed, understanding life in some other way would have been difficult for Martín and others to imagine, for it would have entailed the making of a different common sense and, more profoundly, the making of a new psyche. What I am suggesting here is that the emergence of a new thought from within a frozen ideological interpretation may entail a shake-up of old emotional patterns, for I am trying to describe the emergence of a new style of thinking and, deeper yet, a new gut response to life itself. Indeed, such changes, in all likelihood, will be resisted at first. My experiences with Martín and others suggested that those who wagered certain life decisions on "the way things are" did not want to be proven wrong, indeed, would stubbornly resist the loss of that investment. Hidden underneath the logic of violence as a specific ideology, then, are the processes by which it comes into being in the early history of an individual psyche. For Martín, for example, those processes were now outside consciousness, but, I suspect, they entailed the accumulation of violences, small and large, leaving not so much wounds as faint scars, an accumulation that might transform over time into a conviction that life is unstable or unjust. In my interpretive scheme, then, the logic of violence—a tight knot of emotions, real experiences, and ideological beliefs—inhabits individual psyches and, more broadly, street life's cultural imaginary as a kind of guiding ethos, in short, a sensible way (in some cases, a guaranteed way) to handle particular problems.

I realize at this point that my use of the term "ideology" may be an uncommon one. In everyday talk, the word "ideology" typically describes a fairly consistent body of ideas and values that guide an individual, a social movement, or political party. However, within critical theory, the tradition that guides much of my thinking, ideology is more richly conceived. One of my guides here is Antonio Gramsci,[2] and another is the sociologist/ethnographer Beth Roy, whose explorations of "implicit ideology" have proven quite fruitful for my own analytic purposes.[3] In *Some Trouble with Cows: Making Sense of Social Conflict*, Roy studied an unusual riot between Muslims and Hindus that occurred in the 1950s in a village in Bangladesh. What I find superbly insightful in her text is how bodies of ideas (ideologies) can become so internalized that they disappear as ideas but reappear as "emotions and "truths," a sort of commonsense understanding of the world so ingrained as to be beyond question and, much of the time, outside consciousness."[4] This transformation of an explicit ideology into something more internal, something felt, she calls "implicit ideology." The latter gets forged in the very core of an individual, in his or her emotional life, and the end result is that one possible picture of the world becomes, in effect, the "real" world of rights and wrongs, of felt obligations, of injustices to be endured and injustices to be resisted, and of distributions of power that seem commonsensical.[5] Her analysis suggests that individual life has a certain potential malleability (agency?) that becomes increasingly rigid as the spectrum of our beliefs and emotions become one with those of a politicized world.

In addition to Roy's explorations of implicit ideology, I also owe a debt to critical theory's persistent attention to what I call the "hidden." Whether in the work of such critical theorists as Pierre Bourdieu and Jean-Claude Passeron (the "science of society" [sociology] is the science of exposing the hidden but "efficacious mechanisms" by which vested interests reproduce and conserve the status quo[6]), or Gramsci, who understood the "critical" as "knowing thyself" as a "product of the historical process . . . which has deposited in you an infinity of traces, without leaving an inventory,"[7] the idea of the hidden remains salient. In the work of Roy, of course, implicit ideologies represent a distinctive kind of hidden in which national ideologies have insinuated themselves into everyday life, for instance, morphing into communal memories of small localities and, deeper still, into private emotions of individuals. At these latter levels, an ideology has become so well hidden that it no longer appears ideological. It has become a mode of thinking, indeed, a gut response to life itself. It may even be virtually equivalent to a person's identity. And so it is that my examinations of Alberto, Martín, and, more generally, the logic of violence have been my attempt to unpack a structured hidden that was quite invisible to their eyes and to my own as well for a number of years.[8]

In order to unpack further this structured hidden, or what I called earlier the skeletal structure of the logic of violence, let me examine more richly its first four assumptions: life is tough; most people are not to be trusted; always be wary; and defend yourself or get beaten up. In what ways might these be called an ideology, particularly the sort of internalized, "implicit ideology" described by Roy? All four assumptions have as a common denominator a core presupposition, namely, the disorderliness of existence, which is itself deeply intertwined, and reasonably so, with emotional anxiety. Whether the presupposition is, indeed, accurate is another issue and, perhaps, not a necessary one to settle, for, in these matters, just the perception of disorderliness is quite sufficient. (As I will argue later, the logic of trust rests on another presupposition, namely, the orderliness of existence and thus represents a different sort of ideology.)

A second and closely related presupposition might be stated this way: Because all networks of individuals and all systems that might make justice are also unstable, one can only fall back upon oneself to create a semblance of or-

→ *on your own*

der. This second presupposition supports the important mandate of taking care of one's own "business." It also supports the mandate of righteousness by which one might take the moral high ground and justify the punishment of others. Both presuppositions act as gut responses to create a distinctive kind of actor who, amplified beyond any community, might gain freedom by asserting his or her own definition of order over innately disordered conditions. Such actors need to assert their own authority over the otherwise uncontrollable in order to settle matters once and for all. Certainly, in so doing, such actors are profoundly swollen. They believe that they need to take matters into their own hands because all other possible systems for making things right or just are unreliable, unstable. In other words, the foundations of such a person are deeply anxious because existence itself is perceived as disorderly and because other available ordering systems are themselves unreliable. It seems to me that the brittle street language ("you gotta show 'em they can't fuck with you") or Martín's fears of being thought a "pussy" and his subsequent reactions were instantiations of a definitive ideological position that was not merely the perversion of an individual psyche but, indeed, a distinctive *topos* in a larger cultural imaginary, a guiding ethos that solved real problems in a very real way. But hidden within that clichéd language and in the hyperbolic melodramas that constituted the plotting and realization of vengeance, there lay, for Martín and others, a snakelike ideology whose first bite might well poison an offending party but whose return bite might also catch, in a deadly way, the offended party.

If, as I have been maintaining, ideology was knotted up with emotional life, it might be helpful here to describe further this underlayment of anxiety that I started to describe above along with the "real" events to which the anxiety was attached. "Anxiety" is a particularly useful word for summarizing the innate linkage of fear, pain, and anger. These words became important in my fieldnotes that were written shortly after the night with Martín, but I should say here that they did not encompass any sophisticated psychotherapeutic understanding—and they still do not pretend to do so.

In my interpretive scheme, then, the appearance of pain leads quickly to fear, namely, the fear of subsequent pain; and anger functions as an important mechanism for protecting oneself from future pain. This innate linkage of pain, fear, and anger is the emotional core that, as described earlier, is grooved to a specific presupposition, namely, the disorderliness of existence, from which the logic of violence can emerge as a commonsensical response that might, once and for all, order the disorderly. But pain, fear, and anger cannot erupt without some sort of connection to real events—or, at least, the perception of real events—that might validate an ideological interpretation concerning "the way things are." What then might constitute real evidence and how is this bound up with pain, fear, and anger? If Martín was a good example of these complicated processes, one might examine familial discourse as a site for continuous put-downs, put-downs that were themselves, perhaps, borrowed from the ideological structures of the outside world. For instance, I had seen Martín move through his teen years to become a man, and during all that time and before, he had been considered by the family stupid, overweight, disorganized, and *vago*, "lazy" or "good for nothing." Indeed, if there was anyone in the family who had been marked as the scapegoat, it was Martín. There were moments when he received psychic bashings from his brothers, sisters, and parents that made me squirm. The arguments and sarcasms typically concerned his failing grades. It seemed to me that the recurrence of pain or humiliation had made Martín and others jittery in the world and suspicious that all around lurked the next insult to body or psyche. Martín may have been good natured but he was also hungry for status and respect. Over the years, he had chosen with some self-parody, but also seriousness, a series of names for himself that were fashioned from his ever-changing interests. For example, when he became interested in painting, he fancied himself Michaelangelo; when he became interested in wrestling, he nicknamed himself the Hulk; when he started to sell dope and form his own gang, he adopted the name Godfather the Sequel. If fanciful self-naming offered him a kind of ironic respect, I also saw him on occasion choose suspicion and anger in order to create another kind of respect that might shield him from the attacks of the world. In short, it seemed to me that fear entered most easily and deeply those, like Martín, who had been weakened by humiliation (pain) or the perception of humiliation, and this idea should recall earlier comments in which I described a kind of systemic humiliation operating in the neighborhoods where I worked. Under these conditions, pain and fear often relied on anger as a mode of self-protection.

The more I examined Martín's pains, fear, and angers in the fieldnotes that were written after 10 April the more it occurred to me that the violence that had erupted between Martín and Fidel was due to shared pains and fears. I have to be careful here, however, because although I have spoken confidently of the humiliations that had marked Martín's life, I must speak much less confidently of Fidel's history of anxiety because I knew him much less well. At any rate, Martín's reactions to the rumors were laced with the following fears: Even though he knew the rumors were not true, he feared what the neighborhood might think. He feared losing respect in the eyes of others, of being considered a "pussy" and a betrayer of one's friends. Similarly, he could not make the first move to reconcile his split with Fidel. To make such a move would have ap-

hide behind the meanness

peared to Martín as a loss of face. After all, he knew he was *right* and *deserved* an apology, and these convictions gave him the moral ground from which to judge and punish. Hence, his fear of losing face and his assurance of being *right* congealed into a tough, stubborn, and self-righteous anger, a demand that Fidel, not he, make the first move toward reconciliation. Fear and anger had stolen his potential for suppleness. But Fidel, similarly, could not apologize partly because he too would have lost face in taking back what he had spread throughout the neighborhood and partly because he continued to believe that Martín had, indeed, betrayed him. He too, then, was operating from a similar moral high ground, imagining himself to be the *truly* offended party. In short, Martín and Fidel chose the same effective mechanisms with which to protect themselves: fear, self-righteousness, and anger. Martín and Fidel were, for all practical purposes, frozen images of each other. They were unable to see how their own pains, fears, and angers helped to invent—and eventually make real in the world—each other's wrongdoings. To melt the standoff, both would have had to recognize that the life-pain of the one was similar to the life-pain of the other, that one's fear was similar to the other's, and in this acknowledgment of a kind of partnership in pain and fear, they might have constructed a letting-go of their self-protections. For, in simplest terms, the logic of trust postulates that insidious fears and pains saturate all steps in the logic of violence and that the surest way to derail the gathering of one's own violence is to let go of fear and pain and to acquire (or reacquire) trust.[9] Returning to my earlier language, trust is inserted into the middle of cause and effect, absorbs and erases the cause so that its effect is not inevitable. To interrupt pain, fear, and anger with trust in these ways is, on the one hand, to no longer cower and, on the other, to no longer posture. It is the discovery of suppleness: the body without tension, the mind without anxiety.

But suppleness of this sort does not come easily. Indeed, if anxiety, as I have been describing it, is part of an implicit ideological code that is itself grounded in real experiences of day-to-day life, suppleness is part of another implicit ideology with its own evidence. In short, the basic doctrine or presupposition upon which the logic of trust resides might be described as the orderliness of existence. I need to speak hesitantly here, however, for the logic of trust is not so much a condition I observed amply in Angelstown as it was an invention that helped me to articulate the logic of violence. Like any invention, then, it runs the danger of being a simplistic idealization. It should be clear by now, however, that if I admired the clarity, starkness, and swiftness of the logic of violence, I could not admire its endless anxiety and that within my fieldnotes I conducted a kind of philosophical search for some relieving truth that might interrupt the emptiness of vengeance and argue against Martín, Humberto, and others without becoming arrogant. It was out of this need, then, that the logic of trust spoke to the divisiveness of the logic of violence. Its implicit ideology could not justify an amplified actor, for its doctrine of orderliness did not need an overly powerful actor to make things right. After all, if existence is already ordered, it must be mostly self-sufficient. If it needs anything, it needs a more supple actor characterized by compromise rather than resistance, by security rather than alienation. Indeed, according to the logic of trust, a compromise is not a loss of self; if anything, it might lead to a different sort of gain. But, of course, mobilizing this sort of guiding ethos does not occur easily inside a life history accustomed to real events that constantly seem to steal something from the self, leaving it with a kind of endless, anxious wariness—and anger.

There was a crucial moment, however, when Martín seemed to choose the logic of trust, in short, the welfare of others over his own. The moment occurred after the drug bust when the police separated Martín, Fidel, and Gonzalo and began to work on them individually. In Martín's case, an offer was made: Work for us, the police told him, set up a drug deal with other drug-dealing friends so that we can bust them too, and we'll give you protection and let you off. Martín refused and continued to refuse similar offers from his lawyers. He said that (1) he was afraid that whomever he betrayed might seek future vengeance against him or a family member, (2) he wanted to end the nervousness and anxiety that had overtaken him the last few years, and (3) he wanted to end a certain shame by taking his punishment and, hopefully, finding pride in that. I heard all this as a kind of woundedness seeking a healing, and it fit neatly into the schemes I had been groping toward about the logic of violence and the logic of trust. Quite simply, Martín wanted to free himself from the cycle of violence, wanted to stop its wheel even as the forces of law and order wanted to keep spinning the wheel.

In order to understand more richly the deals that the police and lawyers were offering, I need to elaborate the larger social context. The mayor and his new chief of police had both pledged to "clean up the streets." They had recently intensified drug and gang surveillance, argued for stiffer sentencing of drug dealers and gang members, set up satellite police stations in the neighborhoods where I worked, and encouraged the displaying of blue ribbons in order to show support of the police, an idea borrowed from the display of yellow ribbons by some Americans during the Iraqi War.[10] Moreover, another acquaintance of mine, the officer in charge of the street-gang task force, had earlier told me about the methods of harrassment used by the police to keep street gangs and drug dealers offguard. One of the most common methods was to pressure suspects into becoming informers. As the police intensified the suspect's fear of punishment, they simultaneously intensified the suspect's self-centeredness. If the police could get the suspect to put himself or herself first, they had an informer, someone willing to betray others. In this sense, the forces of law and order and criminals operated through similar logics of violence, but with this difference: Law and order saw itself as representing the moral high ground of the majority of citizens, whereas criminals had individually determined their moral high ground. At any rate, law and order was not interested in fundamentally ending the logic of violence. In fact, it had to keep the logic of violence spinning in order to catch more criminals. The catching of criminals, particularly gang members, had become a major pressure emanating from a nervous public, mayor, and city council. This social context, then, was part of the net that had ensnared Martín, Fidel, and Gonzalo, who, although they were not gang members, were certainly part of the same youth culture. Indeed, as we have seen, Martín often bragged about creating his own larger-than-life street gang. At any rate, I admired Martín's decision not to cooperate with law and order's version of the logic of violence.

During the next few days after Edmundo's and my early morning conversation with Martín, I began patching together in my fieldnotes a view that might link a microworld to the macroworld, or, as I called it earlier in this text, a persistent innerscape to a persistent outerscape. In the neighborhoods where I worked, the core condition of the outerscape, the macroworld, was, as I have said, systemic humiliation. The humiliation was omnipresent but part of the backdrop rather than the foreground. As a result, the numerous moments and events of everyday life were rarely dramatically humiliating partly because individuals always had their own agency and a certain power over their emotional lives. Nevertheless, reminders of one's lower station in the socioeconomic context of the United States were always available. For instance, even as Martín talked to Edmundo and me, his parents had already been told that they would soon not have jobs, for the company where they both worked was transferring all its operations, ironically, to Juárez, Mexico. Both parents were frazzled by their upcoming loss of jobs, lawyers' fees for Martín's case, the need to borrow money from a number of people (including me), their son's possible jail term, and the embarrassment he had caused them.[11] Even when joy mitigated humiliation, as it usually did, humiliation persisted in the background of the mundane: in the look of one's house or its size, the look of one's neighborhood, the clothes that one wore, the car that one drove, the language that one spoke, the color of one's skin. Any marker of difference might springboard someone toward feeling humiliation if he or she was already predisposed to feeling it, and I understood these markers as consequences not only of local conditions but also of the persistence of a history that long ago had deemed Euro-American modernity as enviable and in so doing had created the markers by which to spot those who were trailing behind. If, for me, the markers of modernity had much to do with the "neat and clean" as a symbol of regulating the unregulated, of control over the forces of death and decay, then the markers of "trailing behind" had everything to do with those who seemed less regulatable and, hence, symbolized the potentially irruptive forces on the margins of that system. (As will be discussed in chapter 7, city ordinances encoded the "neat and clean" with particular fervor.) At any rate, at one point in American history, European immigrants had worn the markers of "trailing behind," but from the perspective of Angelstown's leadership, it was now members of the new laboring classes—Latinos pushing north primarily from Mexico, Puerto Rico, and south Texas as well as African-Americans, and "white trash"—who were the primary bearers.

If systemic humiliation, then, was part of the persistent outerscape or macroworld, an understanding of the persistent innerscape or microworld was provided through such terms as the "logic of violence" and the "logic of trust." In this innerscape, there occurred the intensity of individual feeling and interpretation that registered and responded to the outerscape. This patching together of both worlds helped me to understand how social conditions might predispose individuals, particularly youth, to structured responses that might include pain, fear, self-centeredness or "righteousness" anger, and vengeance, all occurring with lightning speed. The story of Martín, Fidel, and Gonzalo's drug bust seemed to summarize so many stories and events that I had heard and seen as well as so many innerscapes. Stories of this sort are often interpreted in the mainstream media as well as the popular imagination as more signs of the pathological breakdown of families and a shredding of the moral fabric of American society. In contrast, I increasingly read their stories as part of a larger ideological formation. Indeed, I saw the ideology as utterly embodied, as a kind of transformation of belief into something muscular. For this same ideological formation was being performed within a certain pose that many young males struck, with many variations, on street corners or on the few occasions when I asked a young male if I could take his picture. The pose sometimes consisted of feet firmly on the ground, arms folded across the chest, torso and head tilted slightly back, and no smile. The pose was formidable, defiant, and meant to instill fear. It was the logic of violence inhabiting the body, for it said, "You damn well better not show me disrespect or I'll climb over your face." Of course, the response to such a pose was either to back down and, thus, expose one's humilation—or to strike a similarly confrontational pose. Metaphorically speaking,

Martín and Fidel had struck equivalent poses during their standoff. But the pose itself, in my interpretive scheme, masked a depth of pain and fear. In order to keep that depth a secret, the body chose what was most opposite, a kind of hyperbolic toughness and coolness. Perhaps the amount of exaggeration was equivalent to the amount of pain and fear.[12]

At any rate, the pose was part of a larger street semiotic, a code. For someone enveloped in the passions of the code, the pose was a threat, a put-down, a sign of superiority, hence, of disrespect. Those receiving the message of someone else's pose might feel their entire history of pain and humiliation suddenly co-alesce into a fireball. At this precise moment, such a person would have had to summon a special courage, a postponement of his or her pain and fear to read the secret beneath the pose and to find compassion for it and to feel a kind of brother/sisterhood of shared pains, fears, and humiliations. Such a person would have had to summon the logic of trust, but, as I have been saying, how difficult it is to find such a logic in one's innerscape when the persistent out-erscape has so thoroughly taught violence, large and small.

conclusion: fear is an emotion/bad is an attitude

I saw the statement which entitles this conclusion printed on a T-shirt during a visit to a medium security prison in October of 1996. A large woman was wearing the shirt, a woman whom I had seen on a number of occa-sions on those days when I visited El Duque, a street gang leader who had the responsibility of controlling the members of his organization that were incar-cerated with him. When I saw her shirt, I knew how deeply it explained much of what I have been trying to describe in this chapter and what I had been strug-gling to understand for a number of years. "Fear Is an Emotion/Bad Is an Atti-tude" were her words, or, better yet, the words of a particular cultural imagi-nary. On another visit to El Duque, I asked him what these words might mean. He described fear as something that one must hide but that attitude was some-thing that you acted out and that didn't show fear. The words of her T-shirt and his words of interpretation, when run through the wringer of my interpretive scheme, might mean something of the following: Fear as emotion is something to be hidden from others because it is a sign of weakness. In an unreliable, ag-gressive world, showing weakness encourages others to take advantage of one. In contrast, "badness" as attitude hides fear, occults it behind a public persona of toughness that protects one from the challenges of others. The T-shirt, then, exposed an important dialectic in which the hiding of fear and emotion was paired against the display of badness and attitude, and it was this dialectic that seemed to fuel Martín's vengeance and to explain his need to face down the challenge of being thought a "pussy" after being slandered by Fidel. But Martín's public pose of "badness" and "attitude" was fragile at best, for the hidden world of emotion, fear, and layered pain that the public persona was paired to was dangerously close to the surface. Here in these spaces rendered dark by the sometimes hyperbolic performances of toughness, one might find the sorts of emotional experiences that I have been trying to explain throughout this chapter. At any rate, emerging from conditions of both real and symbolic violence, a logic of violence or a decision to take vengeance could travel through a network of assumptions with lightning speed or, phrased in the language of critical theory, emerge as a commonsense decision. In short, the ideology and guiding ethos that circulated through Angelstown's particular cultural imaginary were not just ideas; they had become embodied as felt truths. Speaking from an internalized ideology, then, certain individuals, such as Martín or Alberto, wielded their realist effects to conjure what seemed to be a brazenly real world that occulted other interpretive schemes. Under such conditions, the named world was not some nominalist's fancy but, indeed, "the way things are," something that might determine belief and action and become the basis for creating a most satisfying, if short-term, sense of moral righteousness.

6

GANGS AND
THEIR WALLS

"Thee Mystics rule," one of them yelled from the other side of the
school fence. . . . I froze as the head-stomping came dangerously my
way. But I was also intrigued. I wanted this power. I wanted to be able
to bring a whole school to its knees and even make teachers squirm.
All my school life until then had been poised against me: telling me
what to be, what to say, how to say it. I was a broken boy, shy and
fearful. I wanted what Thee Mystics had; I wanted the power to hurt
somebody.
–Luis J. Rodriguez, *Always Running, La Vida Loca:
Gang Days in L. A.*

There are no other gang experts except participants.
–Sanyika Shakur, A.K.A. Monster Kody Scott, *Monster:
The Autobiography of an L.A. Gang Member*

street-gang graffiti: lexicon and syntax

The above quotation of Shakur is an important critique of
anyone presuming to comment, as I will shortly, on street gangs and their
graffiti.[1] I will discuss street gangs even though, at most, Edmundo and I along

with Dan Anderson, a second research assistant who worked with us most particularly on this project, scuttled along the periphery of a few gangs. We interviewed those individuals who accepted us and became friends with a few, and
occasionally we stumbled onto caches of information that we had no right to
see. I never aspired to be a gang expert. I turned to street-gang members, however, because, in my interpretive scheme, they embodied the question of how
one creates *respect under conditions of little or no respect* with an intensity that
acted like a searchlight revealing the rest of the community. Street-gang members explicitly wrote out their needs for respect, and the more I realized this particular fact, the clearer it became to me that the Don Angels, the Valerios, the
Juárez, and the Martíns were expressing, perhaps in more muted fashion, similar needs. My point might be phrased this way: This entire book is, in one sense,
a collection of ways by which a variety of people created *respect under conditions
of little or no respect*. Obviously, there was not just one way but many, and many
of these ways were not acceptable to different members of the neighborhood.
Each way, then, reflected someone's desire and someone else's rejection. In order to understand and integrate the stories of this book, then, I turn to the most
glaring manifestations of desire and frustration, and the appeal of the hyperbolic so as to highlight the common structure, the single story under the many.

What is necessary to understand first are the syntactic elements and lexicon
of Angelstown's graffiti and how that syntax and vocabulary operated in a variety of other media to create a thick semiotic full of redundant messages. I will
concentrate on the lexicon of the Almighty Latin King Nation because I know
more about their organization. The emblem of the Latin Kings was either the
five-pointed or the three-pointed crown with the five-pointed being more
common. Members of the nation referred to the crown as *la corona*. Each point
of the *corona* was jeweled and represented a particular ideal. Oftentimes the
figure of a man with longish hair, trimmed mustache, pointed beard, and a tear
drop was drawn wearing the crown. This figure was called *el rey*, "king," and associations with "Christ the king" or the "king of kings" were not uncommon.
(The term "king of kings," however, was also used for the highest leader of the
King Nation, a leader who was rumored to have visited the area at least once.)
Not appearing in graffiti but still an important emblem of the Latin Kings was
the lion, the *king* of the jungle.

The colors of the Latin Kings were black and gold. Of course, all street
gangs in Angelstown used black as one of their colors, but for the Kings, black
signified the "dominant color of the universe," the "darkness of the immense
night," and the "alpha and the omega." Gold represented the sun and the "bril-

liance of the mind." Black and gold were described as the two colors of creation, "existing since the beginning of time and enduring forever."[2]

The number that ruled over the Latin Kings was five (five-pointed crown, for instance), and their abbreviations were ALKN (Almighty Latin King Nation), LKN, and LK. Again, not appearing in graffiti but still an important part of "representing" oneself as a Latin King was the left side of the body, as in wearing an earring in the left ear, cocking one's baseball cap to the left, or folding one's left arm over one's right. The number five, the phrase "All is well," and "representing" to the left were also used by a larger alliance of gangs called the "People," which in Angelstown consisted primarily of the Kings, Vicelords, and, for a while, the Insane Deuces. The other gangs in this alliance, however, had different colors and symbols. For instance, the colors of the Vicelords were red and black, and their symbols were typically a pyramid, a crescent moon, a cane, a top hat, and a martini glass. The Insane Deuces, in contrast, used green and black as their colors, and their symbols were dice, the spade playing card, and the number two.

Battling against the Latin Kings were rival gangs belonging to another confederation called the "Folks." In Angelstown, the Folks gangs were primarily different branches of Disciples, and these included Black Gangster Disciples, Satan's Disciples (sometimes called Spanish Disciples), and Maniac Latin Disciples. These gangs all "represented" to the right and used a variety of symbols such as pitchforks, 6-pointed stars, a devil's tail and horns, and a heart with wings.

**Lexical Items Most Common to
Angelstown's Major Street Gangs**

Almighty Latin King Nation:
alliance: people
major symbols: 5- or 3-pointed crown (*la corona*), *el rey* (king), lion
colors: black and gold
number: 5
abbreviations: ALKN, LKN, LK
phrase: "All is well"
direction of representation: left

Vicelords:
alliance: people
major symbols: pyramid, crescent moon, cane, top hat, martini glass

colors: red and black

number: 5 and/or 7–4-11

abbreviations: VL, VLN

phrase: "All is well"

direction of representation: left

Insane Deuce Nation:

alliance: folks (formerly people)

major symbols: dice, spade playing card

colors: green and black

number: 2

abbreviations: IDN, ID, D

Disciples (including Black Gangster Disciples, Spanish or Satan's Disciples, and Maniac Latin Disciples)

alliance: folks

major symbols: pitchfork, 6-pointed star, devil's tail and horns, heart
  with wings, swastika

colors: blue and black; other colors with black also designated
  specific disciple groups

numbers: 6, 7–4

abbreviations: BGDN, BGD, SDN, SD, MLD

phrase: "All is one"

direction of representation: right

As I said earlier, graffiti was only one medium to make use of the basic lexicon. Hand signs, tattoos, jewelry, clothes, oral language, and miscellaneous objects used the same vocabulary to signal one's gang affiliations and to insult other gangs. For instance, the hand signal of the Latin Kings consisted of the thumb, index finger and pinky extended outward with the middle fingers folded into the palm. One way to shake hands with another King was to extend one's hand in the described position while clasping only the thumbs, thus forming a five-pointed *corona* across both hands. In terms of jewelry, one of the leaders of the Kings was known for a very large gold crown that he wore on a chain around his neck. Other Kings wore gold rings containing the design of a lion or belt buckles with the appropriate symbols. Among the Deuces, a small but vivid green stone placed in the center of a black braided cross hanging from a black braided necklace was popular.

The most conspicuous way to mark one's affiliation, however, was to wear one's colors. A goal of a young Latin King, for instance, might be the assembling of as many clothes as possible referencing the colors and emblems of the Kings. The referencing could be enormously elaborate, the only limit being the inventiveness and willingness of the King. Basketball shoes worn with five holes left open (five being the ruling number), Pittsburgh Pirates baseball hats (black and gold with a P signaling "People"), a sports jacket from the Iowa Hawkeyes (black and gold) or the L.A. Kings hockey club, or any item from Miller Genuine Draft Beer (black and gold) might be used. Other gangs, of course, appropriated their own mainstream symbols according to their special lexicons. For instance, the red and black of the Chicago Bulls were suited to the Vicelords, and the green in Notre Dame and Oakland Athletics paraphernalia was suited to the Insane Deuces.

In short, the possibilities for appropriating mainstream symbols and recontextualizing them into new meanings were almost endless.[3] These appropriations pointed to one of the most important characteristics of Angelstown's street gangs and, I believe, American street gangs in general. In the public sphere, street gangs and particularly "hard-core" gang members may be viewed as a kind of antisociety,[4] as barbarous and verminlike, so completely outside the fold of the human community that they deserve to be removed. Indeed, as I will show, street gangs for very understandable reasons sometimes played with this very rhetoric creating from it hyperbolized images in which the mainstream could witness its deepest fears. In gobbling up the images, the mainstream felt that it had the evidence that proved the legitimacy of its views. But, I would argue, constructing such legitimacy was based on the same logic of violence outlined earlier, in so far as the mainstream positioned itself atop a moral high ground from which to judge and punish. What quickly disappeared in this moral scenario was a more accurate and complex picture, namely, that, even as a street gang adopted its transgressive pose, the gang was structured with numerous appropriations from the mainstream. In other words, the appropriations of mainstream material, so visible during a gang member's display of his or her colors, might be understood as a kind of synecdoche of an entire system of appropriations through which street gangs constructed themselves. Therefore, to understand the display of colors was to understand that the mainstream's cultural material was the very fund that a street gang tapped in order to make its meanings. The mainstream may have circulated its fund of cash and iconography,[5] but the street gang performed a symbolic conquering of the mainstream when mainstream meanings gave way to gang meanings. For the most part, the mainstream could not interpret gang meanings, and thus a secret, esoteric, subterranean world was made. Here, then, in this most common of gang gestures, the display of colors, was the ambiguous structure of the street gang, borrowing from the mainstream even as it formulated a radical departure.

Such an analysis of the relationship between mainstream or dominant society and its antisociety suggests that a culture might be understood as a fund of topoi, any of which might be a foundation for building a systematic idea. Such a fund can as easily supply arguments and beliefs for the creation and maintenance of, for instance, a democratic state as it can for the destruction of the same state. Of course, the persuasiveness of any particular idea at a particular moment in a culture's life depends on numerous factors such as the socioeconomic contexts through which the idea circulates. At any rate, a society and its antisociety—or, more individually, the "conformist" who maintains the status quo and the "deviant" who tears it down—are, in some sense, hinged to each other. The spine of such a hinge may very well be a cluster of related topoi. Through a variety of examples beyond the displaying of gang colors, I hope, in time, to show the strength of this analysis.

Thus far, I have used linguistic metaphors to describe much of the "lexicon" of Angelstown's street-gang graffiti and how that lexicon became "articulated" across a wide variety of "communicative" strands that conveyed largely redundant "meanings." I have argued that all this resulted in a kind of thick semiotic. I have also suggested that these meanings were appropriated from the mainstream, but that they underwent a translation to emerge as gang meanings that, for the most part, could no longer be read by the mainstream. Moreover, this process of appropriating conventional meaning followed by a translation into esoteric meaning was a synecdoche for gang life itself.

Continuing the linguistic metaphors, I will turn to the "syntax" of graffiti. The most prominent syntactic elements were a group of markers that might be called "negative morphemes." To a certain extent, these morphemes also operated across media. Two of these morphemes were reversals and upside downs. For instance, to reverse a letter in a rival gang's abbreviation or to draw a rival gang's symbol upside down was to disrespect that gang. A reversed "K," therefore, beside an upside down *corona* meant that someone was disrespecting the Latin Kings. Similarly, to "throw down" the hand sign for the Latin Kings was to disrespect the Kings. Or, taking another example, to disrespect the Insane Deuces one might draw an upside-down spade alongside an upside-down 2 (the spade and 2 being two of the primary symbols for the Deuces) alongside a reversed "D." Similarly, one could disrespect the Deuces by "throwing down" their hand sign (index and adjacent finger extended as in the symbol of victory). Because the Deuces and Kings were battling each other, one would expect to see alongside the disrespected symbols the other gang's symbols drawn in conventional fashion.[6] Disrespect, therefore, was syntactically marked through reversals and upside downs—negative morphemes, if you will, "non," "un," or "not"—whereas respect was unmarked. Indeed, the notion of respect relied on the conventions of standard writing insofar as street-gang graffiti was typically written linearly from left to right and followed standard spelling. This last point is important, for it suggests that convention in signaling respect was the baseline on which a transgressive order was manufactured. This structural dependency of the transgressive upon the conventional, of the markers of disrespect upon those of respect, was similar to what I argued earlier about gang meanings being dependent upon and appropriating mainstream meanings. (And this structural dependency recalls the dependence of the transgressive *albur* upon conventional talk discussed in chap. 3.)

Two other negativelike morphemes characterized graffiti. These consisted of "K," meaning "killer," and a squiggly line that canceled a rival gang's graffiti. To draw such a line was to "crack" the graffiti. For instance, imagine that the Latin Kings had drawn their *corona* and written beside it their initials, ALKN. A rival gang member could disrespect the Kings by "cracking" the *corona* with a squiggly line drawn through its middle and by adding a "K" after ALKN. In short, such a gang member would be announcing himself or herself as an Almighty Latin King Nation Killer. Or imagine a member of the Insane Deuce Nation writing out the abbreviations IDN and a Latin King adding a "K" to make IDNK, in short, Insane Deuce Killer.

Four Negative Morphemes

reversed letters

upside down letters/symbols

addition of "K" (killer)

cracking (drawing of a squiggly line through the letters and symbols
     of a rival gang)

The term "killer" is worth exploring further, for it functioned not only in graffiti but also in everyday talk and in the throwing of hand signs. "Killer" and "love" were structured opposites equivalent to the "throwing down" of a rival gang's hand sign and, in contrast, the "throwing up" of the hand sign of one's own gang. Indeed, when a gang member "threw down" a rival gang's hand sign, he or she was often labeled as a "killer" of that gang: "King killer," "Deuce killer," "MLD killer," or whatever. In contrast, when a gang member "threw up" his or her hand sign, the person would be saying implicitly, if not explicitly, "King love," "Deuce love," or whatever. The term "love," then, was the structured opposite of "killer"; however, "love" was not written out and, hence, was the unmarked term in Angelstown's graffiti, whereas "killer" was the marked term.

Even though the conventions for using the four so-called negative morphemes (upside downs, reversals, K or killer, and cracking) were mostly standardized and even consistent across other media, there were subtle rules or habits in gang graffiti that were, for me at least, hard to explain. Most of these puzzles concerned reversals and upside downs. For example, the opportunity to reverse every initial in a rival gang's name was, as far as I could tell, never taken advantage of. Why not reverse or throw upside down, for instance, each letter in ALKN of the Almighty Latin King Nation or the MLD of the Maniac Latin Disciples? Instead, the typical reversal was on the "K" and the "D" respectively, and the other letters were left alone. These observations suggest that the marking of disrespect may have had a set of subtler rules or habits that I have not adequately discribed. My inability to explain why some letters were vulnerable to disrespecting and others were not suggests that the full system (if there is one) for using the negative morphemes has not been fully displayed here.

So far, I have been examining the "lexicon" and "syntax" of gang graffiti. But also very observable in graffiti were certain stylistic elements. Those who put up graffiti, as I was told often, had special talents. Sometimes the authors of gang graffiti would sign their names, but it would be a mistake to take such signings as only self-acknowledgments of the authors' talents. Such an interpretation would overshadow the major purpose of graffiti, which was to explicitly enact a degree of violence against another gang or to implicitly do so by celebrating the power of one's own gang. At any rate, much graffiti went unsigned, but, signed or not, at times there were stylistic characteristics performed with flair that garnered for the graffiti writer considerable respect. One such characteristic was called "Old English script" by gang members and entailed a considerable amount of fancy lettering reminiscent, perhaps, of that found in illuminated manuscripts. Stylistic elaboration, then, of the core symbols and abbreviations of one's gang was at the heart of the very decorative Old English script.

However, I know of at least one example of another kind of elaboration that did not follow the "look" of Old English script. This particular example of elaboration used conventional lettering to create visual puns to amplify a set of redundant meanings. This piece of graffiti was particularly frightening on first viewing. It was drawn by a Latin King (King Sinister, I presume), whom I did

Example of Old English script.

5 Kings Gunning/ 10 Deuces Running.

not know, at a time when the Kings were being gunned down by the Disciples, the Spanish Disciples, the Insane Deuces, and the Maniac Latin Disciples. Done in blood red with a thick application that sometimes dripped, this stretch of graffiti seemed to stylistically capture in ways that I had never seen before the violence and paranoia of the moment. In the left-hand corner, as if introducing the graffiti, was a jingle: 5 King's Gunning/10 Deuces Running. (I presume "Deuces" was meant, but since the lettering only provided a reversed "D," it is possible that "Disciples" was also being punned.) The juxtaposition of this structure, a kind of childlike rhyme, with such a violent semantic amplified the haunting and threatening quality of this stretch of graffiti. Further, both in the lettering of the jingle and other words throughout, there occurred certain visual puns that created redundant meanings. For instance, throughout the graffiti the "i" was typically dotted with five pointed stars, the number "5" being one of the numbers identified with the Kings. In fact, "5" occurred in various places: for instance, below the *corona* and in various arrangements of red dots above the *corona* and other places. In other words, the number "5" echoed throughout the stretch of graffiti, thickening one of its central, if implicitly understood, messages: *King love.*

Simultaneously, put-downs of at least four gangs (Deuces, Spanish Disciples, Maniac Latin Disciples, and Gangster Disciples) were just as thickly and redundantly placed.[7] Since these four gangs constituted the strength of the Folks confederation, King Sinister was saying, in effect, that he or she was a *Folks killer.* Of the four gangs, the one most singled out for disrespect was the Deuces. Almost every letter "G" in this stretch of graffiti, for instance, had a trailing flourish, an upside-down "2." Moreover, two of the prominent symbols of the Deuces, the "2" (followed by a "K morpheme" explained earlier) and the spade, were drawn upside down in the main "text." Also singled out were the Maniac Latin Disciples whose initials were also followed by the "K morpheme." Thickening the message of disrespect was the drawing of the letter "T" in a variety of words. Its top bar was bent downward forming an upside-down pitchfork with red dots below each of the three prongs. This flourish on the letter "T" echoed, of course, the upside down pitchforks in the "main" text and elsewhere by which the author boldly announced himself or herself as disrespecting all Disciples. In short, these flourishes or visual puns elaborated, indeed, saturated, in novel ways the two central meanings in this stretch of graffiti: *King love* and *Folks killer.*

Most graffiti lacked the stylized elaborations of either Old English script or the idiosyncratic visual puns just described. Since this stylized, ornate work was especially respected, it deserves further comment. So-called Old English has a long precedent in American street-gang life. Luis Rodriguez, for instance, talks about "old English" among Latino street gangs in the 1960s and 1970s in Los Angeles: "I had on a T-shirt, cut off at the shoulders, with 'The Animal Tribe' in old English lettering on the back written in shoe polish . . . " He also describes the use of the word "Thee" in such street-gang names as Thee Impersonations and Thee Mystics: " 'Thee' being an old English usage that other clubs would adopt because it made everything sound classier, nobler, *badder.*"[8] For Rodriguez and other gang members, then, this oral and written style they called "Old English" was classy and noble, and this representation sounds my earlier argument about persistent innerscapes linked to equally persistent outerscapes. Old English in the context of the 1980s and 1990s in Angelstown was also classy and noble, and in both eras, I would argue, Old English, as emblem of a romanticized past, allowed its purveyors to rupture the humiliation of the present. In this sense, Old English was a site for creating the stylized difference of street-gang life. In appropriating this style, gangs made it their signature writ large. Moreover, Old English was part of a larger iconography that included thumpers, Too Low Flows, hair and clothing styles, and so on, each one a special site for creating an exaggeration that might be awarded respect. This iconography, then, represented a kind of confluence in which Old English as evocation of the past blended with other styles that evoked the modern. Each style was a site that could offer the remaking of one's world—or at least a rhetorical remaking behind which lay a version of the real world, biting hard, insisting that it be made over through any means necessary. It should be obvious that what I have discussed concerning Old English script is equally true of the idiosyncratic visual puns of "5 Kings Gunning/10 Deuces Running," for, in my interpretive scheme, both exhibited ornate, precise styles, which were versions of the "neat and clean" that redeemed, so to speak, an outerscape that was neither neat or clean.

If Old English script and other ornate visual styles were important elements in the public display of graffiti, there were other physical characteristics that need further discussion. Graffiti, as part of the warfare between rival gangs, was the use of language in the place of—although, at times, as a kind of—weaponry. It could be used, for instance, to proclaim a particular gang's territory or the courage and audacity of a rival gang member who had dared to enter enemy territory to disrespect the local gang. Under these conditions, inscription often led to erasure either by a property owner or rival gang member often followed by another round of inscription and erasure. In short, the ephemeralness of graffiti meant that an evening's work could disappear only to reappear again the next night. When graffiti became layered in this way, one message atop another, a wall became dense with authors. Authors had found a way to scribe themselves over each other in their need to make themselves individually and socially known. This system of inscription and erasure resulting in layered messages, then, was the physical trace that one could read, if one knew how, of the system of respect and disrespect that could rightfully be called the emotional origins behind the warfare of graffiti. Or phrased in the language of the prior chapter, it was the logic of violence, the need to take the moral high ground at the expense of another, written out on the walls of the city.

Other physical characteristics of graffiti included its size as well as the varied surfaces that it could occupy. These characteristics helped to create a special presence in the midst of public space. Often, graffiti was hidden in alleys that offered protection to the graffiti writer, but many times it boldly occupied a more visible public space. The occupation of public space—better yet, its domination—might be compared to what I argued earlier about the domination of public sound spaces through thumper sound systems. Both were "loud" and operated within the same system of respect and disrespect. Graffiti, of course, could occupy a variety of surfaces: interior or exterior walls, fences, dumpsters, concrete supports of expressways, garage doors, doors, and so on. It could even turn the corners of buildings. In taking over these spaces, it created a kind of "rulership"—a loaded and potent term in the context of gang life. Such rulership declared through the medium of graffiti not only who controlled the hood, but simultaneously and implicitly established a new set of rules that violated those of conventional print space. (Conventional print space might be understood here as a sheet of paper, a store sign, a billboard, in short, any space that has been designated for the use of print by some authoritative system and hence regulated by that system through ordinances, systems of standardization, and so on.) Graffiti in minimally observing these conventions, indeed, in writing over them, declared itself outside the law, an eruption that was potentially uncontrollable in the midst of public space. Graffiti implicitly declared metaphorical ownership wherever it desired and in the face of property owners whose own system of rules was being rendered impotent. It is no wonder, then, that graffiti in Angelstown quickly became an issue in the larger battle for control of public spaces. Indeed, while I was doing research, graffiti surfaced during city council meetings. Council members discussed graffiti resistent paints, youth agencies that might be used to remove graffiti, and, finally, passed an ordinance that compelled, among other things, property owners to clean up graffiti on their premises.

graffiti, street gangs, and the public sphere

Recent discussions of the notion of the public sphere provide a theoretical framework that yields a wealth of insights into graffiti and street gangs. The notion of the public sphere was richly conceived by Jürgen Habermas in such works as *The Structural Transformation of the Public Sphere: An Inquiry into a Category of Bourgeois Society* and *Lifeworld and System: A Critique of Functionalist Reason* (volume 2 of *The Theory of Communicative Action*). Despite the value of this concept, however, Habermas's specific model of the public sphere raises considerable doubts. Stanley Aronowitz, for instance, argues that because Habermas's model is dependent on rationality as a "presupposition of public communication," the public sphere is understood as a "restricted space" rather than a participatory one. Aronowitz clarifies how Habermas's model asks the citizenry to transcend their material conditions as well as their emotional states and to become like Habermas himself, someone who has undergone the "rigorous training of scientific and cultural intellectuals. For only those individuals who have *succeeded* in screening out the distorted infor-

Kings vs. Deuces:
Graffiti as War.

Upside-Down Rey:
Disrespecting the
Kings.

mation emanating from the electronic media, politicians, and the turmoil of everyday life are *qualified* to participate in social rule."[9]

This notion of the public sphere as restricted space is of major importance when considering street gangs and their graffiti. Within a restricted public sphere, not even contesting parties represent the entire realm of contestation that cycles throughout a society. The breadth and depth of contestation does not become aired partly because not all the varied voices have been certified, sometimes literally, to speak in such a public sphere. Without such voice, the ability to have some say over social rule becomes difficult, and this situation compels both individuals and groups to develop a series of, as de Certeau suggested, tactics. For de Certeau, a tactic is mobile; it makes use of the cracks that appear within the "surveillance of the proprietary powers. It poaches in them. . . . It can be where it is least expected. It is a guileful ruse. . . . an art of the weak." In short, de Certeau's interest in quotidian practices acknowledged the power to act in everyone, regardless of his or her place in the hierarchy and despite the fact that tactical actions are always framed by the dominant power. From the perspective of a de Certeau, street-gang graffiti in Angelstown was a particularly interesting tactic.[10]

It was as a tactical action, then, that street-gang graffiti claimed metaphorical ownership (or, to use one of the street terms, "rulership") over public spaces.

In other words, when graffiti declared ownership of a particular neighborhood by a particular street gang, that ownership functioned as part of a "shadow" system that had no legitimacy inside the system world. Since ownership in the system world was certified during the exchange of cash, the ownership that graffiti declared was, in comparison, metaphorical, or what might be called a tactical response to the system world. In this sense, street-gang graffiti and its inherent bravado and the willingness to back up that bravado with force were substitutes for cash, its metaphor so to speak—but a metaphor that individuals willingly spilled blood for.

Interestingly, a "shadow" system, as the metaphor implies, depends on themes and models provided by and circulating through the system world. Using the metaphor heuristically, which is how all metaphors work, one might say the following: the system world is the "substance" that casts the shadow, a shadow that has the shape but is not equivalent to the system itself. The result is that the shadow system mimics the system world through the many appropriations of and improvisations upon the system world's material. One example of mimicry was that most street gangs that I knew preferred to label themselves as "organizations," and I remember members of the Vicelords pointing proudly to the buildings owned by Vicelord chapters in Chicago as proof of their organizational status. At any rate, mimicry rarely wishes to be exact, for its own artful dodges or tactics maintain a difference that the shadow system celebrates as its identity, its own space sheltering and nourishing its guerrilla life against a public sphere that is, as Aronowitz said, "exclusionary"—or at least perceived to be "exclusionary."[11]

The more Dan Anderson and I looked at street-gang graffiti, the more we were convinced that it was not only a tactics of action (metaphorical ownership) but also a tactics of language. By "tactics of language," I mean that graffiti was an important narrative "tactic" available to gang members for the public expression of their subjectivities, subjectivities that were constantly being suppressed by the public sphere.[12] Indeed, if my earlier descriptions of street-gang graffiti relied heavily on linguistic terms such as "syntax" and "lexicon," it was to prepare the foundation for describing graffiti as a special kind of narrative genre whose deeper meanings were not explicit but which rested on a large substratum of related but private oral and written texts. In short, graffiti was the condensed narrative of more subterranean narratives and the only one to enter broad public spaces. *(A caveat: Granted, graffiti as a genre allowed for only a limited range of subjective thought to be communicated, and so it cannot be compared to more flexible and powerful genres that are synonymous with subjectivity; but this comparison of genres misses the point. Graffiti, as I have said, was all about passion-*

ate utterances of respect and disrespect. As it was so often described to us, graffiti was an expression of "heart," a potent street term that conveyed one's courage and love, indeed, one's identity with a particular street gang. As a genre, then, it delivered the turmoil of these subjective feelings in a method, style, and content that functioned outside the communicative and economic rules of the public sphere, and so graffiti was suppressed. This is the rather narrow but precise understanding that I claim when describing graffiti as gang members' subjectivity, or "heart," made public.)

In order to clarify the point that the Angelstown graffiti might be interpreted as condensed, public narratives whose roots reached into subterranean texts consisting of more elaborated, private narratives that circulated through the shadow system of street gangs, I will turn to the fact that the term "nation" appeared in both kinds of narratives. The term "nation" or its abbreviation "N," as in ALKN (Almighty Latin King Nation), was commonly written out in the graffiti of Angelstown. Moreover, I have already explained how major gangs referred to themselves as nations or organizations as in the Insane Gangster Satan's Disciples Nation (also known as Spanish Disciples) and the Maniac Latin Disciples Nation. It should be no surprise, then, that terms such as "nation," "empire," and "organization" were part of the daily talk and the official written documents that circulated among gang members. To make my point, I take the following example from a letter authored by a gang leader and widely dispersed to gang members in other chapters of the same gang: "All sections of our Nation must come together to form this structure of power, to put all minds, hearts, and dedication to help this organization structure grow stronger." And notice the word "empire" and continuing emphasis upon solidarity in related documents: "My brothers, this is just the beginning of our Empire. This is a new era of the 90's, which we shall improve with time, to become a great organized power. That we will use to build a predominant (having superior strength, influence, or authority,) Empire." (All quotations from street-gang documents, their spelling, syntax, and so on, are exact.)

Why should the trope or topos of nationhood hold such a special place in the shadow system of street gangs? In my interpretive scheme, the topos of nationhood provided the shadow system one more way to mimic the system world. But why should the same trope be so important for both the overarching nation as well as the many gang nations in its confines? What sort of need does this shared trope satisfy? What sorts of imaginings does it rhetorically conjure? An illuminating set of essays collected in *Nation and Narration* (1991, edited by Homi Bhabha) makes a case for the discursive construction of nationhood among nation states of the system world. (It would seem ironic and significant that insights derived from such studies can be applied also to the construction of nationhood in the shadow system, but this, indeed, is one of my assumptions.[13]) A shared perspective of these authors is that authority busily composes "its powerful image" by constructing such "national objects of knowledge" as "Tradition, People, the Reason of State, High Culture," and so on and represents these "as holistic concepts located within an evolutionary narrative of historical continuity."[14] Ernest Renan in 1882 discussed the strategy that such narratives might take:

> The nation, like the individual, is the culmination of a long past of endeavours, sacrifice, and devotion. Of all cults, that of the ancestors is the most legitimate, for the ancestors have made us what we are. A heroic past, great men, glory (by which I understand genuine glory), this is the social capital upon which one bases a national idea. To have common glories in the past and to have a common will in the present; to have performed great deeds together, to wish to perfom still more—these are the essential conditions for being a people. One loves in proportion to the sacrifices to which one has consented, and in proportion to the ills that one has suffered.[15]

It may be that the topos of nationhood incorporates something of Renan's strategy wherever it is found. At any rate, one can hear it fully inherited in a street-gang document describing the annual picnic honoring the birthday of the gang's founder, their "Beloved King," as if the distances of time, culture, and socioeconomic context could not separate Renan's heroic, historical Europe from that of an American street gang in the 1990s:

> On this day we shall all give thanks to our Beloved King, the day in which the heavens had sent Him down among us, to bring us together as a family.
> This very Special Day is when all of our family comes together, to show the Honor, Love, Respect, and Greatfulness, we all have for the Beloved King. Having Him among us is a blessing, because it's Him who loved us enough to show this Nation the way to a key, which opens the door to Life.
> He never gave up the struggle or hopes of this Nation to become as great as it is now. Holding on was a must, and holding on He has did, never letting the Family fall.
> As we, given Him the power and strength, He in return gave us the

knowledge and understanding to believe in who and what we can become. The one powerful Nation of an Organization, and a Great Loving Family of Sisters and Brothers.

The topos of nationhood—perhaps, in whatever context it should appear—would seem to be, at best, subtly coercive, for its task is to have disparate, individual wills voluntarily meld themselves into a community (brotherhood/sisterhood). At worst, for instance, in a totalitarian state, the coercion is far more blatant. At any rate, in the enumeration of nostalgic legends, heroes, and a common lineage, of shared sorrows, sacrifices, cultural topoi, institutions, language, rituals, honor, and so on, the past is constructed as a kind of animus that continues to—or ought to—inspire the present and make it virtuous long into the future. In short, a dedicated community—a "Loving Family of Sisters and Brothers"—can span the continuum of time and transcend the forces of decay, and it is this dedication that the topos of nationhood tries to instill in the very depths of the individual will as an identification that is more than merely persuasive. If the topos of nationhood can evoke such dedication, then the human longing for continuity, cohesion, stability, and power becomes satisfied, and in this forming of an enduring community we abate our aloneness and our fear of chaos so that even death, particularly in the case of war, can be reinterpreted as sacrifice. It is in these ways and others that the topos of nationhood attempts to create a kind of single photograph of countless people that is passed around as everyone's reality.

At some point, however, if the topos of nationhood should cease to inspire dedication, then the many fault lines hidden below its coercive efforts begin to stir. Some of the most disturbing fault lines would be those invented by street gangs: declarations of independent nationhood via rival geographies, laws, traditions, and systems of authority in the very belly of the overarching nation. In making such declarations, the shadow system mimics or turns itself into a metaphor of the system world, and in that mimicry the system world sees the chaos that its veneer of continuity, cohesion, stability, and power were meant to seal. The irony is that in having pursued the topos of nationhood, the system world set the stage for its own attempted assassination. For the topoi of a culture are available to everyone, and during those times when the rhetoric of the overarching nation fails to inspire some of its citizenry with the mystique of solidarity, the rhetoric of a gang nation is ready to work out its version of the same magic as one response to the increasing organizational status of rival gang nations. It is at these moments that the system world becomes terrified. One of our gang-member friends captured it this way when talking to Dan. Interestingly, our friend described the picnic/celebration day of his gang, a gang linked to but not the same as the one whose documents I quoted from earlier. (Incidentally, all the major gangs that I know have their picnic days, and these moments seem to be a show of strength when the fault lines hiding below the overarching nation become quite public.) Our friend spoke of 2,000 of his brothers and sisters wearing "a sea of baby blue and black" at a state-wide gathering. The police had the area circled but kept their distance, knowing they were outnumbered. Meanwhile, the gang members and their families ate free food and played games provided by the leadership. From the perspective of the lifeworld of the gang members, the scene was "righteous" in so far as it asserted a defiant and just empowerment of their nation over and against the system world's more bankrupt authority.

I have been describing marginalized groups in American culture as fault lines. I have also described how the topos of nationhood has been appropriated by street gangs and others as a kind of mimicry of the overarching nation, and, thus, how the overarching nation finds its very nationhood threatened by independent systems of authority, laws, traditions, and even geographies and weaponry. However, such a view of gang nationhood appears to be mostly oppositional, as if a shadow system had specifically emerged to oppose the system world. Such a view, I believe, is misleading for two reasons. First, gang nationhood in the Chicago area, it seems to me, was a formidable response to the threats posed by rival gangs who had been amassing over time their own organizational status. In short, it was largely within a system of gang rivalry—rather, than a way to defy the overarching nation—that street gangs imagined their nationhood. This view of nationhood as rivalry was particularly true for young gang members, who, in my view, were politically self-conscious only intermittently. However, the gaining of a kind of political self-consciousness might occur through the experience of jail. For some, the experience of jail could function as a kind of rite of passage in which one could get, as one gang member told me, "wisdom." "Wisdom" and "360 degrees of enlightenment," which was a concept that circulated through at least two gangs, might lead to seeing one's gang nation as specifically opposed to the overarching nation. To experience imprisonment was to experience the oppressions of society in their most concentrated form. In addition, jail provided one the opportunity to read the politically sophisticated lore that had been written over the years by the more mature brothers from one's gang. (I have already quoted from some of this lore.) In short, I am trying to avoid the suggestion that all gang members saw their nationhood as explicitly opposing the overarching nation. Second, and more significant, is the fact that opposition is rarely whole and seamless, and thus characterizing street gangs and others as necessarily and defiantly opposed to the overarching nation misses important subtleties. The term of choice in this text has been "appropriation," more so than "opposition." For instance, in contexts of power differences, "opposition" suggests only resistance and its strategies, whereas the term "appropriation" suggests a use of "tactics," in de Certeau's sense, as well as envy felt by the less powerful toward the more powerful. In short, mixed into the oppositional soup concocted by the shadow system of gangs were degrees of envy and desire of the system world. It is from such an understanding that one can make sense of how being a policeman or a Marine or, I have no doubt, fighting in a war defending the United States, might be seen as desirable occupations and actions despite the fact that one's gang nationhood expressed implicit opposition to the overarching nation.

Or take the fact that at least one gang saw its nationhood largely, although not entirely, in the context of improving its efficiency in organized crime, and, thus, urged its members to get an education. I quote from official documents again:

> The gangbanging, getting locked up, or getting high on hard drugs, isn't the way anymore. Education is the key to our success, in everyway. All organizations have become powerful with this key to knowledge. Now it's time for us to reach out and take hold of this key, that will open all doors to give opportunities to the Organization as well as yourself.
>
> What we are trying to accomplish, they call it organized crime. There will be those that will try to stop us . . .

These examples suggest that in the construction of gang nations in Angelstown the topos of nationhood seemed to have functioned with different ends in mind. For instance, it functioned rhetorically by mobilizing the rhetoric of menace, strength, and independence for at least two audiences, other gangs and the overarching nation. But it also mobilized the rhetoric of solidarity and status for a third audience, the gang's own membership. Similar rhetorical conjurings are evoked, for all practical purposes, by nations of the system world. In short, it was as if the shadow system, during its mimicry of the system world, had found the topos of nationhood and in so doing fashioned for itself a kind of hyperbolic pose that could be aimed at three audiences.

Other important topoi cycled through the names that gangs had chosen for themselves. For instance, among the Vicelords and the Almighty Latin King Nation, images of royalty were evoked in the very names. Members were either "lords" or "kings," and, at least among the Latin Kings, female members were called "queens." In some of the gangs, the imagery of royalty was even institutionalized so that in one gang two of the highest offices were titled King of the Nation and Prince of the Nation, and, in another gang, Inca and Cacique (the first term references a ruler or member of the ruling family from the preconquest Incan empire, and the second term is a Spanish word meaning "local political boss" or headman of an Indian people). In addition, we have already seen the leader of one gang addressed as the "Beloved King." What is important to remember in all this, however, is that the topos of royalty existed alongside another organizational structure, that of a corporation, and this latter topos was consistent with how gangs thought of themselves as organizations and nations. This interchangeability of the corporate model with the courtly suggests that both topoi were not contradictory but simultaneously served the same end, which I took to be a rupturing of the relative powerlessness of one's social conditions. One gang phrased it this way: "We . . . have the blood of royalty in our veins. We are the guiding light of our people, place wisdom in our minds, love in our hearts and fortitude to withstand the trials of time. . . . Our ultimate goal, the awakening of our people to their oppressed state, that [the gang's symbol] may lift our heritage to its rightful place among the thrones of Kings and Queens."

If gangs used numerous topoi to construct their power (the topos of royalty and its romanticized vision of the past alongside the topoi of nationhood and corporation"hood" and their romanticized visions of the modern), there remains an important evocation that must be considered, that of madness, disorder, and irrationality. Returning, again, to the very names of some of the prominent gangs in Angelstown—The Insane Gangster Satan's Disciples Nation, The Insane Deuce Nation, The Maniac Latin Disciples Nation—it is clear that the theme of madness and disorder played a special role. Not only did the names of gangs rely heavily on this theme, but individual members sometimes adopted its imagery in naming themselves. The acquisition of street names, as Dan and I were told several times, typically had something to do with a personal characteristic that was noticeable to others. For instance, one of our friends came to be called "Draggin'," a name that he did not like because it suggested how long he had flirted with joining a gang without making a committment. "Rico," whom I talked to inside and outside of jail, got his name by being of Puerto Rican descent, and he began to call me "Smiley." Not even the majority of names were associated with madness and disorder, but those that were—and here's a small selection: "Psycho," "Loco," "Mental 2," "King Sinister"—were significant, for these names, in my interpretive scheme, were important elements in an overall topos of madness/disorder that, along with the other topoi already discussed, helped to construct gang power. Moreover, the topos of madness/disorder was not limited to the Latino gangs of the Chicago area. In California, Sanyika Shakur, for instance, described his own gang name as "Monster," described many similar names for other gang members, and talked often of cultivating a "mad-dog stare" to frighten potential enemies.[16] The topos of madness/disorder in all these instances helped to project unpredictable, menacing violence. Such a projection could protect oneself or one's gang from future threat. The topos of madness/disorder helped to create a "rep" that no one wanted to "mess with"; hence, this topos was integral to the "pose" and the ideo/logic of violence desribed in the preceding chapter. In mobilizing this system, one acquired respect *under conditions of little or no respect*, and such power was to be envied, for in making others afraid, one had acquired a kind of freedom from challengers.

But there is more behind the topos of madness/disorder that can be uncovered. In our culture, the topos of madness/disorder is paired to the topos of rationality/order. They form a kind of Janus figure. Or they might be called inseparable twins since birth. Pursuing this twin birth, of course, is a formidable endeavor. It would entail spinning off into the depths of the many histories of many cultures where we might find versions of Apollonian and Dionysian imagery very much in place. In *Madness and Civilization*, however, Foucault has limited himself to the modern world and traced the emergence of a "caesura that establishes the distance between reason and non-reason; reason's subjugation of non-reason, wresting from it its truth as madness, crime, or disease, derives explicitly from this point."[17] For Foucault, only a recent "caesura" separates the two topoi, but, over time, madness had no truth to tell—or so it came to be seen. Madness became confined to the asylum, in part, because much of European society during the seventeenth century began to evolve a new social order based on rational principles. The keepers of such a social order saw themselves as men of good sense and enshrined a bourgeois morality that regarded laziness, crime, poverty, and unreason as differences to be eradicated. In ceasing to be the "sign of another world," madness lost its ancient value as a kind of irruptive truth-telling except in those curious and special instances where it reappeared in such figures as Nietzsche, Van Gogh, Artaud, and so on.[18]

Of course, what Foucault little appreciates is the possibility that the evolution of psychiatry also represents the good intentions of curing a special form of human pain. By not appreciating this possibility, his analysis is less complex than it might be, for is it not possible that in the making of an evil there is also the making of a good and vice versa? This shortcoming aside, Foucault's rigid critique is important, for it has exposed a Janus figure in the social imagination. When historically the management of society justified the confinement of unreason (insanity, criminality), the preservers of the social order firmed up the topos of disorder in the social imagination. In other words, for those who perceive that the management of society has failed them, the topos of disorder can be both uttered and even worn bodily in order to express disbelief, frustration, anger, and rebellion against the keepers of the topos of order. The topos of order, constantly reinforced by the institutions of society, acquires a kind of nebulous but pervasive dominance that mobilizes a set of counterdiscourses, also nebulous and not necessarily consistent.[19] Here in this mix of dominant discourses and counterdiscourses, we have the emergence of a kind of Janus figure each side of which has its own seductive appeal capable of luring the same individual with either face depending on the needs of the moment. In short, one face of the Janus figure does not fully define a particular gang member or gang. On the one hand, the rhetoric of madness is but one face to be worn—the face of resistance—one choice to be made in order to create a dramatic (sometimes flamboyant) distance between its own counterdiscourse and the normative discourses of the social order. On the other hand, the rhetoric of the corporate organization is another choice, another face to be worn—for marginalized conditions set up a variety of responses to normative discourses, two of which are resistance and envy.

It is important to remember that the topos of madness/disorder precedes any group or individual who chooses to mobilize such a topos. It is part of the fund of a society, and so it is deeply ingrained in that society's history, hence, the consciousness, if one can use such a term, of the society itself. In this sense, it is constantly incarnating, its particular appearance largely determined by the context or social scene in which it appears. For instance, there is little doubt that the topos of madness/disorder has been one of the fueling sources of the Euro-American avant-garde of the nineteenth and twentieth centuries, fascinating its artists, writers, and thinkers. The contemporary marketplace, however, offers a striking incarnation of the topos of madness/disorder. In a dynamic marketplace such as ours, the topos easily sells. Hence, "gangsta" rap and some of its associated iconography has become a commodity not only in its place of origin but also elsewhere.[20] Its successful marketing weakens its ability to be an effective counterdiscourse, for it is now in cahoots with the normative discourses of national and international buying and selling. All of this reinforces, perhaps, my earlier claim about counterdiscourses embodying resistance and envy simultaneously. My central point, however, is that the street gangs of Angelstown, even in their marginalization are part of a continuum, a thought system, if you will, that is more than just the history of gangs in the United States. In their appropriation of a variety of topoi, gangs represent a contemporary incarnation of thought systems ingrained in the society at large. The reaction against the topos of madness/disorder, particularly when it becomes embodied in gang-related shootings, is that it represents both a threat to life as well as a withering away of the social controls that shore up the strongholds of the system world. Tracking such reactions to graffiti and gangs in the context of Angelstown is my next project.

limits of the public sphere

Nancy Fraser wants to believe that a subaltern counterpublic has emancipatory potential. She puts it this way:

> I do not mean to suggest that subaltern counterpublics are always necessarily virtuous; some of them, alas, are explicitly antidemocratic and antiegalitarian; and even those with democratic and egalitarian intentions are not always above practicing their own modes of informal exclusion and marginalization. Still, insofar as these counterpublics emerge in response to exclusions within dominant publics, they help expand discursive space. In principle, assumptions that were previously exempt from contestation will now have to be publicly argued out. In general, the proliferation of subaltern counterpublics means a widening of discursive contestation, a good thing in stratified societies.[21]

In so far as a counterpublic of this sort represents an oppositional interpretation to the status quo and its concentration of power, Fraser would hope that here lies the fertile ground for the emergence of a dialectic between the subordinated world and the system world. Even though she is careful not to romanticize such counterpublics, she finds value in the ways in which these counterpublics act as public spheres bubbling up through the layers of a stratified society with, perhaps, a lack of "decorum." It is through such means that they may articulate and act out their conditions of subordination in order to secure greater participatory privileges and dissolve the pernicious concept of a comprehensive public sphere.

I am not certain that Fraser and others would allow street gangs to be called a subaltern counterpublic. Indeed, maybe here is the test case, a most difficult one, for a Fraser-like interpretation of the public sphere. In short, at what point do well intentioned theorists defend and honor a subaltern group as a legitimate "counterpublic," and at what point does a group become labeled criminal and lose almost all participatory privileges? Or the problem might be phrased this way: How expansive can any participatory democracy be when, lying at the farthest limits of its embrace, there exists criminality that is, at least, partially determined by the same socioeconomic and power differences that give rise to subaltern counterpublics? For instance, I have described gang graffiti as "condensed narratives" that emerge from a "shadow system" to occupy public spaces. Graffiti is the evidence of an intense need to acquire power and voice. From this perspective, then, gang graffiti might be considered part of the public evidence of a larger subaltern counterpublic formed as one response to socioeconomic disparities. Graffiti becomes criminal, however, because it functions outside the economic and message-making rules of the system world. Its illegality, of course, is not particularly serious, but the shadow system from which it emerges, the subaltern counterpublic, so to speak, is, in the eyes of most people, seriously illegal when it entails killings and drug dealing.

For the most part, the public sphere—Fraser's "actually existing democracy"—in Angelstown is fundamentally closed to gang graffiti writers and street gangs. As evidence, I offer a series of events that occurred between the summer of 1990 and early fall 1991 while Edmundo and I were conducting intermittent fieldwork. On 4 June 1990, a Black member of one of Angelstown's primarily Latino street gangs was shot and died a day later. Two other members were shot during the episode. A few days after the shooting, a street ceremony was improvised by gang members who had lost their "brother." The ceremony was staged at the location where their comrade had fallen. The ceremony included flowers that were the same colors as the gang's, large memorial candles, flower-covered crosses, and a placard with a religious saying as well as the street names of other gang members. The local newspaper reported the event, interviewed some of the participants, and took a picture showing about four gang members crouched before the shrine and wearing "hoodies" (street term for sweat shirts with hoods) that helped to cover their faces. Many of the gang members were clearly throwing down (disrespecting) the hand sign of the rival gang responsible for the shooting. The picture and article appeared on the newspaper's front page on 7 June.

The newspaper received numerous complaints, and letters were published in the "Letters to the Editor" section. One letter was from the departing president of the local chapter of Mothers Against Gangs.[22] (I have changed the name of the town as well as the name of the newspaper and have not included the actual names of the letter writers).

> As if the city of Angelstown does not already have enough problems with gangs, the *Gazette* has to go and promote gangs with a large, front-page photo and story concerning the death of a gang member.
>
> We are shocked that the *Gazette* would lend credibility to a pack of vicious hoodlums by printing their hateful nicknames and colors.
>
> Sure, a young man is dead, but he made his choice to belong with the criminal faction of this city. The *Gazette* does not need to glorify his death or his friends. At most, all this story rated was a few lines in the obituaries.
>
> What the *Gazette* should be printing is photos and stories of the innocent victims of senseless gang warfare. How about the reactions of grieving parents or the horror of wounded small children?
>
> Come on, *Gazette*, we need your support in ridding Angelstown of vermin, not promoting their evil ways.

Another letter carried thirty-eight signatures. I have edited some of its less relevant sections in order to make its arguments stand out more clearly:

> We, as members of the Angelstown area and an even greater community of Christian believers, express outrage at the publication of "Slain teen remembered" and the accompanying full-color photo on June 7.
>
> Publication of this piece amounts to little more than free advertising for one of Angelstown's street gangs and the violence for which it stands and appears to represent the slain teen as some sort of "religious" martyr in the abhorrent gang warfare that plagues our community.
>
> Allowing this to be published shows tremendous journalistic and civic irresponsibility on the part of both reporters, the photographer and, indeed, the entire administrative staff at the *Gazette*.
>
> Publishing this picture of and quotes by admitted members of a gang served not to curb the violence but to perhaps fuel it.
>
> [the] symbolism . . . amounts to a living-color, front-page death threat to the rival gang.

. . . As Christians, the juxtaposition of a "memorial"—complete with crosses, flowers, candles, and references to prayers and God—with the gang members and all they stand for, including the death threat, amounts to blasphemy. While it is not the *Gazette* which planned the "memorial," to cover it in this manner shows tremendous insensitivity to Christian believers of all denominations.

It is indeed unfortunate that this young man and others have fallen prey to gang violence, but we do not condone the representation of this teen as a martyr of gang warfare. The "colors" that gangs live by are also the colors that they kill and die by.

May it not be that another human being (innocent or otherwise) dies because the *Gazette* has chosen to glamorize, and thus promote, participation in street gangs. If so, may it forever be on your conscience.

A variety of letters before, after, and much later conveyed a sense of dismay concerning street gangs and a general lack of awareness about the natures of gangs. For instance, the following letter suggests that what the prior writers feared concerning the newspaper's role in promoting the death threats of one gang actually came to pass. The connection, however, is highly suspect since the writer seems to be unaware that the gang rivalry in Angelstown at that time was not primarily between Blacks and Latinos but, in fact, between two primarily Latino gangs (the Latin Kings and the Insane Deuces). Moreover, it is not even certain which gang the accused men belonged to or if they were, indeed, even gang members. The letter is lightly edited in order to convey its central points more efficiently:

I read an article in the *Gazette* on June 7 about a young black man killed by two Hispanic men, members of a rival street gang, on June 4.

. . . The next day, a group of black men, members of a street gang came to the Century Lane neighborhood, romping the street at night and terrifying the neighborhood. The new screen door to my house was destroyed.

I am not a member of a gang, I am not Mexican or Puerto Rican, and I do not have any business with them.[23] I would like to know why I have been included in their hate. Why do gang members destroy property of innocent people?

If someone can explain this to me, I am ready to listen.

The incident mentioned above is not the only incident that has happened in this neighborhood. These are common incidents that happen frequently throughout the summer months.

On June 20, the newspaper published as an editorial the following apology in response to the complaints that had been received.[24] I have edited the essay in order to sharpen its main points.

... We strive continually neither to sensationalize nor underplay the news we report.

Occasionally, however, we stumble. That, in essence, is what happened June 7, when we published a front-page article about a makeshift roadside service conducted in memory of youth gunned down in an apparent gang-related attack.

The problem was not so much the written account—a narrative we hoped would bring home the senselessness of the loss of life it connoted—as it was the photo, containing both gang "colors" and symbols, which accompanied it.

... Since our error went public, our entire news staff has sat down with the police, and we have reviewed and given further definition to our gang-coverage guidelines.

In the process, we have learned just how much both we and, we suspect, many of you didn't know about street gangs and the many pitfalls into which any of us unwittingly can fall.

We'd be willing to bet, for instance, that few law-abiding citizens are aware that such commonplace terms as "people" and "folks" are gang terms that bear no relationship to the definitions most of us associate with those words.

... We are better prepared, now, and we will continue to endeavor not to do anything that can be construed as either glorifying or specifically recognizing any gang.

... Gang activity is a problem for all of us, and it will take all of us working together to minimize, if not eradicate completely, this blight upon our own home turf.

"All of us," of course, includes the mayor, the City Council, the police, the courts, the schools, the churches, groups like Mothers Against Gangs, every other community organization, parents, every law-abiding citizen and this newspaper.

During the next year, numerous articles, editorials, and letters to the editor concerning street gangs were published in the newspaper. One particular editorial published thirteen months (July 1991) after the above editorial stands out because of how it defends the social order. My editing eliminates only important identifying markers.

Park District Sends Gangs Good Message

An ounce of prevention, as Ben Franklin's "Poor Richard's Almanac" reminded more than two centuries ago, truly is often worth a pound of cure.

Thus, . . . Park District Board recently tried to give area park goers their own ounce of prevention, by means of a new set of policies designed to ban gang activity at all of its family recreation areas.

To be sure, parks, trails and other facilities under the district control generally are not overrun by members of street gangs.

Neither are Park Board members and district administrators foolhardy enough to think that mere words on a paper are going to put a stop to those few incidents of gang activity, begging by street people and other potential nuisances which do occasionally occur.

Those words do, however, strengthen the hand of park district police—with the full weight of the law behind them—to physically remove so-called "undesirables" in the scattered instances where they do cause problems.

New rules ban gang colors, insignia, signs

Primarily, the new security rules prohibit all who are wearing known gang colors, emblems and insignia, or who attempt to communicate with gang-related hand signs, from entering and loitering at any park district property.

This is nothing particularly new in what park district police have long sought to accomplish.

However, with so much negative feeling seemingly so rampant about the overall status of the social order these days, it is good to see the district's trustees formally codify what long has been standard practice.

The next step, of course, is to ensure that these new official policies translate into the same kind of aggressive enforcement effort that thus far has marked the first weeks of operation of the park district's beautiful . . . Family Aquatic Center at Howell Place and Montgomery Road in Angelstown.

Indeed, a fine control and enforcement effort there has kept the facility free of incident and helped ensure it remains the inviting family recreation center it was designed to be.

It also, of course—as do the newly passed anti-gang policies—sends a loud and clear message to society's less-desirable elements that this is indeed our community, and they are not welcome.

That's a good message to send.

During this same year, the newspaper reported disagreements between the newly hired police chief and the mayor. In time, the police chief lost the confidence of the mayor and city council and eventually resigned. The mayor was paraphrased as saying that the police chief had come under criticism for not effectively attacking the "city's gang crime problem" and for not addressing the "morale problems within the police ranks." By August 1991, a new police chief had been chosen, and by early September the new chief had installed a "zero-tolerance" crackdown on gang violence. One measure raised the number of officers assigned to "full time gang patrol" from eight to twenty-five. This new unit represented "about one-sixth the department's combined patrol officers and investigators." Other measures included special tactics such as "street-reclaiming neighborhood sweeps" and the promise "to seek aggressive prosecution of gang members accused of crimes—and stiffer sentences for those who are convicted." These measures and others were seen as fulfilling some of the pledges made by the new police chief, pledges that were meant to appease a very nervous city council whose agitated constituencies, concerned about crime and street gangs, had already influenced recent elections.[25]

What, if anything, does this selection of newspaper articles spanning more than a year's time provide? I suggest that it provides one kind of window unto the public sphere, but the view through this window is of dramatic events whose depths remain hidden. Whereas real people lived out these events with anger, fear, sorrow, dismay, and so on, the newspaper—trapped by advertising revenues, deadlines, economic pressures, the need to respect conventional morality, and who knows what else—never entered the emotional turbulences that coursed through a variety of opposing voices, *including those of gang members*. The result is washed-out life and a bleaching-out of the potential of a participatory public sphere. If the public sphere is that "theater in modern societies in which political participation is enacted through the medium of talk,"[26] the *Ga-*

zette could not open its pages to the full range of talk—much less the emotional life behind the talk—so as to begin opening the possibility of political partici- pation. The public sphere as institutionalized openness was not the *Gazette*'s goal, even though it could have helped in this role. Instead, its editorials at- tempted to shape the public sphere according to conventional views and thereby glossed over the potential critiques of the conventional that might have emerged.

The best example of not undoing the conventional was the *Gazette*'s will- ingness to bend to the pressures of those who protested the publication of the photograph of the street-side funeral. I will offer my summary and interpre- tation of the public arguments that eventually led to the *Gazette*'s apology. According to the letters to the editor and the apology itself, the two central ar- guments were (1) that gangs were being glorified and (2) that the *Gazette* unwit- tingly had become a conduit for sending a death threat from the Kings to the Deuces and in so doing were intensifying gang violence. These arguments were coded in such terms as gangs being given "free advertising" and "credibility." The "Christian believers" made a third argument, namely, that the depiction of a fallen gang member as a kind of "religious martyr" was blasphemous and in- dicated the newspaper's insensitivity to Christians in the community. This ar- gument, however, was not mentioned in the *Gazette*'s apology, hence, my claim that only two arguments were central.

Did the credibility and death-threat arguments have weight? On the one hand, both arguments seemed viable. The media, for instance, are sometimes accused of promoting the social ugliness that they witness. Hence, American television audiences are never shown the innocuous streaker who crosses the baseball diamond. More seriously, television stations during, say, a riot may have to determine the fine line between reportage and their potential contribu- tion to incitement if it is possible that nearby viewers may participate. Current practices and policies, therefore, seem to acknowledge that the media may en- courage certain actions. On the other hand, it is probably impossible to deter- mine the amount of encouragement, glorification, or credibility that the media might induce. Certainly, the power of the media to encourage streaking and ri- oting is not as potent as the personal and social conditions that motivate streak- ers and rioters. Moreover, the media do not stop reporting wars, suicide at- tempts, terrorist bombings, and so on because they are fearful of encouraging these actions. Was the street-side funeral a significantly different event? Not re- ally. Hence, it is doubtful that running the picture of the funeral had any long- lasting effect on the intensity of the gang wars, or that it encouraged a young person to join a gang.[27] Gang-related actions emerged more from particular emotional frameworks and social conditions than from pictures in the *Gazette*. It is also doubtful that the *Gazette* conveyed a significant death threat that the rival gang didn't already know about. The Deuces, for instance, did not need a newspaper to tell them that the Kings were disrespecting them. Any argument that maintains that the media glorifies, gives credibility to, or encourages the social nastiness that they report on—in short, that some individuals imitate the news, and some do—has to coexist with the equally or more powerful argument that consumers of the media also interpret, discard, ignore, or remain significantly unaware of whatever spectacles the media may present. The bridge that runs between the media and individual consciousness is full of obstacles and detours so that public consciousness remains multiple. Indeed, some of its variations perversely resist the shapings that power of any kind would like to fabricate.

But is it not a tedious and unfair project to judge as false or irrelevant the arguments belonging to people one disagrees with, particularly if this means failing to understand the emotional frameworks that are attempting to speak through the arguments? From this perspective, arguments cannot be lightly discarded as illogical or groundless. Indeed, they are more like indirect pathways through emotional life, and they can be traversed so that they no longer hide what needs to be heard. In this sense, the argumentive talk that comprises the public sphere and from which policy making emerges is less an arena of rationality than an arena of obscured fears. At any rate, in my view, the arguments made in the letters to the editor and the editorial apology can be traversed so as to reveal important aspects of how real public spheres work. For instance, the funeral occurred in a small and already deeply concerned, even perplexed, community, for the city had never experienced frequent street-gang slayings. The letters and apology, then, seemed to reflect a kind of emotional overload neatly captured in the July 1991 editorial: "so much negative feeling seemingly so rampant about the overall status of the social order these days." And, as if to retrieve some semblance of social order, the same editorial evoked numerous stable icons: for instance, a founding father of American tradition, Ben Franklin, and his "an ounce of prevention . . . is often worth a pound of cure"; the hallowedness of family; and the idea of a community as cordoned-off from "nuisances" and "less-desirable elements." These evocations of stable order helped to justify the enforcement policies of the park district. The irony, however, was that in protecting *public* property in the name of the status quo, the property no longer seemed so *public*. In short, the maintenance of social order is also the maintenance of exclusion. In these letters and editorials, the public—and by extension the public sphere—remained exclusive because at the limits of any defined public lies a fence line of fear electrified by a need for self-preservation. The boundaries of the fence line remain murky because public liberalism may espouse a code of tolerance whereas public conservatism may espouse less tolerant measures. Wherever the fence line lies, however, many who are excluded are magnetized to it, for in testing it one derives power, a power that is otherwise ensconced among those who maintain or abide by the social order. Power derived from testing the fence line might be called reversed power. Hence, those who test may be represented in the public sphere as wild-eyed mavericks toppling the social order, and the self-representations devised by the excluded, as I have suggested among street gangs, oftentimes hyperbolize the maverick label through the topoi of nationhood and madness/disorder in order to test with even more power the very fears that limit the public sphere.

What is important to remember is that the public sphere of modern stratified societies, whether imagined as impossibly comprehensive and bourgeois or imagined as sets of feisty subaltern counterpublics with their own argumentive styles and ways of being, is constrained by whatever becomes its collective fear. Locate the anxiety of a public sphere, and one will have located the limit for engaging in rational discourse and, hence, for constructing a participatory democracy. In this sense, a public sphere cannot "think" beyond what terrifies it. And certainly it is the very stratification of society itself that fosters the emergence of systemic fears, for fears tend to consolidate around divisions and differences and to make these more "real" than what might otherwise be the case. Fear in these instances, then, becomes a kind of touchstone, deriving substance from vagueness, invisibly infecting the possibilities of policy making, and shaping, also invisibly, much of the style and substance of resistance. From all this, I am left with two conclusions. First, the articulation of virtues that occurred in the pages of the *Gazette* were a kind of circling of the wagons by which Angelstown's "law-abiding citizenry" began unconsciously to consolidate communal fears in the guise of virtues and thereby passed a flurry of anti-graffiti ordinances and police actions claiming "zero-tolerance" of gangs. Second, in articulating those virtues, the nonvirtues were simultaneously, if sometimes implicitly, articulated. Thus, on the one hand, those in power could now more easily recognize (and sometimes over-recognize) what they hoped to prevent; and, on the other hand, those most deeply alienated from majoritarian power could now more easily mobilize the styles and substance of hyperbolic resistance. Did any of the new city policies work? Given the fact that gang-related homicides increased in the following years, one might say that the policies did not, but such a reply is probably too much of a generalization. What I am left with instead is a metaphorical interpretation that is grounded somewhat in the complexity of city life but not as completely as one might like: The city's policies nourished in their cores cancerous fears that were never eradicated and thus consistently prevented other policies from emerging, and because of this incomplete understanding of what was happening inside its social body, the city could not realize the cure that it desired. What specific policy might have worked? I am approaching quicksand on this one, but if I were to maintain the faintest of hopes in broad public discourse, and I doubt that I do, I would argue for pushing further back the fence line electrified by fear by encouraging gang leaders and membership to participate in public forums with majoritarian society, by insisting on careful documentation of the assumptions and beliefs of all parties so that they could be later deconstructed, and by insisting that these forums move toward concrete truces, programs, and proposals. Such an approach, I realize, tumbles back into the optimisms of Fraser and the more recent writings of Habermas.[28] In the Angelstown of 1990 and 1991, such an approach would have been outrageous. The approach then and continuing through 1996 has been the unremitting enforcement of powerlessness upon those whose actions speak of a need for power. The assumption behind this approach, of course, has been to not recognize the maverick or to give him/her voice because in doing so maverickness itself will be encouraged across the entire social body until all icons of stability collapse. Better to stamp it out until it is extinguished.

conclusion

Here at the end of this chapter I encounter, it seems to me, one of the central conundrums of critical ethnography. The approach taken by the city, that of unremitting enforcement, offered itself as the only "real" solution. Other solutions run the danger of appearing anemic, eccentric, or groundless. For instance, my reading of street-gang graffiti through the lenses of linguistic metaphors (lexicon, syntax, condensed narratives of subjectivity) runs violently counter to any "commonsense" understanding grounded in the property rights of law-abiding citizenry. I also realize that my interpretations of street-gang culture butts heads with a "commonsense" understanding of criminality. My analyses derive from and argue for a big-picture version of social justice. In this picture, one can all too easily afford generosity and compassion. But there is also a more immediate picture, a local picture, and when we find ourselves in it, we often quickly discard the big one, for the local is urgent and pressing. It squeezes us painfully, annoyingly, and it disciplines us into a kind of honesty concerning the limitations of ourselves and others. From its perspective, the big picture looks like a waste of imaginary labyrinths, a sense of social justice that has never been and never will be. Angelstown's experience with graffiti and street-gangs is a powerful example of a local picture shrinking any possibility of a bigger picture of social justice. Are there ways to dodge the conumdrum? Can one argue critically for a big picture of social justice and simultaneously find solutions that make sense from the perspective of the local? I think so. The rhetorical trick might be to find insights and solutions that are not inconsistent with the reigning ideology but whose implementation has the slow-moving power to alter insidiously the existing institutions and ideologies that constitute the local. The solution presented in the prior paragraph lacks the necessary subtlety, perhaps, and yet rhetorical invention must begin somewhere.

7

BLACKTOP

BE CONSIDERATE . . .

Keep weeds and grass cut.

Keep rubbish and junk off your property.

Keep your garbage contained so that it can't be scattered about and don't put garbage out for collection before 7:00 p.m. the night before pickup.

Keep leaves bagged—don't burn them.

Keep loud music and parties inside—not outside.

DON'T LET CARS WRECK YOUR NEIGHBORHOOD

Automobiles . . .

Should Not Be Parked:

—in the front yard

—on the parkway

—across the sidewalks

—in front of driveways

—on the street or alley after a 2-inch snowfall

REMEMBER!

It is against the law to park a car in the front yard in order to sell, grease or repair it.

DON'T LET YOUR NEIGHBORHOOD GO TO THE DOGS

Pets . . .
Should Not Be Allowed To:
–disturb your neighbor's peace
–foul your neighbor's property
–run loose in your neighborhood

REMEMBER!

It is against the law to keep farm animals or zoo pets inside the city limits.

BE NEIGHBORLY . . .

Welcome new neighbors and get to know the old ones.
Protect your neighborhood by watching for strangers and unusual activity, by keeping lights on and by forming a Neighborhood Watch.
Join with neighbors to clean up local streets, parkways and vacant lots and help plan other neighborhood projects.
–from the pamphlet "Want to Live in a Better Neighborhood? . . . Then Be a Better Neighbor Where You Live!" prepared by the League of Women Voters of Angelstown, Spring 1987

At various times after conducting some specific bit of fieldwork (or running into some obstacle that would not permit me to do so), I would return to Don Angel's apartment to record the day's activities, and after a while my writing would move toward an area of speculation that became loosely lumped under the term "the neat and the clean." The neat and clean was very much about the making of order, and the fieldsite seemed to be swollen with interesting versions of it: an occasional front yard marshaled by a chain link fence that protected mowed grass, flowers, trimmed hedges, and sometimes a bathtub buried to make a grotto for the Virgen de Guadalupe or an assortment of lawn ornaments as menageries and whirligigs; or the neat and clean as a highly polished van with an elaborately decorated interior; or a car converted into a Too-Low-Flow or a thumper with an Alpine sound system and hydraulics; or a stretch of graffiti drawn in Old English lettering; or the neat and clean of a gang member sharply dressed in all his colors. True, a sensibility from, more than likely, outside the neighborhood could interpret some of these examples as gaudy or tacky or, in the case of street gangs, as evidence of the loss of parental control. Nevertheless, those who placed their beings for safekeeping behind these highly designed spectacles and surfaces were *not only finding satisfaction in the making of the sort of order that was sanctioned by immediate others but also using the "languages" of exterior spaces to announce one's accomplishment, indeed, one's person as a maker of order—and all this as if it were a kind of human proclivity.*

As I continued to write about the neat and clean in my fieldnotes, I recalled Mary Douglas's *Purity and Danger* and her discussions of "dirt" as symbolic disorder.[1] Her text focused upon primitive religions and rituals and the persistence in contemporary life of a kind of primitivism, but what I most kept was her notion of symbolic dirt and how humans are both drawn to and repelled by it. Important aspects of the fieldsite, it seemed to me, could be structured between the symbols of dirt as disorder and the neat and clean as the making of an order, and, further, that there were historical trajectories underlying these symbols that, if explored, might illuminate some of the most common practices and discourse habits that mark the modern. The rest of this chapter will attempt to understand certain fieldwork experiences through an analytic lens that relies heavily on such concepts as dirt versus the neat and clean, disorder versus order and, most importantly, the "discourses of measurement," a term that I will slowly unwrap.

ramón's story

One day, Mr. and Mrs. Carranza blacktopped the packed dirt beneath a worn-out tree that shaded the parking spaces for four cars: the family's van, the eldest son's car, Don Angel's car, and his roommate's. I was not there when the work was done. Edmundo and I were there, however, when the Carranzas started planning it. The Carranzas had watched the open lot that bordered their property suddenly become landscaped and later blacktopped. The *Iglesia Pentecostal, Cristo Es El Señor* had recently bought the lot and its small, abandoned, cinder-block building (which at one time had been graffiti-covered) and had started fixing up the area. Don Angel complained fussily that he did not like non-Catholics this close to him, and he feared that they would come to his door preaching. He put up a Spanish sign on his door announcing that those who lived inside were Catholic. At any rate, the blacktopping of what proved to be a sizeable lot went on for several days. Over several evenings, while leaning over the fence that separated the lots, Mr. Carranza got to know Ramón, the man who was laying down the *chapopote*, "asphalt," "tar." One evening, Mr. Carranza asked Ramón to take measurements around his tree and to make a bid for the cost. Ramón pulled out his tape measure. In a kind of hysteria of short bustling legs and numbers yelled out in the closing dark and toward the general direction of Mr. Carranza, he tossed out three or four bids based on different options. Eventually, the project cost the Carranzas eight hundred dollars. The blacktop spread out from the base of the tree to accommodate comfortably approximately five cars. It rose off the packed dirt about six inches or more, and this elevation caused quite a jolt if one's car tire fell off. But everyone was happy. At last, things are looking nice around here, someone said. *Todo parece más limpio*, "Everything looks cleaner," said Mrs. Carranza. When I asked Don Angel, he said that now there would not be any mud when one washed one's car, an outcome that was very satisfying to him because he was so picky about keeping his apartment spick and span with cleaning products conveniently lifted from his janitorial job. *La mugre se acabó*, "The filth is finished," said someone else. The neat and clean around the tree, the recently remodeled Carranza kitchen and dining room, and the new wooden steps that led up to a platform that connected to the front door were small images of getting one's life under control.

Ramón was a strange character. He too wrestled with the neat and clean, only in his case his livelihood depended on it. Edmundo and I talked to him in July of 1990, and he seemed to us to be frenetically chasing stability. He was from the Mexican state of Zacatecas, had gone to school there until the sixth grade, and crossed the border illegally when he was sixteen to arrive in Angelstown in the early 1970s where an uncle and aunt were already living. After a series of factory jobs, which seemed always to end with a power struggle which Ramón described as involving different sorts of wrongs committed against him that justified his quitting in anger, he began to work for himself. He bought a small truck and started doing odd jobs, first on a condemned house that he had purchased and then elsewhere. Laying blacktop full time was an occupation that had emerged over four years after first laying it for himself and later for others. By 1985 or 1986, his blacktopping company was underway.

Ramón's life was a kind of buzzing confusion of entrepreneurial ambition, failure, disorganization, laziness, and cleverness. The surface of his life seemed a series of rambunctious maneuvers to stay afloat by cutting corners, while underneath was an apparently sincere desire to do a good job. The evening Edmundo and I talked to him, he was eager to ask questions about the business of business, of how to make money, of how to handle workers, and particularly of how to organize oneself. He asked these questions even as he frankly admitted that he often did not wake up early enough in the mornings to arrive at the job site on time; but, of course, he required his workers to be on time. At one point, he opened his glove compartment and then pulled at his pockets. Important telephone numbers of clients, creditors, and others came spilling out. At another point, he told us a story of how he had recently purchased a truck he couldn't afford and how even his cousin at the time told him: *Usted piensa con las patas,* "You don't think with your head." Edmundo, who for some time had been working as a counselor, saw in Ramón an opportunity to help someone whose life was in disarray. For a while, Ramón responded to Edmundo's suggestions as if they were manna, and so the three of us talked and talked late into the dark, our conversation occasionally interrupted by the shrieking wheels of a freight train headed east for Chicago.

He owed lots of people money, including back pay to his brother who sometimes acted as his foreman. The reason for his lack of money was the scarcity of jobs, but also his Latino clients often did not pay on time. (In many ways, he preferred white American clients.) In addition, he often did not charge for the finished work because the job had been poorly done. The reason his work was shoddy was because he could not afford to hire people who knew what they were doing. The people he could afford to hire could not be relied upon to remain in his employ, sometimes because his instructions were not clear and sometimes because he made requests that irritated his workers. Ramón, for example, once told his then foreman to lend his car to one of the workers so that the worker could get to the next construction site. The foreman quit. Another reason for Ramón's substandard work was that he did not have enough money to buy a sufficiently large dump truck, one that could carry fifteen tons of hot asphalt. Without such a truck, the first layer of asphalt would cool before he could bring in the next one, and this way of working left noticeably different layers. On large projects, Ramón could rent a large truck, but because his drivers did not have the correct licenses for driving large trucks, they risked possible arrests. His lack of sufficient funds had also prevented him from getting permits from the city, and so for a long time he was unable to enter bids for city projects. Ramón felt he could not compete with larger companies who had more equipment and more cash, and conceded that they did better work. However, he also insisted that all of his small disasters had taught him how to lay blacktop correctly, how to lay it on dry, level dirt, how to lay the gravel properly, and so on. His seemingly endless circle of troubles had led to a series of dodges to escape his bad reputation. Several times he had changed the name of his company, revised his business card, and altered the color of his truck. He claimed that all these changes had given him the chance to learn from his experiences and start anew in a different town or area. "If I don't get some relief this year, I don't know because things are shitty." *Ay carajo, la vida no es fácil,* "Damn, life is tough."

One of Ramón's intriguing abilities was his facility for handling contracts and bids despite his limited English. He carried attached to a clipboard a number of sheets that were titled "Contract" and "Estimate." The sheets contained a considerable amount of official-sounding terminology. At first, I doubted that such a panicky man, who claimed to know little English and who seemed to be skating just a foot or two ahead of creditors, clients, and perhaps even the law, could have created a set of documents that seemed so legitimate. But I had underestimated him. He described going to an office supply store, examining a number of boilerplate contracts, and eventually copying and tailoring what he needed, *le quitaba y le ponía,* "I took out and I put in," until he arrived at his current contract sheet. He did the same thing with his estimate sheet, which for a long time he had titled "Proposal." Ramón had used the same process of copying and tailoring in creating the company sign that appeared on the side of his truck as well as in front of his house. In fact, he described a special interest in looking at signs around town, copying things that he liked and making adaptations here and there. I presumed that because he had had to make changes to escape his bad reputation, these were practices that he had engaged in several times. I never specifically found out if he had to ever write or read extended stretches of English text. However, because most of his clients were Latino/a, I assumed that many of his estimates were written in Spanish.

As I listened to his rapid-fire explanations of his troubles, explanations that were not lugubrious but comically frenetic and amazingly frank, I glanced now and then at his shirt. It was a blue shirt, and after a few glances I realized that it was a kind of uniform that might be worn by a custodian or a mechanic. Neatly scripted on a white patch over one of the pockets was "Ramón." As disorganized and inventively makeshift as he was, Ramón had created an image of competence and professionalism by adopting certain distinguishing details: the uniformlike shirt with his name, the contract and estimate sheets, his business card, his truck labeled with his business sign. Through such details, he created what he wasn't (a reliable blacktopper) and covered up his very real struggle with impending chaos. If his talent for business was modest, his talent for not desiring perfection and idealism, for surviving, making do, and not feeling guilty in the face of messing things up was commendable. Moreover, in laying down his blacktop for the Carranzas, Ramón was the middleman between Carranza dirt and Carranza neat and clean. Ramón's company, somewhat shoddy by his own admission, was the sort that the Carranzas could afford. The iconography that the Carranzas desired was achievable, therefore, either through their own makeshift work or the work of Ramón or others, but it also remained askew, unpolished, always jeopardized by a lack of capital. And so my use of Ramon's story goes something like this: Even as Ramon covered the raggedy surfaces of his own life and that of others, his lack of capital meant that he never could quite escape raggediness, but, indeed, entailed it in the very processes of covering it up.

pablo

Another story, that of Pablo, businessman extraordinaire. I don't think anyone knew, not even Pablo, how much he was worth. He owned a restaurant, a video store, two very bustling Mexican grocery stores in Angelstown, and a third in a neighboring town. When Edmundo and I talked to him in July 1990, he had purchased a building next to one of his stores and hired an architect to draw up plans for turning the building into a pharmacy and a general store, a kind of "Osco" he called it. Unlike Ramón, Pablo was an excellent administrator. His background, however, was similar to Ramón's in so far as he too had arrived in the Angelstown area as a teenager from a family of poor farmers in Mexico who could not afford to educate their children. Pablo had started as a butcher and meatpacker in the 1970s. By 1981, he had saved seven thousand dollars. After borrowing an equal amount, he started his first Mexican grocery store. Success came quickly. Everyone I knew in the neighborhood believed it came too quickly, and this belief had been floating through the Latino neighborhoods and undermining Pablo's status long before he was killed one day in 1991 in the late afternoon on the sidewalk in front of his newest grocery store. Edmundo and I had intended to talk to Pablo again for two reasons. His success story, of course, was interesting, but at the time Edmundo and I were especially interested in how English officialese had peppered, in particular, the Spanish of neighborhood business people with *pochismos*, or borrowings of English words by Spanish speakers.[2] Instead of further talk, however, we were left with unverifiable rumors, for instance, that Pablo had used drug sales to finance his businesses, that he had become overextended, and that he had been particularly nervous the week before professional killers got to him. At any rate, the case went unsolved throughout 1991 and, to the best of my knowledge, remains unsolved.[3]

Pablo's story was also interesting because of what he said to Edmundo and me about his problems with the city. During the interview, Pablo described at least three problems that he had encountered while trying to operate his newest Mexican grocery store. His intentions to repair the sidewalk in front of his store and the parking lot next to his building had been blocked by city hall. Moreover, his plans to convert the building across from his store into a pharmacy and a general store had also been blocked by city hall. In all three cases, he felt betrayed by the city, complained of discrimination against Latinos/as, and argued that what the community needed was a Latino in city hall *para hacer la lucha,* "to wage the good fight" in favor of other Latinos. In order to understand his problems, however, it is necessary first to understand where the store was located and the social forces that were impinging on the immediate area as well as city hall itself.

Dan Anderson and I conducted a number of interviews with city officials in order to understand their views and attitudes about the Latino neighborhoods in which we were working. The most critical issue concerning Pablo's store was that it was located on the main gateway into the city, a gateway that passed through the city's poorest neighborhoods where African-Americans and particularly Latinos/as lived, where graffiti was prominently displayed and gang wars most frequently occurred. The city was eager to control this gateway as well as the streets that formed the city's commercial center in order to make the city attractive to new investment. The image of these streets could be controlled through zoning, ordinances, block grants awarded to private owners who were willing to restore historic property, and through the sale of city-owned properties to buyers who were willing to conform to city plans. One of the interviews that we conducted was with the neighborhood redevelopment director, who formerly had been the preservation director and present during many of the conversations with Pablo. Because her account of the city's image problem and the specifics of Pablo's case was so revealing, I will quote extensively from it.

> All you have to do is drive down Broadway [not a gateway but the main downtown street] and see what has become of that street with everybody doing their own thing all over the years. . . . It's a marketing issue as much as any. . . . If you don't all work together, we have nothing that the other communities don't have. . . . We will never be an economic force, we will never have the kinds of image that drive the tax base and better your schools. . . . Maybe it's kind of a top down thing, but it's not directed I don't think at any particular culture's aes-

thetic. . . . When you talk about what the city is trying to codify, from
the preservation standpoint what we are trying to codify is to thine
ownself be true. . . . If you're a 1920s building, be a 1920s building. If
you're next door to a 1950s building, it should be a 1950s building.

City hall's most important long-term goal, as I said earlier in this text, was
the creation of an attractive city image that might compete with neighboring
cities whose own histories had never experienced a comparable amount of industrialization or such high numbers of immigrant workers. Angelstown's recent economic downturns and "image problem" were merely the newest developments in its continuing history. The neighboring cities, in contrast, lacked
that history and, therefore, lacked the image problem. In fact, these cities were
boomtowns benefiting from an economic expansion sweeping west along Chicago's western suburbs and founded on, among others, research parks (the
Fermi National Accelerator Laboratory, Argonne labs, and Amoco research
offices were nearby), high-tech industries, and numerous service industries
such as insurance companies. The Angelstown city hall's desire to grab its share
of economic rejuvenation was, thererefore, realistic but constantly thwarted by
the city's image. For instance, in the heart of the downtown, there was for a
while a traditional *botánica* (a store that sells medicinal herbs and religious/
magical treatments) alongside another store that also sold herbal remedies but
in a more modern context. Both stores were raggedy in their image and fre-
quented only by Latinos/as. In the parking lot directly east of these stores,
pimps sold their prostitutes all day long. Two or three blocks to the north, the
itinerant merchant, El Arabe, arranged his tapestries, birdcages, and other
items around his old blue cadillac for a week at a time before rumbling off to
other Mexican neighborhoods in Ohio and the rest of the Midwest. And further east there was Pablo's store along the gateway leading to a downtown that
had too many empty storefronts. All these locations and many more were objects to be controlled, if possible, by the city. Pablo's problems with city hall,
therefore, were largely determined by these social forces.

For instance, from Pablo's perspective, there was no reason why the city
should refuse him permission to fix the sidewalk in front of his store. The disagreement had been going on for two years. He hadn't even asked for money
from the city. His insurance had been cancelled because he had not fixed the
sidewalk. I got the other side of the story, however, from the redevelopment director who replied that the broken sidewalks had to be re-engineered. The slope
that existed dropped eight or nine inches. The engineers thought this slope was

unsafe and determined that the entire block needed to be graded correctly, but the city had had trouble getting the other commercial owners to agree. Pablo, therefore, had not been allowed to hire someone to finish the job.

The parking lot beside Pablo's store posed a more complicated problem. From Pablo's perspective, the city told him that a loan of ten thousand dollars was available if he wished to fix the lot. If in five years the business was not sold, the debt would be forgotten. With this understanding he secured plans and a company to do the job. When he went back to the city, the reply was that the law had changed two months prior. The law now said that if an individual had sufficient funds in the bank to finish the job, the loan could not be made. Pablo refused to believe this, claiming that laws do not change this quickly and that, therefore, something fishy, perhaps discrimination, was at work. But, again, I got the other side of the story from the redevelopment director who explained that the original monies had been part of a federal block grant from HUD. During the time that Pablo took to present his plans to the city, the conditions for allocating loans had been tightened because of abuses in other cities. Congress's closer scrutiny of HUD helped to change the rules. The new requirements did, indeed, stipulate that a for-profit commercial owner could not get a loan if he or she had sufficient funds.

Pablo's problems with the city concerning his recently purchased building across the street from his newest grocery store were more complicated than what I could fully understand.[4] Apparently, however, from Pablo's perspective the head of zoning had verbally approved Pablo's intentions to turn the building into a kind of pharmacy/general store. With that understanding, Pablo hired an architect to draw up the plans, but when these were presented to the city, the city replied that the area was not zoned for such establishments. Again, Pablo believed that zoning regulations could not have changed that quickly, and so he remained suspicious and with a set of plans that had cost seven thousand dollars but were useless. Once again, I got the other side of the story from the redevelopment director who said that zoning had never been the major problem; rather, it had been the architect's ideas. The building was a 1920s storefront on a gateway, but the architect wanted to brick up the front to create an "emotionally threatening wall" to passersby. Such a wall was out of character with the neighborhood. The style of this design did not fit the sort of image that the city wished to create along the gateway. Moreover, there were plans to create a parking lot beside the building, and the city wanted to get rid of the "parking lot, building, parking lot, building mishmash" that it considered part of the city's image problem. In fact, throughout the conversation, the redevelopment director alluded to an architectural style called "American vernacular" and to the recreation of a 1920s feeling replete with old-fashioned sidewalk lighting and awnings on commercial stores that the city hoped to restore to the area.

Dan and I continued talking to the neighborhood redevelopment director in the very heart of a city hall—itself in the heart of the city—that was being directed by a strong-willed, Democratic, activist mayor overseeing a group of very competent, young managers attempting to tame or, at least, organize a wily, unpredictable organism called Angelstown. As we talked, more things spilled out. For the most part, the redevelopment director saw zoning and ordinance restrictions affecting everyone equally so that no particular cultural or socioeconomic group was being unfairly targeted. In her view, citizen complaints about junk cars, oversized signs, graffiti, littered property, barking dogs, and so on emerged from all areas of the city, and the city council had responded responsibly for the sake of all.

> The only thing that I can think of that would have been enacted as a response maybe to something that's probably more indicative in the Hispanic community than another is the outdoor vendor's license . . . because . . . people were waking up on Sunday mornings with eaten corncobs all over their yards and watermelon rinds, and in this day and age with AIDS it's like I don't want to leave it lay there but I'm not sure I want to pick it up and . . . ice cream wrappers and all that kind of stuff. . . . People were waking up with watermelon rinds in their yards and those corncobs with mayonnaise on them, which again is another issue. . . . I guess it's part of Hispanic culture, but it doesn't seem very safe to have like mayonnaise out in the hot sun all day. . . . Should the city be involved with . . . having someone make money on a community that you know might not be selling a safe product? . . . The reason was health reasons . . . but it was also the people that park on the corner down by the Ponderosa and sell Elvis on black velvet paintings and Oriental rugs . . . it was just totally awful. They were all over town and they looked terrible. . . . It was a broad ordinance [covering flower vendors as well and affecting all areas of the city], and it was a response to all kinds of complaints like food and wrappers . . . in people's yards and these things on the corner. . . . And the other problem is that it was in response to business owners who said these people [street vendors] aren't paying any sales tax, which means they

are in competition with me . . . so a lot of it came out of the business community in the sense that that's not fair. . . . There are two things, one it gives a bad image to the community . . . in our estimation, the fact that you can have street vendors peddling all kinds of stuff just out in the open. The second thing is other people have to pay taxes on that kind of thing . . . other people have to pay store rents and these guys don't and so is that fair? . . . The community is losing revenue, there is an image issue that we have fought for years and years to over-come so . . . it's like dying industrial town. . . . [But] I don't think that the bulk of ordinances affect these peoples lives at all. . . . I mean it's true that we are generally a more litigious society and a more regu-lated society, but it's true hopefully that we don't have sweatshops anymore. . . . I guess it's the benevolent government thing gets to be a hassle, but . . . the corncob thing, I keep going back to this, but it isn't sanitary for garbage to be on the street. . . . It's not good for the neigh-borhood because of rats and things like that. It's questionable what kind of condition this food is in. . . . And the other thing is they have ten-year-old kids from Chicago that come out, dump them off in a van, come back and get them up like at midnight, and these kids are out there [selling] all day long . . . without their parents or without any-thing, they're too young to be doing this, they're probably worn out. You don't know what kind of condition the food is in . . . so . . . are we looking out for the Hispanic community or are we preying upon them? I guess we tend to think that, you know, this is an unsafe condition and it is generally deteriorative for the neighborhood and they have a lot of neighborhood problems already. . . . When people come to the United States, it's not because they aspire to a third world culture so . . . if you're talking about assimilating, this is the way it is. This is what every-body . . . aspires to, this this this and this which is why we keep trying to force everyone into this mold. I mean that's the American way.

I need to stress here that it was widely believed in Angelstown that city ad-ministration at this point in Angelstown's history was more progressive than any prior administration since World War II. In comparison, other administra-tions were depicted as either neglectful or impotent as social and economic changes coursed through the city. The current administration, for instance, had advocated the drawing up of new ward boundaries that had helped to elect to the city council an African-American woman but had failed to elect the first viable Latino/a candidate in the history of Angelstown. In fact, the campaign of the Latina had been organized largely out of city hall by Latinos who were acquaintances of mine and prominently placed in the city administration.

However, as I talked in city hall to the redevelopment director or the city planner or other important city officials, I felt an old and personal conundrum resurfacing. This same conundrum a few years prior had made me decide to withdraw from the Image Task Force. The Task Force was a city-inaugurated group that had tried to organize citizens, business people, and city administrators around the same goal, namely, the generation of a new image for the city. (The pamphlet from the League of Women Voters, for instance, that I quoted at the beginning of this chapter represented the mind-set of the Image Task Force, although, in my opinion, the pamphlet was a somewhat crude version of that mind-set.) At any rate, on those days when I wandered around city hall trying to find so and so or some snippet of information—sometimes just trying to keep myself busy so as not to get stuck all day in Don Angel's hot apartment— I felt that old, familiar conundrum reemerge. Its gist: These were good people in city hall with good intentions, but something twisted was happening here. Even these twists, however, and perhaps because they were difficult to identify, felt at times as if they might be my own inventions, the results of my taking a moral high ground that was not sufficiently practical to guide any social policy. So went the circularity of my thought back then. The circularity, of course, was connected to my inability to find a black and white explanation that might prove once and for all that gnawing sense that subtle injustices that did not favor Latinos/as and other poor were firmly structured into the management of Angelstown life. To this day, I doubt that any black and white proof can be retrieved from the messiness of Angelstown, but as I wrote through this conundrum in Don Angel's apartment, a larger interpretation of the neat and clean versus dirt—as embodied in the program of the Image Task Force, for instance—began to emerge. I began to call this larger interpretation the "discourses of measurement," and within the package of this term there seemed to be a set of historical processes that might allow one to understand the emergence of modern, professional life as a set of pervasive practices, styles of thought, and ways of speaking. If the discourses of measurement summarized the practices and styles of the modern, then they also indicated the continous rupturing by which the modern created the obsolete. In short, the discourses of measurement became an important part of my interpretive scheme, allowing me to understand some of the more fundamental tensions between Angelstown's city hall and the Latino communities, and, more largely, between those who practice the more modern versus those who practice the less modern.

the discourses of measurement

Let me state at the outset that I use the word "measurement" as a broad metaphor to imply precision, the sort of precision that is often associated with numbers. Most simply, the discourses of measurement are ways by which a *precise* order (or the fiction of a *precise* order) gets made. Insofar as the language of numbers feeds such a pursuit well, the word "measurement" is appropriate. However, the making of a precise order is possible through many discourses and can never be reduced to any single discourse. Hence, a use of numbers does not adequately define all discourses of measurement. Indeed, as I hope to show, there may not be a discourse that is not somehow, even if only minutely, a discourse of measurement.

In order to provide an initial understanding of what I mean by the discourses of measurement, let me compare it to another term, "instrumental rationality." For most contemporary thinkers, instrumental rationality is seen as something negative. Social philosophers as opposed as Habermas, an idealist of modernity, and Lyotard, a critic of modernity, have similarly negative views of instrumental reasoning.[5] Their work builds, of course, on prior criticisms of instrumentality, for instance, that of Nietzsche, Hegel, Heidegger, and many others. At any rate, I am willing to accept a certain familial resemblance between the terms instrumental rationality and the discourses of measurement. Both terms would seem to point to the creation of precise orderings and the emergence of an expert class nimble in their ability to apply these ordering schemes to individual life and social life in order to manage both better. Both terms, then, might suggest that in order to manage, much less master, one's person or one's society, it is necessary to conceptualize one or the other as a determinable whole. Managers imagine such a whole as a cluster of identifiable elements. If instability should appear in any particular element, expert knowledge is directed to the breakdown so that the element can once again contribute to the whole. Whether the broken element is the kidney of a person, the loss of a manufacturing base in a society—or, as I encountered in Angelstown, certain social instabilities linked to a fast-growing immigrant population—expert knowledge is ready to explain and repair the breakdown and bring order again to the whole. Instability, whose metaphor is rampant disease, whether in the physical body or social body, is not allowed its full power to destroy. Stability and instability, order and disorder are not allowed their pendulum swings. Instrumental reason and the discourses of measurement, then, share the same objective: holding the unstable at bay. Both terms indicate those practices and ways of speaking and thinking that put life under the gaze of specialized knowledge systems until life becomes understood so as to better regulate its operations for the presumed benefit of the individual or the larger social order.

But let me make a distinction between instrumental rationality and the discourses of measurement. The first term, as I see it, refers to a relatively recent occurrence, whereas discourses of measurement refers to the long haul (history) of human experience. For instance, most critics of instrumental rationality point to the nineteenth century as a watershed for the emergence of specialized knowledge systems. Steve Fuller, for instance, sees nineteenth-century positivism (read: instrumental rationality) emerging as a claim that science is a cognitively superior human practice, and that reason in this guise is a "governing principle, one that regulates the growth of knowledge by directing and measuring the path of inquiry" under the supposition that without such a principle "human energies would be dissipated into random motion."[6] Is not reason here a type of neat and clean and "dissipated human energies" a type of dirt? Here is my point: Mary Douglas took the long view, that symbolic dirt in different guises was always present in human affairs and that the neat and clean as an ordering scheme was its recurring antagonist.[7] If my observations have some validity, instrumental rationality (or Fuller's positivism) are recent species of something else, a something else that has worn a variety of masks at different times and places. I refer to this "something else" as the discourses of measurement, and I use it as a broad term that tries to explain how any precise ordering might come into being. For instance, one discourse of measurement would surely be the invention of protowriting systems and, eventually, writing systems themselves as special technologies that facilitated accurate record keeping and the management of wealth among early agricultural civilizations such as those in the Near East starting around 3500 B.C.[8] The discourses of measurement, thus, are practices but also ways of speaking and thinking that create order, coherence, and sets of rules to organize the otherwise random motions of daily life. It may well be that instrumental rationality is a very special discourse of measurement, one that may threaten to elevate precision itself into a kind of god.[9] At any rate, the effects of placing instrumental rationality inside a historical lineage are at least two: (1) the "evil" ascribed to it by, say, Habermas, Lyotard, Fuller, and others becomes attenuated because the rest of history—and not just the Enlightenment and post-Enlightenment periods—is seen as sharing in some fashion a certain kinship in which systems of order are put into place for the "better" management of society; and (2) it is seen as one more human practice, deeply flawed, perhaps, but a human practice whose very reasonableness and legitimate efficacy makes it invisible inside the cores of daily thoughts and actions.

What interests me most about the discourses of measurement, however, are their ability (or at least their hope) to manufacture the new and, thereby, to manufacture modernity as an ever expanding neat and clean. This manufacturing process has a variety of characteristics that I will only briefly document as follows.

(1) The discourses of measurement seem to begin with an identification of a kind of emptiness, formlessness, or ambiguity, and it is to this emptiness, now targeted, that the discourses address themselves. In this sense, the discourses are the marks of human understanding as they first invent the emptiness, formlessness, or ambiguity and then systematically fill that emptiness. (It is important to emphasize that the "emptiness" comes into being through the discourses of measurement rather than having an existence prior to the discourses. Similarly, a particular discourse acquires its character in relationship to the "emptiness" that it fills.) An example would be helpful here. Take the problem of death itself. I was often intrigued by the stories of death told to me by Don Angel and others who had grown up on *ranchitos* in the interiors of Mexico. Oftentimes the causes of death were not particularly clear. Don Angel might say that something went wrong, maybe the head, heart, or some other body organ—or maybe not even a body part could be recognized, and the person just died because they were too old. If the *ranchito* was too far from an urban center, there was also not much hope of getting medical help for the dying person. In other words, when the possibility of death, that most fundamental of human instabilities, came, there would not be much expectation of keeping it at bay. *Ranchito* discourse, then, was a discourse from the past in which the head, heart, some other body organ, or old age represented a kind of vagueness, an emptiness, a formlessness, an ambiguity, a set of conditions and physical attributes that were not yet understood. In contrast, modern medicine, as it faces death, is a particularly powerful discourse of measurement. It has systematically targeted, to take as just one example, the head as a kind of emptiness. The head, then, has become a territory to be submitted to the scrutiny of a discourse of measurement, say, that of neurology, which tells us quite emphatically of neurons, synapses, neurochemical transmitters (acetylcholine, serotonin, gamma-amino butyric acid), and hemispheric organization. Only in recent times, then, have the head, heart, or whatever become objects whose component parts have been analyzed. What has emerged at the end of this analysis are specific bodies of knowledge and technologies with the prodigious ability to change the conditions of the head or heart. There has also emerged, of course, an expert class with the ability of wielding that knowledge and technology.

(2) The discourses of measurement tend to belittle other knowing systems—implicitly, if not explicitly—or at least to make a prior discourse of measurement obsolete. Let me use weather reports as an example. What is the difference between the body "knowing" the temperature and humidity of the day as opposed to measuring these at a given moment by a set of instruments or predicting them three days in advance by calculating a host of variables? The body as knowing instrument cannot achieve the exactness of meterology and its amassing of measurements and interpretations of wind velocities, temperature changes, levels of humidity, amounts of rainfall, ocean currents, particulate matter in the atmosphere, and so on. But imagine a time before wind, temperature, and rain gauges, before barometers, before all the devices that give us an overview of nature in order to give us the discourse that we call weather reports. Before such devices, we had a kind of formlessness whose blunt existence was known on the skin. With such devices, however, a new specialized knowledge capable of knowing remarkably subtle shifts in nature becomes possible, and this knowledge displaces the body as knowing instrument. Weather reports, then, are one of the modern ways by which nature becomes known. They have inserted themselves, along with other discourses of modernity, into the human imagination with a certain officialdom and in so doing replaced other ways of knowing and talking about nature. These displaced ways of knowing and talking represent a precision that may now be taken as one more sign of backwardness when compared to the discourses of modernity. To summarize: weather reports are part of a larger parable of gain and loss in which the rise of the modern world through the mastery of a kind of enormous formlessness ushers in new technical systems and a consequent liberation but also ushers in the marginalization of other "primitive" knowing systems that become part of the larger code that helps mark class and racial difference.

(3) Quite often the discourses of measurement are aimed at the control of perceived death, decay, and instability. Hence, professional life, whose existence is largely justified by its ability to control and manage, is deeply intertwined with the discourses of measurement. To a certain extent, these ideas about control have been partially explored through my elaborations concerning the manufacturing of modernity, but more elaboration might prove helpful. Emptiness, formlessness, and ambiguity are the terms I use for representing that vacuum of understanding, that state of vague existence that characterizes something prior to its becoming understood as a cluster of details contributing to a larger whole. In contrast, death, decay, and instability are the terms I use for representing the potential wrecking force contained inside something not yet

understood. The discourses of measurement are the dialectical partner of emptiness. They represent those practices and ways of thinking and talking that replace the vacuum with understanding and, in so doing, temper (or hope to temper) the wildness of death, decay, and instability. In a larger sense, the discourses of measurement are the actions of culture as they encounter wildness, which is sometimes symbolized as nature. But, as I pointed out in the paragraph above, the discourses themselves create conditions of future instability, particularly when their efficacy starts to wane and a new discourse awaits its turn on the human stage. At any rate, the discourses of measurement offer the human community the hope of controlling wildness or at least keeping it at bay, but in exerting understanding over it and perhaps controlling it, new problems may emerge. The security that a discourse of measurement offers may increase dependency and a certain anxious expectation concerning the power of its control, and both of these may tend to magnify the danger of the most miniscule of aberrations and in so doing set off a new round of instability. In short, systems of prodigious control may be inherently more fragile and filled with crises than systems of less control.

(4) Another characteristic of the discourses of measurement is that they are thoroughly integrated into the economic sphere. As technical systems of knowing demarcate the formless, they create the hope, whether illusory or not, that the forces of death, decay, and instability can be mastered, and in creating that hope, they support the emergence of a capitalist economy ready to satisfy the desires hope breeds. Quite often in a highly consumerist society, a discourse of measurement will manufacture the appearance of instability and secure a quick niche in the economic sphere, resulting in a host of weird gadgetry such as some labor-saving device or a children's toy that encourages early learning and supposedly leads to future schooling success. But more often a discourse of measurement will offer a more authentic hope that will sell ferociously. Let me use another medical example to explain my point. While I was doing fieldwork, the daughter of one of the families that I had come to know was diagnosed as suffering from cystic fibrosis. On a number of occasions, I went to hospitals and clinics with her parents to translate and help fill out bureaucratic forms. During every visit, we were moved along a kind of conveyor belt of interviews with specialist after specialist, each one giving their special advice and extracting the information he or she needed. A typical visit to the clinic consisted of interviews with the cystic fibrosis specialist himself, a specialist in training (a different one every time), a nurse, a respiratory therapist, a nutritionist, a counselor, and, of course, secretarial staff to make appointments and fill out finan-

cial aid papers. In the case of this specialized clinic, the management of cystic fibrosis was a kind of small industry in which various kinds of expertise had found an object, in this case, two Mexican immigrant adults with little education.

Behind the scene of the clinic was an even larger industry including cystic fibrosis researchers with their own labs, support staffs, technical equipment, and manufacturers of that equipment in addition to the pharmaceutical companies and the manufacturers of therapeutic equipment. In this sense, cystic fibrosis is an economic resource, a generator of livelihoods and capital, dependent on the creation and satisfaction of hope. At the time of the diagnosis, a cure for cystic fibrosis did not exist, and so cystic fibrosis still retained some of its original power (formlessness, ambiguity, wildness) to decay and destabilize human life. Because capitalist economic expansion, in medicine at least, is intertwined with the finding of physical objects that lead to decay and instability, the wild unknown of cystic fibrosis has provided jobs. In short, each medical problem, once identified, becomes its own sphere of economic potential, and the consumer who supports a small share of that economy must have at least a portion of his or her hopes satisfied in order to continue participating in that economy. As the formless becomes labeled and shaped, and routine practices that cure or manage are developed, a set of public expectations emerge that fuel a further surge of the discourses of measurement toward whatever still remains formless, hence, causing decay and instability. In contrast, for those who died of cystic fibrosis even a few decades ago in the *ranchitos* of Mexico, the explanation of death may have been supernatural or spiritual. Perhaps a small residue of that belief system lived on in the mother's interpretation of her daughter's genetic disease. At one point, the mother denied genetic causes and said the disease was caused by bad luck; on another day, however, she admitted heredity but gave it an interesting interpretation by remarking that the disease had caused different problems in her several families: with her daughter it had appeared in her lungs, but in her uncle it had manifested as craziness, and in one of her husband's brothers it had caused him to be *torcido*, "twisted," and confined him to a wheelchair. Her explanations were a collection of ways by which she translated a particularly modern discourse of measurement (genetics) into a discourse more familiar to her. One might call these translations "cultural improvisations" so as to indicate how the stuff that flows between cultures adapts to new contexts. More importantly, however, notice the different kinds of economies that have been associated with these discourses. Not so long ago the acceptance of death was part of *ranchito* economy, but today's medical economy relies on the public demand that decay and instability be postponed; and the lawsuits and other legal entanglements that occasionally trip up the medical industry are further signs of that same demand.

At any rate, as I wrote out my thoughts on the discourses of measurement in Don Angel's hot little apartment, the fertile possibilities of the term became clearer and clearer. The term offered a metaphor by which to link global issues to local ones. I came to understand the so-called image problem of the city and the city's widespread desire to change dramatically the socioeconomic conditions of Angelstown's poorer neighborhoods as an example of a historical tension between the neat and clean and dirt. With this tension in mind, then, I wish to return to the local, to the lives of Don Angel and other *cheros*; to the thumpers and Valerio; to the Juárez and their oldest son, Andy, who was shot apparently during a gang-related argument; to those who drew street-gang graffiti in Old English; to Ramón, Pablo, and the Carranzas and the latter's desire to create a blacktop parking area in their yard; and to the mayor, city planner, redevelopment director, and other city officials, which included Latinos/as. There on the little stage of Angelstown, it seemed to me, the discourses of measurement as a conflict between the neat and clean versus dirt played out a particular kind of unifying drama. I return, then, to interpretations of specific scenes and to certain reservations concerning city policies.

Scene 1: The so-called image problem of the city represented a widespread desire to alter the appearance of Angelstown's poorer neighborhoods, where most of its Latinos and African-Americans lived. Such a change entailed a sincere humanism to help others, but it also entailed more coercive elements. For instance, the possibility of a larger tax base to raise city and school district incomes was of major importance to the city. Indeed, as a member of the East Side School District's Ad-Hoc Finance Committee, I became very aware of what school administrators called their "landlocked" tax base. The term referred to the fact that the district lacked new land that could be commercially or residentially developed; moreover, there were no signs of economic rejuvenation within their already established boundaries. With economic development not on the horizon, the school district became an advocate of rezoning the residential areas within its district from multiple family to single family dwellings. Such a move, the school district hoped, would shrink the student body as well as encourage new home buyers and the gentrification of old neighborhoods. Interestingly, zoning changes had a special history in Angelstown. The city planner and all other city officials pointed to the 1957 zoning measures as being the crux of contemporary social problems because in 1957 the city responded to industry's call for more labor by zoning much of the east side for multiple family dwellings. The packing-in of families did, indeed, provide a larger labor force, but after a decade or so, the packing-in of recently arriving Latinos/as and African-Americans took off. By the 1980s and 1990s, increased densities of poorer people coincided with a concentration of social problems. According to the city planner, whose views were consistent with city policy, the solution was to rezone back to single family and, in so doing, halve the density, and, over time, increased property values would push the lower-income citizens out. Eventually, gang problems along with school district and image problems would start to fade. I listened to this magic wand version of zoning that, supposedly, in 1957 had created one of the foundations for future social problems and that, supposedly, in the 1990s could begin to dissolve those problems, and I thought of control. Gangs wanted to control their streets, their hoods. In response, the city had overt forms of control, namely, the law and order of the police, but subtler and more powerful forms of control were also available, namely, those who could not afford to stay would be pushed all the way out.

Scene 2: It was never clear to me if the city seriously thought that it could restore its "American vernacular" look, or, as the redevelopment director phrased it, "to thine ownself be true." Certainly, the effort was highlighted as the city fought one downtown store owner who advertised discount furniture and appliances with an enormous, gaudy neon sign of late-1950s/early-1960s vintage. The sign was a kind of visual noise historically related, perhaps, to hawkers and peddlers vying for the attention of customers. The city's argument, as it was explained to me by a Latino city official and a friend of mine, concerned how the store's sign and false front covered nineteenth-century architecture. Here was the "mishmash" of design styles that city officials objected to. In effect, the city wished to replace visual noise with bourgeois decorum, but getting downtown store owners to remove the architectural accumulations of decades so as to return to the purity of "to thine ownself be true" was hard work. Pablo's buildings, not on this main street but on a gateway leading to this street, had been caught in this same vision of restoration and image-making. Pablo told Edmundo and me that he didn't care what his buildings looked like. Hence, when the city encouraged him to place a 1920s awning and sign on his newest grocery store because the building had been built circa 1920, he complied, but with his own awning and sign. In short, the city only had limited power to encourage Pablo and all other store owners to follow the city's restoration ideas. Hence, "to thine ownself be true" was not coercive policy. At most, it was the city's support of a self-conscious style that invented an Americana that never was, that sandblasted the "dirt" of American commercialism off its buildings to establish a neat and clean whose safe sentimentality was highly marketable among the contemporary, Anglo middle class. The city's efforts, therefore, seemed not so much coercive as incongruous in Pablo's context. Why should he care or even know about this invention of Americana, particularly when he sold almost exclusively to recently arrived Mexican working-class folk like himself, to raggedy blacktoppers like Rámon, to janitors/dishwashers like Don Angel, to factory workers like the Carranzas, Juárez, and Martínez—all of whom were frequent buyers at Pablo's stores?

Scene 3: One of the questions that I asked of every city official concerned the increase of city regulations on the civic life of working-class immigrants from the middle of the nineteenth century to the latter part of the twentieth. To what extent, for instance, had the obvious increases in ordinances since that time and the emergence of zoning regulations in the 1920s curbed the expression of urban life so that the newest arrivals to the American city faced far more complicated and puzzling restrictions than prior waves of immigrants? Moreover, was this increase a significant hindrance? Any convincing answer to this question would have to entail both a broader and more fine-grained analysis than what I can attempt in this text. Moreover, it would have to balance the negative side of restrictions with its positive side, namely, arguments, well articulated by the redevelopment director, concerning the improvement of life. In the process, it might also discover that many contemporary restrictions are innocuous. (For instance, the itinerant merchant's ordinance did not stop the selling of *elote*, "corn," and *paletas*, "Mexican-style popsicles." It merely required the vendors to purchase licenses. The vendors whom I talked to after the passage of the ordinance remarked that licensing had not affected their sales.) And yet I was always intrigued by the complaints of almost all the Latinos/as I knew who talked of the innumerable controls that American society represented in contrast, say, to Mexican society. Of course, these individuals quickly continued that Mexican society was fundamentally corrupt. When Mexican authorities attempted to control, it was, in effect, an attempt to get a *mordida*, "bribe"; thus, regulations were continually being undermined. My friends appreciated the fact that American society lacked these sorts of corruptions. Nevertheless, there was frustration and puzzlement among business owners such as Rámon and Pablo and among the Carranzas—who periodically sold snow cones on the street corner where they lived and homemade Mexican meals at the factory where they worked until they were told to stop because of health regulations controlling the sale of food items—and among the Juárez, who wanted to fix up their basement and attic and stuff even more renters, illegal or not, into their two-story house. Everyone, seemingly, was trying to make one more buck through improvisations of these sorts or by cheating on taxes. Depending on the interpreter, the increased regulations of American society either protected my friends and others from their own excesses or stifled their accumulation of cash. At any rate, it was clear that increased regulations of civic behavior created conditions, both positive and negative, that were different from those at any other time in American immigrant history.

Scene 4: The reservations that I have been articulating might be understood, in the end, as a strong suspicion that American urban sites have increasingly attempted to tame public life by corraling it into domestic spaces. Issues of crime, graffiti, itinerant merchants, city image, young males loitering on street corners, and corncobs/watermelon rinds in yards—whatever serious or innocuous problems each one might represent—can also be taken as a broad sign that street life has represented a kind of "dirt" that threatens the idealized neat and clean of easier-to-control domestic spaces. The street has become a site of the unpredictable, but interior spaces—whether those of home, school, or office—have framed and confined life into rooms and, thus, become a site for the exertion of authority. The boost in income levels that has characterized industrialized societies has been a major factor in spreading the imagery of modern domestic spaces as distinctively substantial, as both safe and stuffed with comforts.[10] It takes cash, therefore, to generate these signs of the modern, but the drawback of witnessing the rest of the world (worst yet, determining social policy) from the vantage point of safe retreats has been that social distance has become amplified. The desire to tame street life, to place authority and control over it, and the felt need to protect the comforts already accumulated inside domestic spaces are, thus, linked responses, themselves signs of social distances and structured fears whose realities most choose to preserve rather than dissolve.

I wish to particularize scene 4 with specific scenes from Angelstown. A drive on any summer evening through the more middle-class and white neighborhoods of Angelstown revealed mostly empty streets. At most, one might see on occasion a gardener in a large front yard or dog owners walking their pets or older couples strolling and talking. For the most part, however, life was being lived privately, either inside the home and invisible to a passerby or somewhere else. On the near east side, however, where most of my research was done, street life was far more visible and voluble. Particularly if the evening was hot at Don Angel's, none of us stayed inside for very long. The Carranzas too flowed in and out and around. The younger children played different ball games with the regular troop of kids from the neighborhood, or all played on their scooters and bikes. The older children visited whomever had gathered on the steps of the grocery store across the street. If a *paletero*, "vendor of Mexican-style popsicles," walked by, someone might buy a round for everyone. When a thumper drove by and if the kids knew him, they might yell his name. Within a few blocks of us, certain street corners were favorite locations for the gathering of young males, whether gang members or not. Differences in street life between different neighborhoods had been noted by one of the teachers of one of the children I knew. The teacher saw this difference as a sign that Latino/a parents did not create curfews for their children or insist that their children be in bed at a certain time or keep closer controls over the whereabouts of their children. Based on my experiences, I thought his observations were misinterpretations.[11] I took his perspective to be a continuation of nineteenth-century observations of the working classes by the middle classes. Within that ideology, the domestication of street life, which is the making of a neat and clean, starts by encouraging parental authority over children until it instills a certain privacy and self-consciousness that helps children monitor themselves so that social authority might more easily assert its will to civilize public intensity.

Toward the end of fieldwork, I became increasingly interested in the notion of electricity as a sign of the modern and the making of a neat and clean. It was a strange notion, perhaps, given the focus of my research, but I intuited the idea from the fieldsite and modestly explored it through a set of limited interviews and speculated about it in my elaborated fieldnotes. Electricity, emerging after industrialization was well underway, not only transformed the means of production but also, in time, helped to create private, domestic space. Electricity liberated industry from individualized power sources—for instance, running water, steam, and coal—and literally connected all industries to a web of standardized electrical impulses that could be tapped anywhere along the line. Electricity continues to be a sign of the modern insofar as the electronics industry—its computer chips, circuit boards, superconductors, and more—represents one of the major foundations of the economy of the future. But it is the use of electricity to help create domestic space that interested me the most. Bringing electricity to the home has helped industrialized societies expand the role of domestic space and, consequently, to reconstruct the experience of public life. Electricity has converted real events into visual images to be displayed on a TV screen, has provided entertainment through impeccable sound systems, has extended the ability to store fresh food, has changed one's immediate environment through air conditioning, has enabled individuals to wire themselves via computers to sources of information. One result may be a kind of insidious reengineering of the relationship between public and private life. The possibility of experiencing private life either alone or through an insular family has expanded, and, consequently, public life can be experienced less directly.

Domestic space, for those who can afford it, has become a kind of cocoon aglow and animated by electrical impulses that automatically modify room temperature with unprecedented exactness, entertain and inform us with simulacrums, and, significantly, provide a shell of surveillance and security to protect domesticity and its contents. The result is that life outside the cocoon is lived more indirectly. The experience of these rather privileged conditions heightens the urge to domesticate public life in order to reduce that shudder of difference between exterior and interior spaces. Hence, in my interpretive scheme, making the two locations look more similar through the sorts of admonitions that began this chapter or by restoring the streets to a 1920s look that never existed becomes a sign of middle-class domesticity extending its styles of control over the life of the streets. Perhaps as electricity and other aspects of the modern have helped to enlarge the possibilities of domestic space, society in general has become ever more urgent about shrinking those pockets of exterior space that remain out of reach.

Let me correct, however, what may seem to be a simplistic interpretation, namely, that the predominantly white middle class of Angelstown through a kind of generalized neat and clean was, so to speak, colonizing the more raggedy style of Latino/a neighborhoods without Latino/a permission. In many ways, both areas of town maintained the same desire to establish in their work and home life the values of the neat and clean and to possess the iconography of the modern. I have already elaborated the various ways that the neat and clean revealed itself in daily life. Further, and as one might expect, electrical gadgetry as a sign of the modern—for instance, VCRs, TVs, cordless phones, and sound systems (but not air conditioning and security systems)—was enjoyed as readily in the lower-income neighborhoods it was in the higher-income neighborhoods.

For me, one of the more revealing moments for understanding the strong magnetic pull of the more modern upon the social imaginary occurred late one evening when my teenaged friends Cecilia and her older brother laid out a continuum of the neighborhood from the least modern to the most modern. In their distinctions, one could hear the social forces of the neat and clean versus dirt and how each one helped to define the other. Even though they located a distinctive power on the side of the modern, that power was compromised, for any move toward the modern entailed a simultaneous loss of some cherished belief or value. Their observations about this ambiguity brought into focus what I had been hearing and seeing for a number of years, particularly among the younger people I knew. What follows, then, is their ranking scheme starting from the least modern to the most modern: ·

1

Rural *cheros*: ex., Don Angel

2

Urban *cheros*: ex., specific young males known to all three of us

3

Conservative, old-fashioned parents: ex., virtually all Latino/a parents

4

Young *cheros*: ex., Dancers from the local Mexican Folkloric Ballet

5

Gangs, thumpers, hip hop music, and heart throb: ex., Martin

6

Alternative music crowd: ex., Cecilia and her crowd

7

Whites: ex., preppies but not burnouts

Like any ranking scheme, this one was heavily biased. It was produced by two teenagers who felt both moderately alienated and sentimental about their Mexican origins, and both angry toward and envious of the White middle classes. For the most part, their views seemed representative of that large collection of youth that constructed their identities somewhere in the in-between spaces that borrowed from and rejected both Latino/a traditions and white middle-class traditions. Frankly, I felt considerable sympathy for their views because they entailed subtle degrees of pain, resentment, and noncooperation without going to the limits of alienation that some gang members may have felt. The bias of their ranking was most evident in their handling of such volatile terms as *chero* and "gangs/gang members." For instance, young *cheros* who belonged to the dance troop, and many of whom I knew would not have accepted their place in this ranking. They had a special aura and poise about them as if they were quite consciously moving toward the American mainstream via the maintenance of Mexican traditions. The ones I knew were successful leaders in school, and at least two of them went on to college while I was doing research. They saw themselves directly opposed to gangs, as was evident on the afternoon I described previously when the director of the dance company during a public performance berated gang members, who had been laughing at the dancers from the front row, as the embarrassment of the community. In contrast, some gang members of this same gang saw themselves as "knights of the round table." In short, members of different groups would have disagreed with Cecilia and placed themselves higher and others lower.[12] Moreover, Cecilia's interest in alternative music was rare in the neighborhood because hip hop and heart throb (the latter being contemporary popular music with a Latino beat) were more widely listened to. Another difficulty concerned the placement of "white burnouts" who seemed to represent a style of alienation that differed considerably from that of, say, gang members. "Preppies," of course, referred to those despised young Whites who were moving toward college and, eventually (it was imagined), the future management of American society.

At any rate, in the eyes of Cecilia, her closest friends, and her brother, the young *cheros* of the dance company represented "goody-goodies" whose successes implicitly humiliated others but who, in particular, represented old-fashioned traditions that were embarrassing. These critiques, constructed, perhaps, in self-defense by Cecilia and her friends, provided a certain distance from the markers of tradition that were implicitly humiliated in the larger society. However alienated these young people felt, they simultaneously maintained their distance from gang members whose seemingly deeper alienation went further than Cecilia and her friends wished to go. Alternative music, therefore, represented a sharp break from Latino/a origins, but it also broke from hip hop and heart throb (themselves breaks from the same origins) of most of the neighborhood youth culture. Moreover, alternative music, in the view of Cecilia, represented yet a third break, this from White society and "preppie" culture. Indeed, Cecilia and her friends stood alone, and I was curious as I watched Cecilia take up guitar lessons if she would ever find the truly in-between space that might settle her disquiet, something that would break from hip hop/heart throb and yet embrace something Latino/a while simultaneously breaking from alternative music and yet embracing something white.

Let me return, however, to my central point concerning the ranking scheme. I considered it to be revelatory despite its shortcomings. Its central insight was to contrast tradition and change. Both tradition and change had their strengths and weaknesses. For Cecilia and her brother, the Mexican was the embodiment of tradition, always making things last, repairing things, conserving, making-do with what one had because there wasn't sufficient cash to shop and waste. Here was the jerry-built, make-do, escape-artist world of Ramón and the raggedy neighborhood that he both covered up and helped to produce. As a result, tradition was also the embodiment of embarrassment, the humiliating marker of one's lack of power, socioeconomic and more, to change rapidly with the times. But here also was a certain poignancy and loyal fierceness that connected one to one's neighborhood and family.[13] Increasing the poignancy, perhaps, was the sense that tradition itself was fleeting, for no matter how much one desired it, the most one could do, as Cecilia's brother so eloquently stated, was to "hold that culture in your hand for a minute or so." Here then, too, was the brevity of tradition, the always fleeting moment threatening to replace what one loved.

But the modern, as one of the results of change, was another focus of desire. Again, Cecilia and her brother were quite clear about the markers of the modern, particularly its electrical gadgets—for instance, cellular telephones, beepers, computers, sound systems, CD players, and electrical instrument tuners—and of how especially desirable they were in the neighborhood. The modern also held out liberation from tradition, the fact that Cecilia wanted to have nothing to do with being treated like a traditional Mexican woman by a "macho" husband or even have the traditional *quinceañera*, "coming-out party celebrated on a girl's fifteenth birthday." Not everyone, of course, in the neighborhood would have agreed with Cecilia and her brother's list. Nevertheless, the appeal of the modern, its allure because of its association with increased income and purchasing power by which one could afford electrical gadgetry as one of the modern's special markers was, with the exception of those like Don Angel, almost universal. Why else had Pablo become a major economic force in Angelstown if it had not been because of his desire to do something other than what his father, an *agricultor*, "farmer," had done, or why else the universal desire among adults that their children should not have to work as hard as they and perhaps even work in an office someday? This steady move from *agricultura*, to factory work or some other form of "hard" labor in the United States, to the hope of professional or office work for one's children was common among the people I knew. A few, of course, were born and raised in urban areas in Mexico, and the life of the *agricultor* was unfamiliar to them. Nevertheless, the progression represents a typical pattern and, more significantly, a kind of ritualistic cleansing of dirt from the family name so that, at last, it might be trained into the professionalizing discourses of measurement and, thereby, enter the neat and clean of domesticated interiors.

In short, the iconography of the modern as well as that of the neat and clean swayed with a special swagger through the imaginations of many and embodied itself in the neighborhood's version of the neat and clean. The result was that the domestication of public life and the intent of city hall to clean up the image of the city entailed degrees of coercion but also implicit cooperation from those being most acted upon. It is important, however, to emphasize the implicitness of the cooperation because on the more visible surface were numerous small examples of explicit noncooperation. I have already discussed a few of these: for instance, that gang members and their graffiti were demonized to the extent that their voices could not enter the public sphere; that Pablo imagined that discrimination from city hall was constantly interfering with his own plans to make things look good, as he said; that Latino/a leaders and business people had formed their own *Cámara de Comercio*, "Chamber of Commerce," despite invitations to join Angelstown's Chamber of Commerce because they felt their very different problems and interests could not be addressed by the mainstream organization;[14] and that over the years that I lived in Angelstown, only Latinos/as attended the very large and lively Mexican Day Parades and Puerto Rican Day Parades. I could list many more public and private moments that would further argue how ethnicity and socioeconomic difference divided Angelstown. However, I would have to simultaneouly insist that an undercurrent of shared values and iconographies, not easily acknowledged by many, kept tugging at the divisions, preventing ruptures more remarkable than those listed, although the potential for such ruptures was ever present.

How, then, might I explain the emergence of ordinances, their functions as a response to "dirt," and the allure of the neat and clean along with its somewhat heavy-handed insistence embodied, for instance, in the quotations from the pamphlet that began this chapter? In my interpretive scheme, ordinances and zoning are further versions of the discourses of measurement. A discourse of measurement exists in dialectical relationship with a specific formlessness; it makes a something out of a nothing, carves an order out of a supposed wildness. In this case, civic behavior is constructed as a kind of wildness so that it can be tamed. In short, a discourse of measurement is aimed at this perceived wildness that consists of the jostling of bodies and egos over limited resources. The proliferation of city ordinances and the emergence of zoning during the American twentieth century resulted from the need for practical solutions, I presume, to straighten out conflicting claims over resources. However, one might also regard civic behavior as a kind of unconscious formlessness that, over time, has become increasingly defined into what is and is not acceptable. For instance, take as one example the Angelstown ordinances controlling peddlers and itinerant merchants: they can no longer "shout or cry out" their wares; they have a variety of spacing regulations that keep the merchants at a distance from retail stores and schools; they have defined hours of operation; they have public right-of-way restrictions; they are prohibited from selling in parks; they require elaborate application forms to be filled out; they require licenses to be paid for and visibly worn; and they cannot sell T-shirts, velvet paintings, and other nonperishable items for reasons of city "aesthetics."[15] At one time, all this was not so, had not even been thought of. Today, however, what was nothing has become a something that exists consciously as formal regulations governing the use of public spaces. Former conditions, over time, became defined as dirt and randomness that were later shaped into the neat and clean by social controls. Whether such controls serve all or mostly a few takes us to the roots of who participates in the public sphere. Do such controls significantly affect the daily lives of people, are they mostly innocuous, do they beautify and enhance public life—these questions, as we have seen, are most difficult to answer. However, what I want to make most clear is that the discourses of measurement have been aimed at social life in order to finely tune the possibility of a better public environment. It may be that the desire for that "better" environment necessitates ever larger systems of management that entail bureaucratic controls that significantly displace self-control and, more significantly, intensify the structures of alienation by making power more entrenched and complicated to access. Moreover, I wonder if these increasing controls over public life, so evident in the proliferation of ordinances mentioned above, have themselves come into being because of the increasing availability of domestic comforts and protections. A special sort of cocoon has become more available to the middle classes. Public life, when defined against those standards, must represent difference, an innate difference of size and volume. In short, the application of the discourses of measurement, via ordinances, may represent an increasing inability to acknowledge the innate texture of public life, its characteristic unpredictablity, its noise and sweat, its "dirt." Judgments that are meant to preserve the system world as opposed to public life, then, may be fragile versions of the neat and clean, versions too accustomed to comfort and protection and, thus, too easily disturbed by the ever-fissioning, protean qualities of public life.

I suspect that public life can never be made into a neat and clean but must always coexist with its dirt. At times, I suppose, the dirt may be truly infectious, but most times the cries over an encroaching dirt probably reflect a special paranoia belonging to those timid enough to become violent. It may be unfair to reduce in these ways our American social crises: our literacy crisis, our economic-competitiveness crisis, our educational crisis, our decaying moral order.[16] It seems to me, however, that the language of crisis results from the discourses of measurement, particularly its failed expectations, and so the many crises of Angelstown cannot be understood outside that falsely manufactured world delivered to us by those many discourses. And, if I can be forgiven my presumptuous desire to see Angelstown as emblematic of something not only local but global, I would like to postulate that this almost primordial tale of the neat and clean versus dirt, which is now being repeated as modernity's tale of unequal development, tells us that the neat and clean is never monolithic, never an agent of homogenization. The neat and clean and its attendant discourses of measurement are always nuanced by the communities and individuals who practice them. We might imagine a variety of societies, then, urging their citizenry toward the modern in a variety of ways—and, therefore, simultaneously defining the backward in a variety of ways. Of course, those defined as backward may also, in turn, resist the modern in a variety of ways. And so it goes, the plethora of ways that modernity can take. But I speak more acutely, or at least I hope I have, about a particular locality, Angelstown, and a few of its inhabitants whose tales represent only a few of the ways by which the more modern and its "neat and clean" has jostled against the less modern and its "dirt."

conclusion

At the end of one of the episodes of the television program *The Simpsons*, Homer turns to his wife, Marge, and says, "Aw Marge, there is no moral to the story. It was just a lot of stuff that happened." Toward the end of José Limón's "*Carne, Carnales*, and the Carnivalesque: Bakhtinian *Batos*, Disorder, and Narrative Discourses," Limón reported what others thought of him and his text. The *batos*, "guys," "dudes," from Mexican-American south Texas, whom he had been "studying" for some time, insinuated that he might be an *antropoloco*, "crazy anthropologist," and that his text might be *puro pedo*, "pure bullshit."[17] To be sure, when Limón talked of the work of even better known intellectuals, *los batos* were convinced that such work consisted of even more *puro pedo*. *Puro pedo* and *The Simpsons* are leveling devices, a stretch of graffiti scrawled against one's house of cards, performers in a Bakhtinian carnival whose incessant joking prevents the consolidation of the centripetal. (Ironically, *The Simpsons* has become an institution within popular culture, and so, rather quickly, its critical power has dimmed.) Limón concluded his essay by sketching his version of the ethnographic text: "At the heart of this gift of the carnivalesque is a reflexive critical self-awareness of our status as ethnographers: writers of people. For, as my friends . . . reminded me, this postmodernity of the carnivalesque must also include the keen sense of critical reflexivity that goes with such discourse, the sense that we must always decenter our own narrative self-assurance lest it be saturated with dominating power."[18]

I like Limón's work a lot. As for myself, I like the idea of skating along fast on a political blade, of making an aesthetic turn somewhere in the program, and then erasing that design, ankles firmly strapped to the political but a willingness to lift one's foot now and again. However, let's consider for a moment the fast moving political blade that, I presume, wants to slice up those thought systems that have given birth to the status quo and its social policies. My own sense is that the human condition is frustratingly ironic, splendidly double-sided, so that the reforms and utopias that emerge from critique become the next round of social disasters. I am reminded here of Angelstown's ordinance changes of 1957 that every city official pointed to as contributing to the current problems of the city. Were the ordinances in 1957 imagined as future disasters? Or take the city's desire to improve its image. If accomplished, who are the people who would most benefit from economic rejuvenation, and, then, what about the others? What rights do socioeconomic outsiders have? It is as if every action, every decision, contains at least two electrical charges: positive and negative. It is the negatives from prior reforms that drive the need for new reforms, and it is the rhetoric of optimism combined with human blindness that obscures the negatives already inherent in the next round of reforms.

But I do not wish to lose my theme here. What is this ethnography, or, as I prefer to call it, this project in the rhetorics of public culture or the rhetorics of everyday life? During the earlier part of this century, the director of the American Museum of Natural History, Henry Fairfield Osborn, a famed paleontologist, is said to have described anthropology as "gossip of the natives." And this was during the time when Franz Boas was associated with the museum and anthropology was becoming increasingly scientific.[19] In 1989, Edmund Leach, in a review of Geertz's *Works and Lives: The Anthropologist as Author,* described the ethnographic monograph as having "much more in common with an historical novel than with any kind of scientific treatise."[20] Between Osborn's moment and ours, there was a considerable amount of realist discourse and scientistic desire. For several decades now, realist discourses in ethnography have been played with, have been encased within the trope of irony for both aesthetic and/or political purposes. Limón's work is only one example, a new performance mode within a discipline whose subject matter has been largely about performance. In this ironic mode, realist discourses have not been abandoned, indeed, cannot be abandoned because they are too embedded in the act of communication, and communication is mostly boorishly deictic, typically pointing to someone's reality. Besides, the ironic mode needs to maintain a foil that can be ironized. In short, realist discourses persist, but their ontological grounding has eroded. Such discourses now are much more self-aware of their own ideological conditions and that of others. This sort of critical ethnography, it seems to me, is the thought system that this book belongs to as it attempts to engage judiciously the mechanics of rhetorical persuasiveness and all the mimetic tools and poetic tools available.

But here at this point in the text, almost at its end, I wish to throw a wrench—and some dirt—into my own machinery of interpretation, for, in the spirit of Limón, I wish to raise questions about the ordered worlds that texts give rise to. I began this book by talking about a specific maker and his makings, who lived somewhere in San Antonio, Texas, more than twenty years ago. From that beginning to this end, I have talked of a variety of makers: Don Angel who took pleasure planting seeds and mixing different colors of flowers together in the grotto of the local church; gang members who, with pleasure and vengeance, drew street-gang graffiti in Old English lettering. An ethnography, of course, is also a making, a politically loaded ordering, that is rarely self-reflexive about how and why it has come to be. My answers to the how and why are rather disturbing. It seems to me that, through writing, the world in all of its variation becomes sorted into a pattern. As a result, both authoring and reading offer a special pleasure: the illusion of control, control over the abundance of language and the world pointed to by that language. Call it a vicious pleasure: written language seems to offer a ruling self, whether author or reader, the special opportunity of reducing language and experience to something manageable and, thus, to create an order. Even if the order sought is that of disorder, as in certain kinds of poetry, what gets created is a domesticated version of disorder, in short, the appearance of disorder, rather than the being of disorder.

Perhaps my thoughts here seem tenaciously stubborn, but I wish to detail a particular perspective, one that emphatically goes against the grain of our more humanistic bias that praises the liberatory capacity of writing and floats like never-never land through both the academy and the general public. I do not doubt that writing is hugely liberatory, but I wish to point to its negative, more disturbing side, and in order to do so I find myself speaking with the voice of a curmudgeon. I wish to point to a special relationship between the space that contains a writing and the writing that inhabits that space. I will claim that the two form a powerful dialectic. Stated simply, the dialectic consists of writing (the making of socially meaningful marks usually related to oral language) and a blank surface (paper, clay tablets, computer screens, walls, and so on). Writing is the making of an order and the blank surface is that space or servant that bears the order. Typically, writing catches the eye, but the surface that receives the writing does not. In this sense, writing contains the stronger presence, and the surface that receives the writing is defined by that presence. The surface, then, is an ordered, limited space cleared of obstacles and ready to be acted upon by an ordering agent wielding a highly routinized tool. I am borrowing heavily here from de Certeau:

> First, the *blank page*: a space of its own delimits a place of production for the subject. It is a place where the ambiguities of the world have been exorcised. It assumes the withdrawal and the distance of a

> subject in relation to an area of activities. It is made available for a partial but regulatable operation. A separation divides the traditional cosmos, in which the subject remained possessed by the voices of the world. An autonomous surface is put before the eye of the subject who thus accords himself the field for an operation of his own. This is the Cartesian move of making a distinction that initiates, along with a *place* of writing, the mastery (and isolation) of a subject confronted by an *object*. In front of his blank page, every child is already put in the position of the industrialist, the urban planner, or the Cartesian philosopher—the position of having to manage a space that is his own and distinct from all others and in which he can exercise his own will.
>
> Then a *text* is constructed in this place. Linguistic fragments or materials are treated (factory-processed, one might say) in this space according to methods that can be made explicit and in such a way as to produce an order.[21]

Let us telescope outward from de Certeau's *blank page* (I prefer computer screen) in order to witness a whole continuum of regulated spaces through which a subject performs a textual ordering. First, the blank page or computer screen has standardized dimensions, say, $8\frac{1}{2} \times 11$ inches or $7\frac{1}{2} \times 5\frac{3}{4}$ inches respectively. Second, the page or computer sits on a desktop, itself a standardized shape (mine is 45×30 inches). Third, the desk sits in an office (mine is $10\frac{1}{2} \times 10$ feet) also standardized with other offices in a single building. Fourth, the building itself has been constructed with standardized tools according to standardized techniques and laws. The entire continuum of spaces is ordered and rationalized and extends beyond the building itself. Long before the writing is to be done, therefore, the empty space on and in which it will occur has come into existence via specific discourses of measurement. Writing, of course, does not have to occur in this kind of serialized arrangement in which textual ordering is encased in ever expanding sleeves of order, but writing, which is a kind of domestication of speech—the word technologized, as Ong put it[22]—often occurs inside domesticated spaces and often enables us to realize our desires to further domesticate and control.

But it is the ordering agent, the self as he or she faces the blank page or computer screen, that I wish to pay particular attention to and that is described by de Certeau. The surface that receives the writing, as I described earlier, is a site for reducing the world to a more personal configuration. It makes no difference if we call this configuration a scientific idea, a personal essay, a poem, a note, or a report. In all cases, the subject faces his or her object, and this object becomes the site of production, the place where one can exercise one's will. Of course, I am not talking about the exercising of a free will, for there are always institutional and genre constraints that limit the writing subject. At any rate, whenever I think of the perplexing conditions of writing, I typically reflect upon my own experiences as a teacher of writing. It occurs to me, for instance, that the goal of literacy training in the United States in the latter half of the twentieth century, as Valerio so glaringly faced, is to produce individuals who can create viable miniature worlds in both their writing and reading. These miniature worlds are molded out of words according to such principles as coherence, insight, persuasiveness, completeness, and even beauty. To perform such work on words prepares one not only as a word user but also as a shaper of self and one's surroundings. This explains, then, de Certeau's claim that the child producing on the page is rehearsing a future economic role, that of industrialist, urban plannner, or Cartesian philosopher. This rehearsal is evident in teacher comments on student papers: "Have you chosen the right word?" "Can this be made clearer?" "Your argument here is inconsistent." "Are you being contradictory here?" Such comments encourage students to shape language in school-appropriate ways, but they also presume a stance toward reality: "If we could just get the words right or straighten out our thoughts," says the presumption, "we might have more control over both language and the reality embraced by our language." The comments encourage a separation between the shaper and that part of the lifeworld being shaped. Writing is one practice, one discourse of measurement, among many that attempts to interrupt or shape an amorphousness that might otherwise melt us into everything else, and we call these interruptions or shapings acts of consciousness or self-consciousness. The discourses of measurement are very much at work here, encouraging deeper and deeper levels of reflection so as to generate a more accomplished shaping. And what is learned at this practice site called school, a kind of minor leagues, is meant to be utilized more ferociously and seriously in the majors, real life. Hence, it is presumed that schooling will operate centripetally upon a society reinforcing what is standard and conventional and sloughing off the dialectical and disruptive.

But there is a saving grace in all this, and I call it the saving grace of critique, indeed, the sweetness of critique that always finds the remainder, the forgotten, the hidden and, thereby, exposes as illusion that sense of control, that sense of a ruling self in control. Writing, then, like other discourses of measurement, is a failed expectation, and I, for one, am grateful, for here is the powerful release that the saving grace of critique gives us. This ethnography, then, if submitted to critique, would reveal what? Like other ethnographies exposed, it would reveal how innumerable particulars were sifted through, leaving most behind, and how the ones that remained were denuded of their contexts so that they could be distilled into a set of tenuous generalities. In all this making of generalities, there is much that remains hidden, even from my view. Hence, there is much that can erupt, like a saving grace, to expose as illusion whatever conclusions I have attempted to make. The ethnographic text, then, is the making of an order, a neat and clean, a gathering of generalities and particularities, of explanatory tropes, personal and professional styles, imagined audiences, borrowings from other texts, and so on. The perceived fieldsite passes through these filters to become the fieldsite of the text. The fieldsite of the text is the one that readers come to know, and its borders are not geographic landmarks but, instead, paper and the imagination of a reader. Can we ask ethnography to be more exact or more complete or more faithful to the fieldsite? Other than demanding honesty and hard work of any fieldworker, I do not think that more can be asked. I realize that some perplexing, if tired, arguments regarding objectivity versus subjectivity are not being acknowledged here, but these distinctions no longer seem to me subtle enough to capture the experience of fieldwork, the sense that I have, for instance, that fieldwork is largely ethos driven, that logos gets made via ethos. Or what about the strong possibility, which I also discussed in chapter 1, that fieldworkers are predisposed to seek out and make conclusions because of a deep reservoir of memories that are no longer remembered even as they continue to function as a sounding board validating some conclusions and not others? And yet despite this seeming acknowledgement of the powerful undertow of subjectivity, I wish to resist that too, for any fieldsite must always be more than a repetition of the fieldworker. The fieldsite is a distinctive other, and its materials resist the repetitiousness of subjectivity. In short, the object of analysis has its own undertow. Here, of course, has been the guiding ethos of ethnography for most of its history, to move beyond the repetitive self toward a clarification of the fieldsite, even if the clarity is only temporary, illusory, or tenuous. This way of imagining ethnography—as something that tries so hard to be exact and complete but remains always a failed expectation and a target for the sweetness of critique—is very humbling, yet it contains, finally, so very much that is worthwhile.

NOTES

PREFACE

1. I use the term "Latino/a" throughout to characterize those of Latin American origin. As de la Garza and his co-authors (1992) indicate, the term is misleading since survey research suggests that "Latinos" prefer to label themselves according to their national origins. Indeed, most of the Mexicans I knew in Angelstown labeled themselves *mexicanos*. In this text, however, "Latino/a" is an efficient umbrella term covering a variety of self-labels. My own *latinidad* is discussed in chapter 1.

2. See Plato (1971, 42–43).

3. See Aristotle (1991, 36, 320, 288–89).

4. My attempt to distinguish the classical era from our own according to differing conceptions of art and skill is probably too sweeping and misleading. For instance, the poet of classical Greece was imagined as very much in touch with divinity, madness, and disorder—and this, of course, was long before the romantic era. And modern culture occasionally talks of the art in mundane skill: for instance, the art of medicine or the art of hitting a baseball.

5. For instance, Nancy Scheper-Hughes, whose literary talents are amply displayed in *Death Without Weeping: The Violence of Everyday Life in Brazil*

(1992), and who, I take it, is at least in sympathy with "literary" ethnographers, invokes the notion of high art and not that of *tekhne* when she writes, "The ethnographer, like the artist, is engaged in a special kind of vision quest through which a specific interpretation of the human condition, an entire sensibility, is forged" (p. xii).

1 STARTING PLACES

1. Mercedes, like other Valley towns before and after World War II, was visibly split between its very large Mexican-American population and its smaller Anglo population. In Mercedes, for instance, there was a small Anglo Catholic church, which I sometimes attended with my mother and sister, and a large Mexican-American church that we more frequently attended. The most visible sign of the split, however, was the railroad track that still divides the town into a Mexican-American side north of the tracks and an Anglo side to the south. Actually, the social scene was and is less crude than my portrait suggests because Mexican-Americans, for as long as I remember, have also outnumbered Anglos on the south side. As an example, both the Anglo and Mexican churches were located on the south side. The point I wish to emphasize, however, is that the north side remains 100 percent Mexican-American. I am not a historian of the Rio Grande Valley, but my sense is that the splits within many of the Valley towns were originally drawn, in

part, during the early decades of this century when fruit and vegetable packing sheds were located alongside railroad tracks that ran along the northern edges of many towns. The packing sheds were major employers of Mexican-Americans. North of the tracks, then, became the site of cheap labor and housing, and eventually the emergence of a separate Mexican economy—or so goes my hypothesis.

2. "We require more intellectual autobiographies to clarify why academics end up studying what they do," says Maurice Punch (1986, 22).

3. For an interesting link between ethnography and ethos, see Stephen Tyler (1987, particularly 202–3). In addition, it is important to be clear about how ethos is differently conceived among rhetoricians as opposed to sociocultural anthropologists. Following Aristotle, most rhetoricians conceive of ethos in the context of persuasion and argumentation. For example, they note that the moral character of a speaker may be more persuasive for a given audience than the actual arguments presented. Think of the ethos of Martin Luther King, Jr., in his "I have a dream" speech, but also of the ethos of President Bill Clinton and his difficulties in presenting himself as a leader of the military, particularly before military audiences. Among sociocultural anthropologists, however, ethos, and I am following Ortner (1984, 129) here, typically refers to one of the most elusive parts of a culture, its sense of being other, its distinctive flavor, its stylistic dimensions as opposed to its worldview.

4. To suggest how logos and ethos are deeply bound to each other, I will turn to current discussions in mathematics. If there is a discipline that has the aura of being logos driven, of its truths being discovered rather than invented, it is mathematics. In comparison, sociocultural anthropology has never had that kind of prestige. Some mathematicians, however, acknowledge that theorems are proven in social contexts and that mathematics is "a socially conditioned body of techniques" (Horgan 1993, 100). If mathematics does have a social component, then it should be possible to talk sensibly about the intertwining of mathematical logos and the ethos of a particular mathematician and perhaps even about how mathematical reasoning reflects the ethos of a cultural moment. (My thanks to David Mandersheid, mathematician and acquaintance, for this last, very controversial point.) For an example of such a possibility, one might turn to David Cassidy's (1992) account of Heisenberg during that remarkable moment in the history of twentieth-century physics when the Copenhagen school fought for the supremacy of its position. Mathematical argument was generated by intense conditions, by individuals seeking or defending their reputations, and namely, by Heisenberg's need to establish an uncompromising position in the context of powerful mathematicians such as Niels Bohr and Erwin Schrodinger. Ethos here, then, may have fueled logos. I interpret

Cassidy's account of Heisenberg as suggesting that even mathematical reasoning owes much to an agonistic context and quirks of character.

5. See Garver (1986).

6. See Clifford and Marcus (1986) and Geertz (1988). See also Sangren (1988), as well as Cintron (1993) for different positions on and outlines of the debate.

7. See Limón (1994).

8. See Taussig (1986) for a sensitive treatment of the notions of representation, display, and performance—hence, *epideictic* rhetoric, although he does not use the term—in the context of clashing cultures. See Burke (1969, particularly 70–72), for a brief synopsis of *epideictic* rhetoric in the classical era.

9. A further affirmation of the importance of ethos in the making of ethnographic logos comes, I believe, from feminist anthropologists. Abu-Lughod (1991), for instance, argues for "ethnographies of the particular." These sorts of ethnographies display the minutiae of the everyday instead of obscuring them behind generalizing conclusions. In such an ethnography, the anthropologist would not say, for instance, that the " 'Bongo-Bongo are polygynous' " but would instead display in detail how the institution of polygyny is lived so that the reader would encounter not only the institutionalized discourse of polygyny but would also gain a sense of how it is interpreted, misinterpreted, and contested, how people strategize, feel pain, and so on (153–54). In this sort of ethnography, ethos does more than saturate the moment of inquiry; it seems also to define the structure and content of the text in so far as these display the details of individual agency idiosyncratically embodying a protean rather than an essentialized institution. An institution understood in this way would seem less coherent and timeless, less a clearly identifiable object of logos-centered inquiry. Hence, the institutions of the Other would seem less frozen in their differences to Western institutions. This kind of ethnography departs from Western anthropology's historical practice of delineating a somewhat abstract divide between Us and Them that mutes the details of daily life and the cultural flows that characterize a global economy. In this sense, then, Abu-Lughod's version of a feminist anthropology seems to be in keeping with my arguments about both the presence of ethos in the history of anthropology and the need to more consciously acknowledge it in our fieldwork and textual practices.

10. The following quotations from the romantic poet Percy Bysshe Shelly and cognitive anthropologist Richard Shweder suggest that ongoing themes of alienation and cultural critique link the early 1800s to the 1990s: "We owe the great writers of the golden age of our literature to that fervid awakening of the

public mind which shook to dust the oldest and most oppressive form of the Christian Religion. . . . The great writers of our own age are, we have reason to suppose, the companions and forerunners of some unimagined change in our social condition or the opinions which cement it. The cloud of mind is discharging its collected lightning. . . . I have, what a Scotch philosopher characteristically terms, 'a passion for reforming the world' . . . " (from the "Preface" to *Prometheus Unbound* by Shelley [1977, 134–35]). And this from Shweder (1991, 55): "Today, anthropology's favorite Nietzschean role is that of the 'ghost buster,' the enlightened critic who steps outside of and transcends his own tradition. Indeed, many anthropologists spend their time promoting free individualism (rebellion and liberation) through the criticism of social institutions and customary practices and by means of the revelatory unmasking of received wisdom, dramatically exposed as phantom culture. Many phantoms have been added to the modernist's list of things that do not exist except in the minds of their beholders: not only the obvious phantoms such as God, sin, sorcery, witches, and the evil eye but also other phantoms such as childhood, mental illness, sex roles, kinship, sacredness, authority, and even ethnographic writing itself . . ."

11. See Rosaldo (1989).

12. Scheper-Hughes (1992, xi–xii).

13. Behar (1993, 337).

14. Lavie (1990).

15. The backdrop to my commentary here is a controversy aired during the 1995 meeting of the American Ethnological Society. The controversy concerned the charge that Renato Rosaldo in *Culture and Truth* (1989), particularly in his discussions concerning grief, had projected sentimentalism into his work. Ruth Behar, as responder, denied the criticism. The arguments and replies, of course, were far more complex than I can manage here.

16. Throughout this chapter, I have followed a, more or less, Aristotelian view of ethos and logos in order to suggest how persuasion gets made in ethnography. However, most traditional rhetoricians also acknowledge two more methods for persuading: *pathos*, "the awakening of emotions inside an audience by a speaker," and *mythos*, "the recurring stories, particularly the cultural values and beliefs, told by a people." If an entire book is needed to flesh out how ethnographies come to be via ethos, logos, pathos, and mythos, I will offer, instead, brief and very speculative suspicions about pathos and mythos.

Pathos, I suspect, carries more of the persuasive machinery than logocentric ethnographers wish to admit. Here is why: most ethnographies are about communities and cultures that are at the margins of

power. In an era shaped by democratic idealism and/or humanism, facts that argue for social justice and that awaken the emotion of indignation become salient in the field and convincing in the text. For instance, surely, the persuasiveness of Scheper-Hughes's monumental *Death Without Weeping* (1992) has much to do with the amount of evidence (logos) mobilized to prove social injustice and the amount of uncompromising indignation (pathos) conveyed. I suspect that the idea of social injustice and the emotion of indignation are so twinned that mobilizing one automatically mobilizes the other. The resulting argument, thus, seems not only compelling but even self-evident. But what would an observer see and feel in an era very different from our own, one not shaped by the global spread of human rights? Would such an observer critique social systems that do not emphasize the welfare of the individual if he or she had never experienced a welfare social system in the first place?

As for mythos, one needs to think about the mythos of sociocultural anthropology itself. Mythos has everything to do with the traditional stories and cherished values told over and over by a people. For instance, one of the stories about fieldsites concerns the emotional disequilibrium that ethnographers feel as they fluctuate between astonishment and boredom. Such disequilibrium may be disappearing as differences between societies dissolve; nevertheless, this phenomenon is part of the mythic representation of fieldsites, one of the markers of "being there" as opposed to "being here" at home (Geertz 1988). More importantly, the fieldsite is also marked by intense analysis that tries to explain the astonishment. The amount of labored inquiry aimed at the fieldsite as opposed to home life, then, marks the fieldsite as different. But why is "being there" such an object of intense consciousness, whereas "being here" is lived more unconsciously? I would argue, then, that the mythos of "being there" is, in part, due to several hundred years of ethnographers talking of their vivid experiences and making knowledge out of them, that one of the results of all that inquiry has been the creation of an almost sacred place called the fieldsite along with the creation of legendary figures who negotiated their fieldsites memorably, and that "being here," in contrast, is a kind of secular place less felt and less intensely quizzed. This difference between the sacred and the secular is but one hint that the fieldsite is part of the mythos of a people, part of a yearning and need to feel and understand life differently, a quest, perhaps, to rupture the dissatisfying routine of "being here" with the intensity of "being there."

In order to enter persuasively the conversation of ethnography with claims about a new fieldsite, one must find ways to be both consistent and inconsistent with the tradition. The new fieldsite must be consistent with the mythos of fieldsites but not too consistent because ethnographic tradition itself requires new findings. Here then are traditional obligations that focus what gets seen and talked about and blur the fieldsite's rawer material. At this point, I do not wish to become overly baroque, but it occurs to me that for every ethnographic project there are at least three fieldsites in constant overlap. There is the real fieldsite where flesh and blood people deal with a flesh and blood ethnographer(s); there is, as I suggested earlier, the fieldsite of the ethnographic text, which is not at all coterminous with the real fieldsite even if the audience imagines it as such; and, finally, there is the mythos of the fieldsite, a mythos that includes all the storied fieldsites. I doubt that these three fieldsites can be purified of each other. Indeed, theirs is an intricate threefold relationship. Of the three, the first is, of course, the most important, but convincing claims about the first require the transformative processes of the second and third.

17. For details concerning fieldwork methods and work prior to the dissertation, see chapters one and three of Cintron (1990).

18. The end results of this project consisted of a number of oral histories collected on audiotape and deposited with the local historical museum. In addition, two essays were published, one by Carr (1992) and another by Cintron (1992).

19. See Heath (1983) and Scollon and Scollon (1981).

20. In the history of anthropology, a constant theme is a deep-seated doubt about the viability of its key terms. Compare the following quotations from Edward Sapir and Roger Rouse. Here are different ideologies and different moments in time; nevertheless, their conclusions are similar. In 1932, Sapir said, ". . . the term 'society' is itself a cultural construct which is employed by individuals who stand in significant relations to each other in order to help them in the interpretation of certain aspects of their behavior. The true locus of culture is in the interactions of specific individuals and, on the subjective side, in the world of meanings which each one of these individuals may unconsciously abstract for himself from his participation in these interactions . . ." (reprinted in Sapir 1949, 151). He continues: "The concept of culture, as it is handled by the cultural anthropologist, is necessarily something of a statistical fiction. . . . It is not the concept of culture which is subtly misleading but the metaphysical locus to which culture is generally assigned" (153–54).

Sapir's construction of the culture concept as a fiction relies heavily on his sense of the individual as a psychological entity whose behavior is not fully determinable by his or her culture, partly because every "culture" has a number of subcultures. Nearly sixty years later, Rouse (1991) also suggests that terms like "community," "culture," and "identity" are fictions, but his postmodernist (or poststructuralist) notions originate from the deconstruction of essentialism coupled with a reading of recent social forces, including the emergence of global economies and the telecommunications industry: "Thus, in the United States as well as in Mexico, the *place* of the putative community . . . is becoming little more than a *site* in which transnationally organized circuits of capital, labor, and communications intersect with one another and with local ways of life. In these circumstances, it becomes increasingly difficult to delimit a singular national identity and a continuous history. . . . But it is not just the image of the community which is compromised. The image of center and periphery is also coming under increasing strain" (16–17).

21. See Sebeok (1991).

22. See Heath (1983) and de Certeau (1988).

23. See Michele Rosaldo (1980, 28).

24. See Appadurai (1993, 269–95).

2 MAPPING/TEXTING

1. See Pratt (1986) and Geertz (1988), both of whom discuss scenes of first contact.

2. Firth (1957, 1).

3. My thanks to Jane Nicholson and Fredric Will, both of whom have helped me flesh out the term "discourses of measurement." The term first emerged during fieldwork as I explored in my field notes a pervasive set of practices, styles of thought, and ways of speaking that seemed to maintain the structures of power, indeed, to divide those who had more power from those who had less. I explain the term in greater detail in chapter 7, but here is an initial statement: the discourses of measurement have everything to do with the emergence and maintenance of modernity and the consequent defining of what it means to be more modern (more powerful) and less modern (less powerful).

Let me provide one example. A characteristic of the discourses of measurement is an increase of precison (or the fiction of such an increase). The evolution of a discourse of measurement first emerges from a kind of unconscious, dumb amorphousness. In circumscribing, articulating, and defining that amorphousness, the discourse of measurement frees itself by making the amorphousness an object of study. In time, the discourse of measurement represents an awareness, an understanding, an improvement, something modern. For instance, Scheper-Hughes in *Death Without Weeping* (1992) describes such folk medical terms as *delírio de fome* and states that this term refers to "hunger before it was understood in the medical academy as 'protein-calorie' or 'protein-energy' malnutrition" (137). She persuasively notes that the average daily caloric intake of the *Nordestino* rural workers is 1,500 to 1,700 and compares this to caloric estimations at the Buchenwald concentration camp (1,750) and a "classic scientific study of human starvation" that gradually reduced caloric intake to 1,570 (157). Hughes would probably agree—even though it is not her point—that *delírio de fome* represents a set of practices, a style of thought, and a way of speaking borrowed from the past, while modern medicine's caloric measurements represent another set of practices, another style of thought, and way of speaking, in short, a discourse of measurement. The juxtaposition of this discourse to a folk discourse is part of a power imbalance, and from that imbalance emerges, among the "folk," structures of magical imitation, envy, humiliation, and sometimes violent resistance.

It is my contention that modern life represents a headstrong push toward ever more complete and powerful discourses of measurement that are themselves fueled by the opportunity of profit. The result is that societies rapidly make and remake themselves leaving a variety of eddies spinning in the wake. Many of our class, racial, and ethnic divisions are loci for the tensions and power imbalances wrought by the discourses of measurement in relationship to "folk" discourses.

4. Compare my statements to Mark Monmonier's in *How to Lie with Maps* (1991) "A good map tells a multitude of little white lies; it suppresses truth to help the user see what needs to be seen. Reality is three-dimensional, rich in detail, and far too factual to allow a complete yet uncluttered two-dimensional graphic scale model. Indeed, a map that did not generalize would be useless. But the value of a map depends on how well its generalized geometry and generalized content reflect a chosen aspect of reality" (25).

5. Dan and I analyzed the 1990 census for Angelstown, examining the percentage of Spanish origin, household incomes, and median home values for each census tract. Our findings indicate that the areas in which we did our fieldwork had the highest percentage of Spanish origin (72 percent), among the lowest of household incomes ($27,315), and among the lowest of median home values ($53,200). Interestingly, there was one census tract to the southeast of where we lived that had a lower household income ($14,036), a lower medium home value ($49,200), and only a small percentage of Spanish origin (14.3 percent). Poverty in Angelstown clearly was not just Latino; it was also African-American and White. In contrast, the census tracts most associated with the rhetoric of meandering streets (located on the far west, the far east, and the far northeast) had negligible Spanish origin populations, median home values well above $100,000, and household incomes of at least $50,000 or significantly higher.

6. Le Corbusier (1947, 28–30). Notice how Le Corbusier weaves such themes as mastery, control, and the power of the elite—themes that I explore in chapter 7 when discussing the discourses of measurement—into his arguments for city grids and rational city planning. But Le Corbusier's rationalism was not sterile. His writings in *The Radiant City* are oddly eccentric, brilliant, and humane—as much of his architecture; nevertheless, his later work in India is "part of the cataclysmic encounter of what we now call the Third World with the West" (Prasad 1987, 286). Closer to home, the work of Le Corbusier is the model for Chicago's infamous Cabrini-Green project (Kiamin 1993, sec. 13, 4) a hothouse that encourages drug sales and gang violence that are closely related to similar activities only forty miles away in Angelstown. In many ways, modernist architecture has been a global project blind to its alienating effects. Nevertheless, I need to note that Le Corbusier was probably wrong to link city grids and rational city planning to modernity. Archaeologists have excavated a number of ancient cities and found evidence of city planning, including, but not limited to, streets laid in grid patterns.

7. My use of the word "colonization" is inspired by Benedict Anderson's *Imagined Communities* (1991), particularly the chapter "Census, Map, Museum." Whereas he considers the "real" colonization of Southeast Asia by Europeans wielding censuses, maps, and museums, I apply the term closer to home to explain the management of people and land. The term "colonization" here, then, functions more metaphorically, but it helps me to construct the shared ground that helps centralized power of various kinds to extend its control.

8. See Cintron (1992) and Carr (1992).

9. During the mid-1980s, city leaders in Angelstown decided to request a special census count. A group, including myself, were asked to help with the counting of Latinos because it was feared that illegal immigrants would not be counted and, therefore, that the census would not report the actual number of Latinos. Whether or not the final count was "accurate" is doubtful, but since the city got the higher count and, therefore, extra revenues, the city was satisfied. We can always raise doubts about the ability of any discourse of measurement "to get things right"; however, a more radical response might admit that even if a discourse of measurement accomplished its goal, would its accomplishment be a significant distortion of the real lives of people? For instance, take the Don Angel after whom this book is named. The Don Angel whom I know exists very differently within census counts. There, he is "Hispanic," speaks only Spanish, has an income that places him among the working poor, and can be used as a statistic to generate for the city grant revenues that he will never see. As we will see, however, even Don Angel, who lives a remarkably simple life compared with others, embodies a kind

of elusiveness and complexity that statistics, which are used for the making of social policy, cannot contain.

10. Gadamer (1992, 350).

11. Fraser (1993, 4).

12. Slang term for *rancheros*. A disparaging term, it is used by young people in the neighborhood to label traditional Mexicans who may or may not have come from *ranchitos*, small farming communities. I explore the term in greater detail in chapter 3.

13. For other discussions of the history of Angelstown, see Carr (1992), Cintron (1992), and Palmer (1986).

14. I quote McCarty from a 1963 publication, which I will call *Angelstown in the Beginning* to mask Angelstown's true identity.

15. Pratt (1986).

16. Again I quote McCarty from *Angelstown in the Beginning* (1963).

17. A notion of "place" was, of course, very much an important aspect of Native-American ideology, indeed, something worth fighting for as is clearly evident in the *Life of Black Hawk*, which is a history of the Sac war leader, Màkataimeshekiàkiàk (Black Hawk), as told to and translated by Antoine Leclair at the request of Black Hawk. It was the defeat of Black Hawk in the early 1830s that opened the region to settlers such as the McCartys. Black Hawk's account is quite clear about the border lines of the Potawatomis, Sioux, and other neighboring groups. His account suggests, again, that embedded inside the term "wandering" was an ethnocentric interpretation that implicitly, if not explicitly, justified a different sort of society organized around the conversion of land and other forms of property into economic livelihood.

18. *Angelstown in the Beginning* (1963).

19. For further information, see Carr (1992) and Cintron (1992).

20. As a teacher of writing, I am tempted to compare further the sort of standardization just discussed to standardized written language. Granted, this is an eccentric comparison, but in making linkages of this sort I hope to expose what may be the ideological roots that nourish more general cultural practices and make these practices coherent with each other. The result of all this coherence is the emergence of a kind of common sense that may operate in onerous ways in daily life.

Here, then, is my understanding of standardized writing, its emergence, and the service it performs:

Standardized writing relies on two systems of order, the second more arbitrary than the first. First, there is a kind of primary order, which consists of linguistic conventions (phonological, morphological, syntactic, semantic, and pragmatic), that underlies the almost automatic speech of a native speaker. The speaker need not place any conscious attention on mastering the conventions or his or her birth dialect. And these conventions continue to function as one becomes a writer of one's speech. However, mastering standardized writing in the American educational setting also entails the mastery of a secondary order that forces an increasing self-consciousness upon the apprentice. In making language visible, a new set of uncomfortable operations (spelling rules, punctuation marks, dialectical and stylistic appropriateness, linguistic brevity and clarity, rhetorical effectiveness, and the insistence that language must bear the burdens of thought and/or emotions) help to convert language into an object that can be manipulated. In conquering language in these sorts of ways, we have created a blueprint for a more complex conquering of the rest of the life world and fashioned a discourse to effect that conquering. Language in becoming disciplined via writing is ready to discipline the world in its own image. But who will do the disciplining of the world? The minds and bodies of each generation are disciplined into and by the discourses of measurement as the raw discourse of each student is submitted to years of shaping.

21. See Carr (1992) and Cintron (1992).

22. Cintron (1990, 42); Palmer (1986).

23. M. A. Schumacher, "Early Settlers Were Founders of St. Nicholas, *Gazette*, Centennial Edition, sec. 6, 73.

24. "Hits Mexican First," *Gazette*, January 1920, 1.

25. See Palmer (1986), Carr (1992), and Cintron (1992) for oral history interviews in Angelstown and Kerr (1976) for Chicago.

26. Information concerning the night school was derived from a series of Reports of Board of Education. The Angelstown school district published these annually for a number of years, and I examined the ones between 1913 and the 1940s. Some of my findings were published in Cintron (1992).

27. For more detailed descriptions of these three waves of Latinos, see Carr (1992) and Cintron (1992).

28. The 1974 date is taken from a 1976 publication by the Angelstown Bicentennial Commission that I will call *The Angelstown Story* to mask Angelstown's true identity.

29. For a fuller account of the tensions in Angelstown, see Carr (1992) and Cintron (1990, 1992).

3 LOOKING FOR DON ANGEL

1. See Clanchy (1979) for an excellent history of the evolution of official documents and the emergence of practical literacy. The following passages do not describe birth certificates, for instance, but they explain the practices of record keeping as they emerged in Europe. Of course, record keeping in the Middle East for taxes, sales of land, and such were already well established thousands of years before the birth of Christ.

> Although after 1300 many private charters still bear no date, forms of dating had become firmly established and commonplace. In general, after much preliminary hesitation, writers had got the measure of time. But because dating had evolved at the slow pace at which literate habits became acceptable, rather than being arbitrarily imposed by Roman law, English methods of dating documents remained complex and inconsistent. From a historical point of view, this variety of methods is a memorial to the formation of literate habits reflecting both feudal and Christian ways of thought. The evolution of the dating of documents is a measure of growing confidence in their usefulness as records.
>
> Everyone agreed that legal documents like charters must be signed, but there was as much diversity of opinion about what constituted a valid signature as there was about what made a date appropriate. As with dating, this diversity suggests that ways were being sought which would prove acceptable both to non-literate traditionalists and to experts in records. By and large in Mediterranean Europe notarial practice was preferred for authenticating documents as for dating them. A notary provided safeguards against forgery usually by writing the document in his own hand and by appending to it his name and an individual *signum* which he drew with a pen (241).

2. Ibid., 7: "It is possible that Englishmen became exceptionally conscious of records as a direct consequence of the Norman Conquest. Making records is initially a product of distrust rather than social progress."

3. Ibid., 56–57: "In the twelfth century to 'record' something meant to bear oral witness, not to produce a document. . . . The spoken work was the legally valid record and was superior to any document. . . . In Henry II's reign Glanvill's treatise provides the text of a writ which orders a sheriff to have a plea 'recorded' (*recordari*) in his county court, and then he is to convey his 'record' (*recordum*) to the king's court by four knights. It is evident that the knights convey the record

orally, as the parties to the plea are ordered to come to 'hear the record'. . . . Fifty years later [1250 or so], however, . . . no longer are four knights required, but only two, as their word is now of secondary importance. This change, from an oral to a predominantly written procedure, appears to have occurred in John's reign."

4. Speech act theory also helps us to understand these documents. "I hereby certify . . ." and "this is to certify that . . ." seem to be performatives (Austin 1978; Wardhaugh 1986, 274–79). Something is not just being said; something is being done. Whereas performatives in speech act theory occur in oral language, the performatives examined here are written. Both Clanchy's (1979) historical analysis and speech act theory, then, have allowed us to understand these documents as having roots in oral language but acquiring, with the shift to writing, a sense of action somewhat independent of the body.

5. See Cintron (1993).

6. Briggs (1988) has recorded a very similar phrase with essentially the same meaning, *los viejitos de antes*, that circulated in the New Mexican communities that he has worked in.

7. More words that have been difficult to track in dictionaries of Mexican indigenous languages: *norni varajini junguni* (in Spanish: ¿Cómo estás? ¿Gusta usted algo? "How are you? May I help you?" or "Would you like something?" and *chuscutas conc tacsines* (in Spanish: *tortillas con frijoles*, "tortillas with beans"). These phrases were told to Edmundo and me by a practicing *curandera* originally from the state of Colima but now living in Angelstown. She memorized these phrases as a little girl, and they had been memorized by a parent. She spelled them out phonetically, having no other idea what they might look like. They were supposedly Tarascan, another indigenous language. This claim is suspect because of their formulaic character as greetings modeled on Spanish politeness forms and the similarity between *con* and *conc*, "with," suggesting that the supposed Tarascan had already absorbed a considerable amount of Spanish. I point out these phrases in order to suggest that Don Angel's stock of indigenous words—if that, indeed, was what they were—was not uncommon in Angelstown. Did their existence as isolated words and phrases in the memories of intimate elders suggest, again, the slow subjugation of indigenous culture at the feet of a more public Spanish culture?

8. These objectifying processes—for instance, the making of transcripts from interviews—by which ethnographers make data of the fieldsite and eventually construct the fieldsite of the text, which is not exactly the same as the actual fieldsite, are worth considering in the light of recent critiques of the experimental turn in ethnography. Wolf (1992), for example, criticized

the current enthusiasm for form at the expense of content that may characterize experimental ethnographers. For her, such enthusiasms violated the "ethical assumptions" of the ethnographers' craft (59). I believe that what she did not emphasize sufficiently, however, was that any ethnographer—even those who do not wish to emphasize form or write "fictions"— must create objects of analysis that are profoundly distanced from the ebb and flow of the actual fieldsite. The result is that ethnographers, more often than not, analyze not fieldsites themselves but a set of mediating objects that are both related to and yet distanced from the fieldsite. These mediating objects inevitably threaten the ethos of all writers of ethnographies whether or not they wish to experiment, emphasize form, or write "fiction." In the face of this gap that will not close between experience and the experience analyzed, I, nevertheless, offer my metaphor of "umbilical connection" so as to acknowledge the importance of maintaining ethos. See also Urban (1991). His distinction is between the discourses of the native and the metadiscourses of anthropologists, the latter including at times the metadiscourses of natives. As with Wolf, he too insists on some sort of alignment (umbilical cord) between the object and its interpretation in order to prevent "chicanery and illusion" (27–28).

9. Nuckolls (1991) explored the use of sound during oral performances among nonliterate lowland Ecuadorean Quechua speakers. Her claim, if I understood it was that the nonliterate performative style is a repertoire that enhances the verbal.

10. The word *chero* was broadly applied and not easily defined. For instance, two girls told me one day that they didn't like *cheros* because they were always "hitting" on young girls. Indeed, *cheros* were often young single males, but many were not. In the last chapter of this book, I distinguish between "rural *cheros*" and "urban *cheros*," a distinction that was provided by another pair of young people from the community. Don Angel, for instance, was considered a rural *chero*. Moreover, those adults in the neighborhood who thought themselves a bit better off or more educated also used the term *ranchero* to distance themselves from the distinctive *chero* or *ranchero* style. At any rate, my understanding of what I have taken to be a very significant street term emerged as a contrast with other street terms such as "with it" and "contemporary," terms that I have further translated as suggesting the "modern."

11. According to Forrest (1984), *matachin* dances have existed among the Pueblo in New Mexico and among the Yaqui and Tarahumara in Mexico, to name a few. Surprisingly, the dances originated in Europe, and one can find references to *matachin* dancers in sixteenth-century European accounts. It is thought that the Spanish brought the dances to the New World where they mixed with indigenous traditions.

Forrest described the dances as religious celebrations, and Don Angel agreed that they were essentially Catholic. Don Angel's regalia, however, was unlike those depicted in Forrest's book. His headgear, for instance, was distinctly Native-American and not reminiscent of a bishop's mitre. Also he held a ritual bow and arrow in his left hand rather than a trident. Briggs (1988, 51) also has pictures of New Mexican *matachin* dancers taken in 1976, and these costumes, again, were distinctly unlike Don Angel's.

12. A possible interpretation of this short passage might claim that Don Angel was referring to "seeing" or hearing the stories themselves rather than the practices referred to by the stories and, most importantly, rather than the efficacy of the practices in which indeed lost animals were found or hidden truths divined or wild animals kept at bay by a *reata*, and so on. That he meant he saw particular people performing particular practices rather than merely hearing about the practices is clear in the tape recordings; however, whether he also saw the efficacy of the practices is less clear, for Don Angel maintained, as I said earlier, his own brand of skepticism that tended to compromise his relationships to *los viejitos*.

13. See Octavio Paz (1988, 12): "New Spain (Mexico of the sixteenth, seventeenth, and eighteenth centuries) was a historical reality that ran counter to the current of Western civilization, that is, against the flow of emerging modernity. The second, the Republic of Mexico, was a hasty adaptation of that modernity, which has distorted our traditions without making us a truly modern nation."

14. Irene Campos Carr (personal conversation) in her work on working-class Mexican women in Angelstown also reported extensive lewd joking. She has used lewd joking and various other kinds of evidence to challenge the stereotype of the passive, obedient Latina.

15. The question of degradation is one taken up by Limón (1989) in his study of similar verbal games among Mexican-Americans in south Texas. Famous observers of Mexican culture, such as Octavio Paz, have also maintained the degradation argument. Limón correctly, in my view, argues against this interpretation because it supports the views of those in power by stereotyping the lower-class male: "This interpretive tradition unintentionally helps to ratify dominance through its negative psychologistic interpretation of the Mexican male lower class and their language" (472).

Limón attempts to construct a more Marxist interpretation that sees verbal play as a "temporary forum of non-alienation" (479). For Limón, during this kind of verbal gaming a variety of lower-class markers become transformed into markers of prestige that explicitly resist the social structures that determine those who have more power from those who have less. It should be clear that my own interpretation of a game of *albures* among *mexicanos* in Angelstown has much in common with Limón's interpretations of similar verbal games among Mexican-Americans in south Texas.

16. I have not said much about things Chicano for the simple reason that the term was virtually nonexistent in Angelstown. Mexican immigrants referred to themselves as *mexicanos*, and the children of the immigrants sometimes called themselves that or Mexican. For instance, I recall hearing the term "Chicano" in the neighborhoods of Angelstown on two occasions among teenage girls who, in fact, were talking about never having heard it before until recently but, nevertheless, liked the term for themselves.

17. See Bakhtin (1988).

18. See Halliday (1978, 36).

19. See Limón (1989).

20. See Bakhtin (1988).

21. See de Certeau (1988).

22. Ibid., 172.

23. For a fuller discussion concerning the statistical methods used for measuring literacy, the wide discrepancy concerning the number of illiterates in the United States, and further case studies that suggest that standardized measurements of illiteracy are unreliable; see Cintron (1990).

24. See Hernadi (1988).

4 A BOY AND HIS WALL

1. Valerio's father worked in the United States, oftentimes illegally, for a number of years before bringing the family north. See Cintron (1990) for further information.

2. A specialty item resembling beef tips and prepared in many of the Mexican grocery stores in Angelstown. For a while, Valerio's father worked in one of these grocery stores and was known as an excellent cook of *carnitas*.

3. See Carr (1992) and Cintron (1992).

4. In making a distinction between a structuralist orientaition and a meaning-making one, I am following the path of writing research and theory as developed in the United States since the late 1960s and early 1970s. Unlike most researchers and theorists of writing instruction, however, I hesitate to say that signifi-

cant reform results from a meaning-making orientation. I elaborate these arguments toward the end of the book in my discussions on literacy training.

5. See Cintron (1990) for details.

6. In my view, reflective and self-reflective languages do not necessarily liberate. When schooling encourages them, for instance, they can become all too easily another set of mystifications that serve to separate those who think reflectively from those who don't, in short, those who are being groomed to manage from those who are to be managed. For instance, those who may become future managers may display success at "critical thinking"—another term, perhaps, for reflective and self-reflective languages—while those who display less success may be on a different route. Such a system, I believe, had already placed Valerio and his family in the to-be-managed category. However, one can never predict the emergence of reflective and self-reflective languages. For instance, they can appear despite a lack of schooling success and certainly outside of schooling. I address these possibilities tangentially in chapter 6.

7. *How does one create respect within conditions of little or no respect?* I am sensitive to the problem of "questions" generating research and answers being the conclusions of that research. In Cintron (1993), I argue that the question/answer structure of researchers is a rhetorical device. The apparent genetic relationship that binds research questions and their answers may be a satisfying bit of artifice, but just outside the hubris of the question/answer structure is the messiness of phenomena, recalcitrant and hard to herd.

8. See Pérez (1991) for a personal account of how he and others earned money in the United States to be used in Mexico.

9. Benjamin (1986) said: "Each epoch not only dreams the next, but also, in dreaming, strives toward the moment of waking" (162). Benjamin was keenly aware that for several hundred years, Western culture has fantasized a future of technological mastery. From such fantasies, it has created designs and images that try to appropriate that future. But, alas, when the actual future arrives, we realize that those former designs and images defined the age in which they were drawn rather than any future. What was once meant to look modern, even futuristic (American car design during the 1950s and 1960s might be one example) comes to look antique.

10. My analysis of the hyperbolic and Susan Stewart's analyis of the gigantic in *On Longing: Narratives of the Miniature, the Gigantic, the Souvenir, the Collection* (1993) have much in common. The breadth of her investigations include Western high and public cultures, whereas I use the term "hyperbolic" in more

limited fashion as a heuristic to uncover certain cultural formations and private imaginings in a particular fieldsite. Nevertheless, when she says that "the gigantic represents infinity, exteriority, the public, and the overly natural" (70) as well as technology, she is wording insights similar to my own but conceiving them more broadly.

11. A large exhibition hall in Chicago.

12. Pachucos were young Mexican-origin males of the 1930s, 1940s, and 1950s who chose to display themselves with distinctive dialects and attire rather than assimilating many of the mainstream conventions. Although Pachucos were a distinctive part of the L.A. scene, the term was also common where I grew up in the south Texas high schools of the early sixties. Low-riders, particularly during the fifties, were distinctly decorated cars, sometimes with elaborate hydraulic systems, that inhabited the same self-conscious space as Pachucos, neither traditional Mexican nor Anglo. Incidentally, there are at least two commercial magazines, one called *Low Rider*, targeted to Latino/a audiences in which some of the continuity between low-riders of the past and thumpers of the present can be seen.

13. Did such posters exist? I suspect so because the styles themselves were highly commercialized, particularly in Latino communities (car exhibitions, contests, magazines), even if the names "thumper" and "Too Low Flow" were more local or regional.

14. At different times, Valerio had also expressed the desire to be a pilot, a Marine, or someone who didn't have to work as hard as his father.

15. One need only point to another kind of iconography, food, to understand my point. For instance, I remember seeing an international recipe book sold for a while on *Sábado Gigante*, a famous Saturday night variety show originating from Miami and appearing on Spanish language television. The reach of the show spans the Caribbean and North and South America. While doing research, I watched the show often with friends, but I have also watched the show with my own family. The recipe book consisted of typical dishes from every Latino country and seemed to invent a kind of pan-Hispanic middle class as its targeted audience. In my interpretation, these *platos* were also local iconographies now internationalized. In so being, they continued the histories of other foods, which have been diffused from original locations and eventually absorbed by distant ones (for instance, spices from the East over many centuries became Europeanized).

16. Examining these images of Arabic culture in the midst of Mexican images was particularly intriguing at this time. Edmundo and I had just completed some interviews with Latino youths who were members of a mostly African-American street gang, the Vicelords, a gang that relies somewhat on Muslim imagery and ritual. For instance, the Latinos described "praying in Muslim," of bowing to the east toward Mecca, and of avoiding the eating of pork. Here too was an example of local iconographies becoming international but, in this case, coming to rest among Latinos in order to express a mostly African-American militancy whose style had become theirs.

17. See Limón (1994) for an incisive account.

18. From Appadurai (1993): "The United States is no longer the puppeteer of a world system of images, but is only one node of a complex transnational construction of imaginary landscapes. . . . The imagination is now central to all forms of agency, is itself a social fact, and is the key component of the new global order" (273–74).

5 THE LOGIC OF VIOLENCE/ THE LOGIC OF TRUST

1. I borrow the term "fight stories" from Shuman (1986).

2. See Gramsci (1995).

3. See Roy (1994).

4. Ibid., 149–50.

5. Ibid.

6. Pierre Bourdieu and Jean-Claude Passeron (1994, 218).

7. Gramsci (1995, 324).

8. My last comment raises a number of ethnographic difficulties that ought to be aired out at least in an endnote. Other ethnographers have made magnifying glasses of these questions and burned holes into their own texts and the texts of others (see Stephen Tyler's infamous "Postmodern Ethnography: From Document of the Occult to Occult Document" [1987] and Steven Sangren's caustic reply "Rhetoric and the Authority of Ethnography: Postmodernism and the Social Reproduction of Texts" [1988]). I speak less operatically, but if, as I have said, a structured hidden is invisible to the eyes of those who appear in ethnographies, how should readers interpret the ethnographer's interpretations of any hidden? In short, where is the hidden? Is it out there in the social scene? Is it part of the ethnographer's fantasy life? Is it in both places? Moreover, how is it that the seer who sees the enigma is more a social outsider than an insider, and how many seers does it take to authentically clarify the enigma? Ethnographies that pretend to some sort of social science realism, and most do, including this one (despite its very pronounced wink), utilize a set of

procedures that will ground them in a kind of real. For instance, one of the classic procedures is to ask informants to comment on one's interpretations: "See, here's what I've found operating inside of you and in the social situation that you inhabit. Do you think I've got it right?" For those readers who wish to critique my interpretations in this chapter, I asked Martin that question, more or less, on a Sunday in 1995 in a crowded pancake house as he ate an enormous breakfast while Edmundo and I waited for him to finish reading an earlier draft of this chapter. I was most surprised when he said: "Yeah, this sounds about right—and I particularly liked the stuff about the light bulb, like a detective story." Was his interpretation transparent with my own? I don't think so. His confirmations were too glib for my tastes. He did see something of himself and his social situation, but, for the most part, he was looking for something easy to read, fast-paced—a detective story. In contrast, I was struggling to unpack what was mostly hidden from his own view and that of others, an enmeshment of innerscapes and outerscapes by which violence, particularly vengeance, becomes logically justifiable, in short, an ideologic. I have no important conclusions to draw about these ethnographic problems that seem to constantly bugger ethnography. I suspect, however, that a theory of the hidden of the sort that I am trying to develop here is at the core of good ethnography, for it is the unpacking of a hidden that compels an ethnographer to forge ahead. Simultaneously, this same hidden remains somewhat unverifiable no matter what procedures or techniques are used, and so if one insists on a dream of social science realism, this obdurate thing called the hidden will, more than likely, bugger it. Better, then, to find some way to accommodate two dreams, that of social science realism and artifice making.

9. See Dentan (1992).

10. An editorial titled "Put up that blue . . . but also keep yellow" (in the 2 June 1991 *Gazette* articulated the sentiments of city leaders: "Deployed to a hostile landscape to do battle against a potentially ruthless enemy, Desert Storm veterans say home support, as evidenced by photographs and news accounts of entire cities and villages decked out in flags and yellow ribbons from coast to coast, helped keep spirits high and motivation at the ready. . . . There is, however, another war—replete with its own armed force deployed to often-hostile landscapes to do battle with ruthless enemies—at hand, and it is going on every day right in our midst. . . . Backing from the Angelstown City Council, Police Department and municipal administration, led to last Tuesday's 'Blue-Ribbon Summer' rally, at which Mayor Jones [a pseudonym], urging broad community support for police efforts to combat gangs and drugs, told a crowd of 250: 'Blue is our color, and we're going to show our color in every neighborhood of the city this summer to show that this is our city.' "

11. The job loss never did manifest but remained an ongoing insecurity for a number of years. Even though this period was particularly hard for family members, I had seen them earlier endure a severe van accident that involved all family members, a constant shortage of cash (each parent earned six to seven dollars per hour, and there were seven members to support), and mysterious blackouts and periods of "nervousness" that overtook the mother and were diagnosed as stress and job related. (She worked in quality control at her factory.) Despite these events, the family was relatively buoyant, and I had seen more complex conditions in other families that I occasionally lived with and still other families that I regularly visited.

12. In his substantial study of street gangs, *Islands in the Street* (1991), Martin Jankowski said: "There have been some studies of gangs that suggest that many gang members have tough exteriors but are insecure on the inside. This is a mistaken observation. Although it may be somewhat disconcerting, in the vast majority of cases, the nut that has a hard shell has a tough kernel too—that is, the individual believes in himself and has strong resolve" (27). My discussion of the "pose" is meant to include a variety of scenes and situations that involved gang members. On the one hand, then, it would seem that Jankowski's observation challenges my own; on the other hand, throughout Jankowski's book there is considerable discussion of the factors that cause gang violence: "fear, ambition, frustration, and personal/group testing of skills" (140). These factors are consistent with my own observations/interpretations. More importantly, however, my description of the "pose" as covering pain attempts to evoke an innerscape from which the reader can understand pain as an important dynamic activating a need for ambition, or a need to test oneself against others, or a need for power.

6 GANGS AND THEIR WALLS

1. Street gangs have been studied by social scientists for a considerable amount of time. The perspective, as one might expect, has been that of social science realism. For instance, the amount of fieldwork behind Jankowski's *Islands in the Street* (1991) has been far more wide-ranging than my own. But the work of Conquergood (1992) in Chicago has been more relevant to my text because it has dealt with street gangs aligned to those in Angelstown and, more importantly, because his approach to culture as performative and my own as rhetorical have been very similar and sharply different from the goals of traditional social science. The work of Padilla (1993) has also been relevant because of its Chicago focus.

2. These quotations come from a variety of conversations and other sources.

3. One weekend someone associated with the Insane Deuces was visiting me in Iowa City, which is about a

four-hour drive from Angelstown and the home of the Iowa Hawkeyes. Black and gold are prominent in the city, particularly on a football weekend. We drove through one area of the town in which different *coronas* were the logos of different businesses including a motel chain. He jokingly remarked that the whole city was owned by the Latin Kings. To be immersed in a specialized language is to translate automatically the world into that system—sometimes jokingly, sometimes seriously.

4. I borrow the term "antisociety" from Halliday (1978), who also analyzed with rich results the term "antilanguage": "An antisociety is a society that is set up within another society as a conscious alternative to it. It is a mode of resistance, resistance which may take the form either of passive symbiosis or of active hostility and even destruction" (164). I would emphasize in Halliday's interpretation the notion that an antisociety is thoroughly imbricated in the dominant society so that its ability to resist may even depend on imitating many of the structures of the dominant society.

5. Street gangs have also been a fund of iconography and a cash resource for the mainstream. A few years ago the *Wall Street Journal* ran an article discussing the marketing of a new beer with ads showing a young African-American male wearing sunglasses and a hoodie (slang term in Angelstown for an athletic sweater with a hood) and throwing up a gang hand-sign. The marketing of gangster rap, certain movies, and clothing apparel also rely on the imagery of street gangs. Such examples reinforce the notion that the mainstream or dominant society is economically enmeshed in its "antisociety" and can utilize it as a source of legal profit.

6. The story about the war between the Deuces and the Kings is an important one because, for all practical purposes, it inaugurated a level of gang violence that Angelstown had never seen before. Traditionally, in the Chicago area the Insane Deuces and the Latin Kings along with other gangs have belonged to the same confederation, the People, and have been aligned against another traditional confederation, the Folks. In the late 1980s, however, a war broke out between the Kings and Deuces. Like any war, a number of specific events led to its escalation. According to those to whom I've talked, an inaugural event was a drug deal that went sour and led to one gang believing that they had been set up by the other. Another event was that a well-known Latin Queen left her high-ranking King boyfriend and began dating a Deuce. Killings ensued that escalated into a number of revenge killings. The Deuces broke ranks with the People and sought aid from their traditional enemies in the Folks confederation. The Insane Gangster Satan's Disciples Nation (sometimes known as the Spanish Disciples) and the Maniac Latin Disciples

Nation were Folks gangs who seriously jumped into the fray. The Latin Kings were left with only one major ally, the Vicelords. At one point, representatives from the People confederation in Chicago were said to have tried to mediate or at least dampen the war, but their actions failed. Rather quickly, Angelstown became known as a rogue city whose gangs had broken traditional alliances and forged new ones. The upshot was a permanent realignment that spread throughout Illinois in which all Deuce chapters broke with their former allies, the People confederation, and linked themselves to their former enemies, the Folks confederation. One result of this realignment was a steady increase in gang-related homicides despite a "no tolerance" police campaign during the early 1990s. The Angelstown library staff compiled the following totals for gang-related homicides in Angelstown based on issues of the local newspaper (which I've called the *Gazette* in this book):

1990: 3
1991: 6
1992: 8
1993: 10
1994: 12
1995: 13
1996: 15

The Angelstown Police Department provided the totals shown in the following table.

Homicide Totals for Angelstown, 1991–95

	Gang-related homicides	Total homicides	Unsolved homicides
1991	7	13	3
1992	8	14	4
1993	9	20	7
1994	12	15	1
1995	13	25	3
Totals	**49**	**87**	**18**

According to the officer that I talked to, a significant number of the unsolved homicides are believed to be gang-related.

NOTE: The totals in the list above and in this table were reported to me over the telephone.

7. This stretch of graffiti contained, for me at least, a certain amont of ambiguity. At first, the upside down "A" throughout the graffiti even in the ALKN—clearly, the graffiti writer's own gang—would seem puzzling. A consistent interpretation was that it was disrespecting a gang called "Ambrose." A less consistent interpretation among gang members and police to whom I talked was that it was disrespecting the entire city of Angelstown.

8. Rodriguez (1993, 51–52, 41–42).

9. Aronowitz, (1993, 91).

10. De Certeau (1988, 37). I am grateful to Dan Anderson for first making this observation.

11. Aronowitz (1993).

12. Terms such as "subjectivity," "narratives of graffiti," and important concepts, such as the relationship between graffiti and the public sphere, were developed in conjunction with Dan Anderson.

13. Indeed, taking this idea one step farther, it would be interesting to consider the topos of nationhood in the narratives of First-Nation Peoples, among African-Americans (particularly the Nation of Islam), and within the Aryan Nation. In short, how does the same topos circulate among different marginalized groups compared to the middle class and elite of a "legitimate" nation? Another helpful source for this perspective other than *Nation and Narration* is Benedict Anderson's *Imagined Communities: Reflections on the Origin and Spread of Nationalism* (1991).

14. Bhabha (1991, 3).

15. Renan (1991, 19).

16. Shakur (1993).

17. Foucault (1988, ix–x).

18. Ibid., 115, 286. Perhaps a longer quotation will clarify further: "There must have formed, silently and doubtless over the course of many years, a social sensibility, common to European culture, that suddenly began to manifest itself in the second half of the seventeenth century; it was this sensibility that suddenly isolated the category destined to populate the places of confinement. To inhabit the reaches long since abandoned by the lepers, they chose a group that to our eyes is strangely mixed and confused. But what is for us merely an undifferentiated sensibility must have been, for those living in the classical age, a clearly articulated perception. It is this mode of perception which we must investigate in order to discover the form of sensibility to madness in an epoch we are accustomed to define by the privileges of Reason. The act which, by tracing the locus of confinement, conferred upon it its power of segregation and provided a new homeland for madness, though it may be coherent and concerted is not simple. It organizes into a complex unity a new sensibility to poverty and to the duties of assistance, new forms of reaction to the economic problems of unemployment and idleness, a new ethic of work, and also the dream of a city where moral obligation was joined to civil law, within the authoritarian forms of constraint. Obscurely, these themes are present during the construction of the cities of confinement and their organization. They give a meaning to this ritual, and explain in part the mode in which madness was perceived, and experienced, by the classical age" (45–46).

19. Richard Terdiman (1989) has grasped the same idea, but emphasized the oppositionality of counter discourses a bit more than I am inclined to, in the following: "For if 'modernity' is the name for a society increasingly regulated by discursive dominance, paradoxically the counter-discourse emerges as its crucially repressed secret, as the alternative whose exclusion defines the apparent stability of the social formation itself. . . . And such a notion redefines the ground upon which contestation—the conscious fore-grounding of otherwise repressed alternatives in the discursive realm—might stage its struggle and attempt its subversion" (342).

20. According to Hirschberg (1996), Death Row Records, started in 1992 and the most successful producer of gangsta rap, grossed more than $100 million in four years (26).

21. Fraser (1993, 15).

22. A week or so before the printing of the letter, it was reported in the same newspaper that Mothers Against Gangs had lost its backing from the county's Juvenile Court Services because of long-standing differences between the letter writer (the president of the group, who was in the process of resigning) and Court Services as well as the mayor of Angelstown. To the best of my knowledge, the arguments in the letter were not related to these political disputes.

23. I do not know whether the following observation is significant, but the writer's name was distinctly of Spanish origin.

24. The letters that I have selected were actually published *after* the newspaper's response. I chose to duplicate these letters, in part, because of the status of the writers in the community or because of the tone and arguments within the letters. The newspaper may have continued to publish the complaints after its public apology because of delays due to already filled "Letters to the Editor" sections or because, as did indeed happen, the front-page story continued to generate criticism even after the newspaper's apology.

25. The paraphrases and quotations for this paragraph have been taken primarily from two front-page articles, dated 24 August 1991 and 9 September 1991. I continue to not name the paper in order to mask the identity of the city.

26. Fraser (1993, 2).

27. I had one friend who collected every *Gazette* article on gangs that he found. He knew everyone who

appeared in the articles, having gone to school with most of the people or known about them on the street. He cut the articles out and pasted them onto paper. Later he became a gang member, but it would be egregiously simplistic to say that these events had a cause and effect relationship. Street gangs, in fact, were very distressing to him. As his old friends became notorious, he did not want to emulate them; nevertheless, he did keep track of them but as a kind of archivist collecting the present so that his memory might not fade. Still another friend, a gang leader close to my age, also collected gang-related newspaper articles. Again, these were stories about people whom he knew. I also suspect, however, that since he often had to investigate the facts behind certain "issues" relevant to his gang, the newspaper was one source, admittedly a poor one compared to his own contacts, for gathering information.

28. In Habermas's "Further Reflections on the Public Sphere," written decades after his inaugural work and incorporating the sorts of revisions inspired by Fraser and others, Habermas acknowledges the influence of contesting, smaller public spheres, and yet he does not let go of the need for rational discourse. Throughout this chapter, I have been describing the power of collective fear, something that Habermas and not even his critics seem to have acknowledged. See Habermas (1992, 421–61).

7 BLACKTOP

1. Douglas (1992).

2. Sometimes borrowed English terms or phrases might acquire Spanish prefixes or suffixes or some other structural characteristic or, more simply, a Spanish pronunciation. These borrowings are called *pochismos*. Examples: "taxas" for "taxes" (instead of the Spanish word *impuestos*), "estimado" for "estimate" (instead of the Spanish terms *cotización* or *presupuesto aproximado*), and an assortment of other terms such as "city hall," "mayor," and "bookkeeper." These particular *pochismos* suggest, to me at least, a certain structure of use among native Spanish speakers who have had to cope extensively and unexpectedly with American officialdom. In Angelstown, it seemed to me that certain aspects of power had become firmly coded in English, and this suggested to me that social dominance had insinuated itself, via the *pochismo*, into the daily talk of Spanish speakers. (See Sánchez [1983] for similar ideas.) As interesting as this interpretation may have been at the time, it is not one that I significantly pursued.

3. Pablo's murder surfaced again in 1996 during a discussion with a street gang leader. According to this man, Pablo's drug business operated at the next higher level compared to his own. Pablo competed with two other operators in Angelstown. The street gang leader, a significant supplier himself, had his own connections, but on occasion he did purchase directly from Pablo. It was clear to him that Pablo's murder concerned a drug deal gone bad.

4. One of these complications concerned Pablo's claim that he wanted to build a pharmacy/general store whereas the city claimed that his architect presented plans for a pharmacy/doctors' offices.

5. See Habermas (1987) and Lyotard (1984).

6. See Fuller (1992).

7. "As we know it, dirt is essentially disorder. There is no such thing as absolute dirt: it exists in the eye of the beholder. . . . Dirt offends against order. Eliminating it is not a negative movement, but a positive effort to organise the environment. . . . In chasing dirt, in papering, decorating, tidying we are not governed by anxiety to escape disease, but are positively reordering our environment, making it conform to an idea. . . . The ideal order of society is guarded by dangers which threaten transgressors. These danger-beliefs are as much threats which one man uses to coerce another as dangers which he himself fears to incur by his own lapses from righteousness. They are a strong language of mutual exhortation. At this level the laws of nature are dragged in to sanction the moral code. . . . The whole universe is harnessed to men's attempts to force one another into good citizenship. Thus we find that certain moral values are upheld and certain social rules defined by beliefs in dangerous contagion. . . ." (Douglas 1992, 2–3).

8. See Martin (1994) and Schmandt-Besserat (1989).

9. Time-keeping would seem to be a particularly interesting discourse of measurement, one that has been on the human scene for an extraordinarily long period of time. Its most recent versions, however, seem to be wildly hyperbolic, for in achieving a kind of prodigious exactness the conditions are set in which the smallest failure to be exact may have enormous chaotic consequences. In short, late modern time-keeping may be not only a technological necessity but also a parable of our times. In 1993, *Science News* reported that a new atomic clock was put into operation. The clock "will neither gain nor lose a second in the next million years" ("Starting up . . . , 276). *Time Magazine* also reported on the clock, saying that it will be twice as accurate as prior models ("Just in Time," 53). The need for this accuracy comes from telephone and computer networks that need "to synchronize the flow of trillions of bits of information," TV and radio stations that need "to time their broadcasts," the armed forces that need help in "satellite-based navigation" and "smart-missile guidance," and scientists that need to measure the "motions of continents across the surface of the earth and galaxies and stars across the sky" ("Just in Time," 53). In this search for exact

time-keeping, I also sense a cultural predilection to give magnitude to the infinitesimal and to use such procedures for knowledge making, indeed, to define knowledge largely as an accumulation of details.

10. My argument builds off of Sennett's in *The Conscience of the Eye: The Design and Social Life of Cities* (1990): "To mold a young human being, you must protect it from destructive outside influences. This belief, self-evident to us, was not at all self-evident to earlier ages, who practiced what would seem to us a shocking disregard of the young. . . . The notion that character develops and reveals itself in an interior marked by the division of labor spoke logically in the nineteenth century from the new importance placed on childhood development; partitioned shelter was necessary for this prolonged, difficult, perilous process. By contrast, the mixed confusions of a crowd, a street, a smoke-filled bar, seemed no place for the protracted process of developing a baby into an adult. The stimulations of the street lacked the sequential order of the rooms of a house. Self-development and the exposure to the city's differences thus became opposed in visual terms: the linear, interior order of unfolding, distinct scenes as in a railroad flat, versus the outside chaos, the street like a collage; the shelter of the sequential versus exposure to the synchronous" (30–31).

11. See Cintron (1990, 143).

12. My own views concerning the folkloric dance troop were aligned to but an extension of Cecilia's views and her brother's. My views ran very much against the grain of my friends who were Latino leaders and helped to promote the dance troop in the area. First, I should say that the dances were authentic in the sense that the teacher had taken folkloric dance courses at a special institute in his hometown of San Luis Potosí. Second, although I cannot describe all the ways traditional dances have functioned in Mexican society, one role has been to sentimentalize and idealize the past in order to create national identity, nation building, historical consciousness, and tourist dollars. Third, the role of the dance troop in the context of Angelstown was also complex. From the mostly adult perspective, the dance troop offered a chance for young people to learn something about their Mexican roots, it kept them "off the streets," and through tours in and out of the state, it provided an elect group of young people a set of professional experiences beyond anything available in the neighborhood. Indeed, it was a group of Mexican nuns from the local church who first organized the troop. I saw the troop as responding to local fragmentation by appealing to an image of quaint Mexico that had never existed. The nostalgia and nationalism of the dances themselves hid the socioeconomic disparities and resentments between Mexican peasants and elites that had forged the dances in the first place. By relying on this image of quaint Mexico, the troop gave

the Latino/a community of Angelstown a bit more focus even as it made the community more palatable and safer in the imaginations of Whites. Nevertheless, more and less alienated youth from the community saw through the illusion of "quaint Mexico" and the troop's aura of moral uprightness. Instead of feeling pride, they felt, as Cecilia said, "embarrassed" by the imagery of the old-fashioned and out-moded. The old-fashioned was the source of Mexico's wealth, its *chero* identity, and this meant, of course, that Mexico provided poor, "backward" immigrants as a labor force for American modernity. Even the dance director told me one day how sad he felt when he periodically returned to Mexico and saw its poverty compared to the wealth of the United States. For him, however, the dance troop was a way by which to recoup worth under conditions of nonworth, respect under conditions of no respect. His dancers, I presume, agreed, but the young people who laughed sarcastially or complained from the shadows were trying to construct their own versions of respect against the troop's "goody goodies" and upright future citizens.

13. If I were to summarize the complex passions behind the poignancy and loyal fierceness, I would say, "This is my raggedy ass and I'm proud of it—fuck you!" The "you" would be an ambiguous pronoun referring both to the neighborhood and to the Whites with money. However, these words, in part, are my artful invention because I never heard them phrased exactly that way. Because of this fact, I have not woven them into the main text but placed them here as a note, even though I feel that they capture rather precisely the complicated emotions not so much of adults but of a broad range of more and less alienated young people.

14. I have not talked in any detail about the *Cámara de Comercio*, also known as the Hispanic Chamber of Commerce. It was a divided group that sometimes split according to those who were involved in service organizations as opposed to real businesses, or according to those who spoke only Spanish as opposed to those who could easily negotiate both languages and cultures. Moreover, some saw the organization as having ineffective leaders not strong enough to get the group to agree. I knew many of its leaders and interviewed some of its members. Most of their stories have not directly entered the text but have, nevertheless, deeply informed it.

15. All of these restrictions controlling the behavior of peddlers and itinerant merchants have been taken from the current Code of Ordinances for the City of Angelstown.

16. The following quotation comes from an ad by the Mobil Corporation that ran on page A25 of the 9 September 1993 edition of the *New York Times:* "Teachers. They're the best and last defense if American hopes to remain competitive in the future. But will they

be able to get America's children ready for the stiff competition on tomorrow's global battlefield of technology when some of the most potent weapons are math and science literacy?" For another thirteen paragraphs, the ad amplifies its war and America-under-siege metaphors. This same issue of the *New York Times* contained a front-page article with the following heading: "Study Says Half of Adults in U.S. Can't Read or Handle Arithmetic." The results of this four-year federal study were discussed by Madeleine Kunin, Deputy Secretary of Education, on the evening of 9 September on a PBS news show. The reporter began the interview by calling the results of the study "a blunt fact." On the evening of 10 September another PBS news show discussed the study with the same gloom and doom.

These happenings on 9 and 10 September, I believe, constitute an example of the discourse of crisis attempting to solidify a national culture. Interestingly, the discourses of measurement are both the subject of the crisis (too many of our citizens have not adequately mastered these discourses) and the means (testing instruments, statistics) by which the crisis is identified. At any rate, fear and a sense of common struggle are summoned so as to whip the citizenry into action in order to preserve national identity (read: economic prosperity). By joining the "good fight," Mobil Corporation and the government are cast as heroic leaders. In my view, the urgency of such discourse is coercive, for the "crisis" suggests that the individual "citizen" must satisfy literacy standards (which become elusive phantoms as they escalate decade by decade) or suffer the humiliation of not earning enough to adequately support oneself. In short, human dignity is no longer a given—as the rhetoric of a democratic state might lead us to believe—but something attainable only after the acquisition of specialized skills. If economic success does, indeed, become dependent on these skills, then the rhetoric of freedom and equality, which, in part, structures the fabric of our nation, will be further undermined, for human dignity will be seen as resulting from privilege and the satisfaction of a set of prior conditions or standards. See Aronowitz (1993, 87) for a similar argument. At the moment, however, these conditions are not frozen: economic success—or, at least, satisfaction—can still be attained with only modest literacy skills. Moreover, such studies as the one reported by

the *Times* are, in part, shams because the discourses of measurement are not able to *measure* what real people do with what they know. During my fieldwork, for instance, Mexican immigrants acted collectively to solve their literacy problems. In fact, all sorts of collective actions—for instance, the use of talk in understanding written texts and society in general—utterly vanish from the gaze of literacy tests that can only *measure* individual action under structured testing situations. The rhetoric of crisis and the policy making that it generates is not built on "blunt facts" when the real world remains largely unmeasured. See Cintron (1990) for further discussion of the sham of literacy tests.

17. See Limón (1989, 482).

18. See ibid., 484.

19. See Mukerjee (1994, 29).

20. See Leach (1989). I largely disagree with the comparison of fiction to ethnographic writing. I believe that comparison to be an artifact of the unfortunate situation that literary studies rather than rhetorical studies largely control both the academy and the public's understanding of discourse. This phenomenon is recent, however, dating roughly from the nineteenth century, and if it did not hold such swagger, the academy would more immediately understand ethnographic writing—tropes, characters, and all—as essentially argumentative rather than fictive. Despite my disagreement with Leach, I quote him more extensively here: "As anthropologists we need to come to terms with the now well-recognized fact that in a novel the personalities of the characters are derived from aspects of the personality of the author. How could it be otherwise? The only ego that I know at first hand is my own. When Malinowski writes about Trobriand Islanders he is writing about himself; when Evans-Pritchard writes about the Nuer he is writing about himself. Any other sort of description turns the characters of ethnographic monographs into clockwork dummies" (140–41).

21. See de Certeau (1988, 134).

22. See Ong (1988).

REFERENCES

Abu-Lughod, Lila. 1991. Writing against culture. Pp. 137–62 in *Recapturing anthropology: Working in the present*. Edited by Richard G. Fox. Santa Fe: School of American Research Press.

Anderson, Benedict. 1991. *Imagined communities: Reflections on the origin and spread of nationalism*. London: Verso.

Appadurai, Arjun. 1993. Disjuncture and difference in the global cultural economy. Pp. 269–95 in *The phantom public sphere*. Edited by Bruce Robbins. Minneapolis: University of Minnesota Press.

Aristotle. 1991. *On rhetoric, A theory of civic discourse*. Translated by George A. Kennedy. New York: Oxford University Press.

Aronowitz, Stanley. 1993. Is a democracy possible? The decline of the public in the American debate. Pp. 75–92 in *The phantom public sphere*. Edited by Bruce Robbins. Minneapolis: University of Minnesota Press.

St. Augustine. 1960. *The confessions of St. Augustine*. Translated by John K. Ryan. New York: Image Books Doubleday.

Austin, J. L. 1978. *How to do things with words*. Cambridge: Harvard University Press.

Bakhtin, Mikhail. 1988. *The dialogic imagination, four essays*. Edited by Michael Holquist, and translated by Caryl Emerson and Michael Holquist. Austin: University of Texas Press.

Behar, Ruth. 1993. *Translated woman: Crossing the border with Esperanza's story*. Boston: Beacon Press.

Benjamin, Walter. 1986. Paris, capital of the nineteenth century. Pp. in *Reflections: Essays, aphorisms, autobiographical writings.* Edited by Peter Demetz, and translated by Edmund Jephcott. New York: Schocken Books.

Bhabha, Homi. 1991. Introduction: Narrating the nation. Pp. 1–7 in *Nation and narration.* Edited by Homi Bhabha. London: Routledge.

Blackhawk. 1994. *Life of Blackhawk.* Edited by Milo Milton Quaife. New York: Dover Publications.

Bourdieu, Pierre, and Jean-Claude Passeron. 1994. *Reproduction in education, society, and culture.* Translated by Richard Nice. London: Sage Publications.

Briggs, Charles L. 1988. *Competence in performance: The creativity of tradition in mexicano verbal art.* Philadelphia: University of Pennsylvania Press.

Burke, Kenneth. 1969. *A rhetoric of motives.* Berkeley: University of California Press.

Carr, Irene Campos. 1992. Mexican workers in Angelstown: The oral history of three immigration waves, 1924–1990. *Perspectives in Mexican American studies* 3:31–51.

Cassidy, David. 1992. Heisenberg, uncertainty, and the quantum revolution. *Scientific American* (May): 106–12.

Cintron, Ralph. 1990. *The use of oral and written language in the homes of three Mexicano families.* Ph.D. diss., University of Illinois at Chicago, Chicago, Illinois.

Cintron, Ralph. 1992. Divided, yet a city: A brief history. *Perspectives in Mexican American studies* 3: 1–29.

Cintron, Ralph. 1993. Wearing a pith helmet at a sly angle, or can writing researchers do ethnography in a postmodern era? *Written communication* 10, no. 3: 371–412.

Clanchy, M. T. 1979. *From memory to written record: England, 1066–1307.* Cambridge: Harvard University Press.

Clifford, James, and George Marcus, eds. 1986. *Writing culture: The poetics and politics of ethnography.* Berkeley: University of California Press.

Conquergood, Dwight. 1992. On reppin' and rhetoric: Gang representations. Unpublished manuscript.

de Certeau, Michel. 1988. *The practice of everyday life.* Translated by Steven Rendell. Berkeley: University of California Press.

de la Garza, Rodolfo, Louis DeSipio, F. Chris Garcia, John Garcia, and Angelo Falcon. 1992. *Latino voices: Mexican, Puerto Rican, and Cuban perspectives on American politics.* Boulder: Westview Press.

Dentan, Robert. 1992. The rise, maintenance, and destruction of peaceable polity: A preliminary essay in political ecology. Pp. 214–70 in *Aggression and peacefulness in humans and other primates.* Edited by James Silverberg and J. Patrick Gray. New York: Oxford University Press.

Douglas, Mary. 1992. *Purity and danger: An analysis of the concepts of pollution and taboo.* London: Routledge.

Firth, Raymond. 1957. *We, the Tikopia.* London: George Allen and Unwin.

Forrest, John. 1984. *Morris and Matachin: A study in comparative choreography.* Sheffield, England: The Centre for English Cultural Tradition and Language, University of Sheffield.

Foucault, Michel. 1988. *Madness and civilization: A history of insanity in the age of reason.* Translated by Richard Howard. New York: Vintage Books.

Fraser, Nancy. 1993. Rethinking the public sphere: A contribution to the critique of actually existing democracy. Pp. 1–32 in *The phantom public sphere.* Edited by Bruce Robbins. Minneapolis: University of Minnesota Press.

Fuller, Steve. 1992. Being there with Thomas Kuhn: A parable for postmodern times. *History and theory* 31: 241–75.

Gadamer, Hans-Georg. 1992. The expressive power of language: On the function of rhetoric for knowledge. *Publications of the Modern Language Association of America* 107, no. 2: 345–52.

Garver, Eugene. 1986. Making discourse ethical: The lessons of Aristotle's rhetoric. Pp. 73–96 in *Proceedings of the Boston area Colloquium in Ancient Philosophy.* Vol. 5. Edited by John Cleary and Daniel Shartin. Lanham, Maryland: University Press of America.

Geertz, Clifford. 1988. *Works and lives: The anthropologist as author.* Stanford: Stanford University Press.

Gramsci, Antonio. 1995. *Selections from the prison notebooks.* Edited and translated by Quintin Hoare and Geoffrey Nowell Smith. New York: International Publishers.

Habermas, Jürgen. 1984. *The theory of communicative action.* 2 vols. Translated by Thomas McCarthy. Boston: Beacon Press.

Habermas, Jürgen. 1987. *The philosophical discourse of modernity: Twelve lectures.* Translated by Frederick Lawrence. Cambridge: MIT Press.

Habermas, Jürgen. 1992. Further reflections on the public sphere. Pp. 421–61 in *Habermas and the public sphere.* Edited by Craig Calhoun. Cambridge: MIT Press.

Habermas, Jürgen. 1994. *The structural transformation of the public sphere: An inquiry into a category of bourgeois society.* Translated by Thomas Burger, with the assistance of Frederick Lawrence. Cambridge: MIT Press.

Halliday, M. A. K. 1978. *Language as social semiotic: The social interpretation of language and meaning.* Baltimore: University Park Press.

Heath, Shirley Brice. 1983. *Ways with words: Language, life, and work in communities and classrooms.* Cambridge: Cambridge University Press.

Hernadi, Paul. 1988. Doing, making, meaning: Toward a theory of verbal practice. *Publications of the Modern Language Association of America* 103, no. 5: 749–58.

Hirschberg, Lynn. 1996. Does a sugar bear bite? Suge Knight and his posse. *New York Times Magazine*, 14 January, 24–31, 39, 40, 50, 57.

Horgan, John. 1993. The death of proof. *Scientific American* (October): 92–103.

Jankowski, Martín Sánchez. 1991. *Islands in the street: Gangs and American urban society.* Berkeley: University of California Press.

Just in time. 1992. *Time Magazine* 139 (13 January): 53.

Kamin, Blair. 1993. Rebuilding the community: New ideas in public housing are a return to the basics. *Chicago Tribune*, Sunday, 20 June, sec. 13: 4, 6–8.

Kerr, L. A. N. 1976. *The Chicano experience in Chicago, 1920–1970.* Ph.D. diss., University of Illinois at Chicago, Chicago, Illinois.

Lavie, Smadar. 1990. *The poetics of military occupation: Mzeina allegories of Bedouin identity under Israeli and Egyptian rule.* Berkeley: University of California Press.

Leach, Edmund. 1989. Writing anthropology. *American ethnologist* 16, no. 1: 137–41.

Le Corbusier. 1947. *The city of to-morrow and its planning.* Translated by Frederick Etchells. London: The Architectural Press.

Le Corbusier. 1967. *The radiant city: Elements of a doctrine of urbanism to be used as the basis of our machine-age civilization.* New York: Orion Press.

Lévi-Strauss, Claude. 1961. *Tristes tropiques.* Translated by John Russell. New York: Atheneum.

Limón, José. 1989. *Carne, carnales,* and the carnivalesque: Bakhtinian *batos,* disorder, and narrative discourses. *American ethnologist,* 16, no. 3: 471–86.

Limón, José. 1994. *Dancing with the devil: Society and cultural poetics in Mexican-American South Texas.* Madison: University of Wisconsin Press.

Lyotard, Jean-François. 1984. *The postmodern condition: A report on knowledge.* Translated by Geoff Bennington and Brian Massumi. Minneapolis: University of Minnesota Press.

Martin, Henri-Jean. 1994. *The history and power of writing.* Translated by Lydia G. Cochrane. Chicago: University of Chicago Press.

Monmonier, Mark. 1991. *How to lie with maps.* Chicago: University of Chicago Press.

Mukerjee, Madhusree. 1994. Profile: Ellen V. Futter. *Scientific American* (July): 28–29.

Monmonier, Mark. 1991. *How to lie with maps.* Chicago: University of Chicago Press.

Ong, Walter J. 1988. *Orality and literacy: The technologizing of the word.* New York: Routledge.

Ortner, Sherry. 1984. Theory in anthropology since the "sixties." *Comparative studies in society and history* 26(1):126–66.

Padilla, Felix M. 1993. *The gang as an American enterprise.* New Brunswick: Rutgers University Press.

Palmer, Susan. 1986. *Building ethnic communities in a small city; Romanians and Mexicans in Angelstown, Illinois, 1900–1940*. Ph.D. diss., Northern Illinois University, De Kalb, Illinois.

Paz, Octavio. 1988. *Sor Juana: Her life and her world*. Translated by Margaret Sayers Peden. London: Faber and Faber.

Pérez, Ramón "Tianguis." 1991. *Diary of an undocumented immigrant*. Translated by Dick J. Reavis. Houston: Arte Publico press.

Plato. 1971. *Gorgias*. Translated by Walter Hamilton. New York: Penguin Books.

Prasad, Sunand. 1987. Le Corbusier in India. Pp. 278–337 in *Le Corbusier, architect of the century*. London: Arts Council of Great Britain.

Pratt, Mary Louise. 1986. Fieldwork in common places. Pp. 27–50 in *Writing culture: The poetics and politics of ethnography*. Edited by James Clifford and George Marcus. Berkeley: University of California Press.

Punch, Maurice. 1986. *The politics and ethics of fieldwork*. Sage University Paper Series on Qualitative Research Methods, vol. 3. Beverly Hills: Sage.

Renan, Ernest. 1991. What is a nation? Translated by Martin Thom. Pp. 8–22 in *Nation and narration*. Edited by Homi Bhabha. London: Routledge.

Rodriguez, Luis J. 1993. *Always running, la vida loca: Gang days in L.A.* Willimantic, Conn.: Curbstone Press.

Rosaldo, Michelle. 1980. *Knowledge and passion: Ilongot notions of self and social life*. Cambridge: Cambridge University Press.

Rosaldo, Renato. 1989. *Culture and truth: The remaking of social analysis*. Boston: Beacon Press.

Rouse, Roger. 1991. Mexican migration and the social space of postmodernism. *Diaspora* 1: 8–23.

Roy, Beth. 1994. *Some trouble with cows: Making sense of social conflict*. Berkeley: University of California Press.

Sánchez, Rosaura. 1983. *Chicano discourse: Socio-historic perspectives*. Rowley, Mass.: Newbury House.

Sangren, Steven. 1988. Rhetoric and the authority of ethnography: "Postmodernism" and the social reproduction of texts. *Current anthropology* 29: 405–35.

Sapir, Edward. 1949. Cultural anthropology and psychiatry. Pp. 140–63 in *Culture, language, and personality: Selected essays*. Edited by David Mandelbaum. Berkeley: University of California Press.

Scheper-Hughes, Nancy. 1992. *Death without weeping: The violence of everyday life in Brazil*. Berkeley: University of California Press.

Schmandt-Besserat, Denise. 1989. Two precursors of writing: Plain and complex tokens. Pp. 27–41 in *The origins of writing*. Edited by Wayne Senner. Lincoln: University of Nebraska Press.

Scollon, Ron, and Suzanne B. K. Scollon. 1981. *Narrative, literacy, and face in interethnic communication*. Norwood, N.J.: Ablex.

Sebeok. Thomas A. 1991. *A sign is just a sign*. Bloomington: University of Indiana Press.

Sennett, Richard. 1990. *The conscience of the eye: The design and social life of cities*. New York: Alfred A. Knopf.

Shakur, Sanyika (Kody Scott). 1993. *Monster: The autobiography of an L.A. gang member*. New York: Atlantic Monthly Press.

Shelley, Percy Bysshe. 1977. Preface to *Prometheus Unbound*. In *Shelley's Poetry and prose: Authoritative texts, criticism*. Edited by Donald Reiman and Sharon Powers. New York: W. W. Norton and Company.

Shuman, Amy. 1986. *Storytelling rights: The uses of oral and written texts by urban adolescents*. Cambridge: Cambridge University Press.

Shweder, Richard. 1991. *Thinking through cultures: Expeditions in cultural psychology*. Cambridge: Harvard University Press.

Starting up an improved atomic clock. 1993. *Science News* 143 (May): 276.

Stevens, Wallace. 1968. The idea of order of Key West. Pp. 128–30 in *The collected poems of Wallace Stevens*. New York: Alfred A. Knopf.

Stewart, Susan. 1993. *On longing: Narratives of the miniature, the gigantic, the souvenir, the collection*. Durham: Duke University Press.

Taussig, Michael. 1993. *Mimesis and alterity: A particular history of the senses*. New York: Routledge.

Terdiman, Richard. 1989. *Discourse/counter-discourse: The theory and practice of symbolic resistance in nineteenth-century France*. Ithaca: Cornell University Press.

Tyler, Stephen. 1987. Postmodern ethnography: From document of the occult to occult document. Pp. 199–216 in *The unspeakable: Discourse, dialogue, and rhetoric in the postmodern world*. Madison: University of Wisconsin Press.

Urban, Greg. 1991. *A discourse-centered approach to culture*. Austin: University of Texas Press.

Wardhaugh, Ronald. 1986. *An introduction to sociolinguistics*. New York: Basil Blackwell.

Wolf, Margery. 1992. *A thrice-told tale: Feminism, postmodernism, and ethnographic responsibility*. Stanford: Stanford University Press.

ACKNOWLEDGMENTS

Rhetoricians tend to overthink the words and genres they use. And so it is that I cannot help but think about the genre of acknowledgments: what purpose it serves and even its history. *A gift was made, a gift in return, an exchange of gifts.*

I am indebted first of all to the people I lived with and talked to in "Angelstown." For too long, you tolerated a nosey person. If you should open this book, you may find yourself somewhere in here, disguised, of course, but between us we know the truth and I hope you will find also my deep appreciation. And for Janis, a special appreciation. Second, I wish to thank my research assistants, Edmundo Cavazos, Dan Anderson, and most recently Anne Eisenberg. More than anyone else the three of you know the inevitable fudging that book writing takes.

Back in the early days, before I started wearing a pith helmet, a certain "crew" helped me shape the possibility of ethnographic work: Anne Doyle, Mary Ann Janda, Beverly Moss, Juan Guerra, Jabari Mahari, Marianthe Karanikas, and Larry Anderson. What I remember most, however, was the hilarity of it all. Along with that group, I need to mention here some other University of Illinois at Chicago friends, particularly Leonard Ramirez of LARES, and Mark Zimmerman, Otto Pikaza, Mary Kay Vaughn, and the rest of the Latin American Studies faculty: all of you reminded me of what I had forgotten, and so I made a U-turn. My very, very special thanks, however, to those who took charge: Martin Steinmann, Thomas Kochman, Shirley Brice Heath (during a couple of visits), David Jolliffe, and most especially Marcia Farr. (Marcia: I only became wayward after I left your hands, so it wasn't your fault—and the CHILL meetings were great.)

Years later and I was still working in the same fields, but now I was a seasonal migrant from Iowa. How can I ever thank sufficiently the Project on the Rhetoric of Inquiry (POROI)—you folks (Dierdre McClosky, John Nelson, Jim Throgmorton, Bob Boynton, et al.) gave me a second education. And I must include all the members of our little Rhetoric Department: Mary Trachsel, Fred Antczak, Dennis Moore, Barb Biesecker, Cleo Martin, Takis Poulakis, Melissa Deem, Donovan Ochs, Carol Severino, Gene Krupa, Doug Trank; and then there are the rhetoricians across the tracks: Bruce Gronbeck, David Depew, Kathleen Farrell, Michael McGee—seeing all of you on a daily or at least monthly basis has changed my life. This book would not look the same without my having absorbed fractions of your distinctive worldviews. And as for the anthropologists that I talk to now and again—Mac Marshall, Margery Wolff, Laura Graham and TM, Virginia Dominguez, and most especially José Limón and Ruth Behar, and then the in-between folks like Dwight Conquergood, Bonnie Sunstein, Rich Horowitz, Jane Desmond, and Kristine Fitch—thank you for your ongoing support.

A variety of organizations have offered at different times some wonderful help in order to complete this book. At the top of the list would be the Rockefeller Foundation and its humanities fellowship offered by the Department of American Studies and African-American Studies at SUNY Buffalo. I would like to especially thank Michael Frisch, Charlie Kyle, Liz Kennedy, Robert Denton, and Charles Fairchild for the best year of my life. My thanks also to the Obermann Center for Advanced Studies and to those long eccentric conversations with Fred Will. Finally, I wish to thank the English Department at Chico State for the invitation and conversation and most especially to that gentleman who asked, "So what makes Valerio's wall any different from any other teenager's wall?"

There is one very special person who appeared seemingly out of nowhere, fishing, it seems, off the bow of Beacon Press. I had been lost in the sea. To Deb Chasman, my editor (and rescuer), to her patience, to her critical and editorial skills, and to her sweet toughness. You knew what the text should look like from the beginning, but it took me a while to catch up. Anyway, we finally got it reeled in. Whew . . . a long haul.

Finally, I wish to thank Jane: We found the breath of life after the world had come to an end. *Your writing, my writing, a dovetail.*

Index